MW01630276

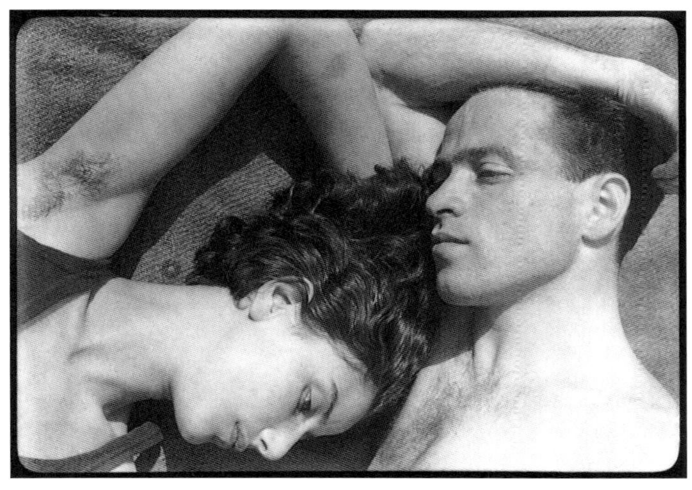

HUNGARY

1908–1937

Irene Sunbathing, 1936

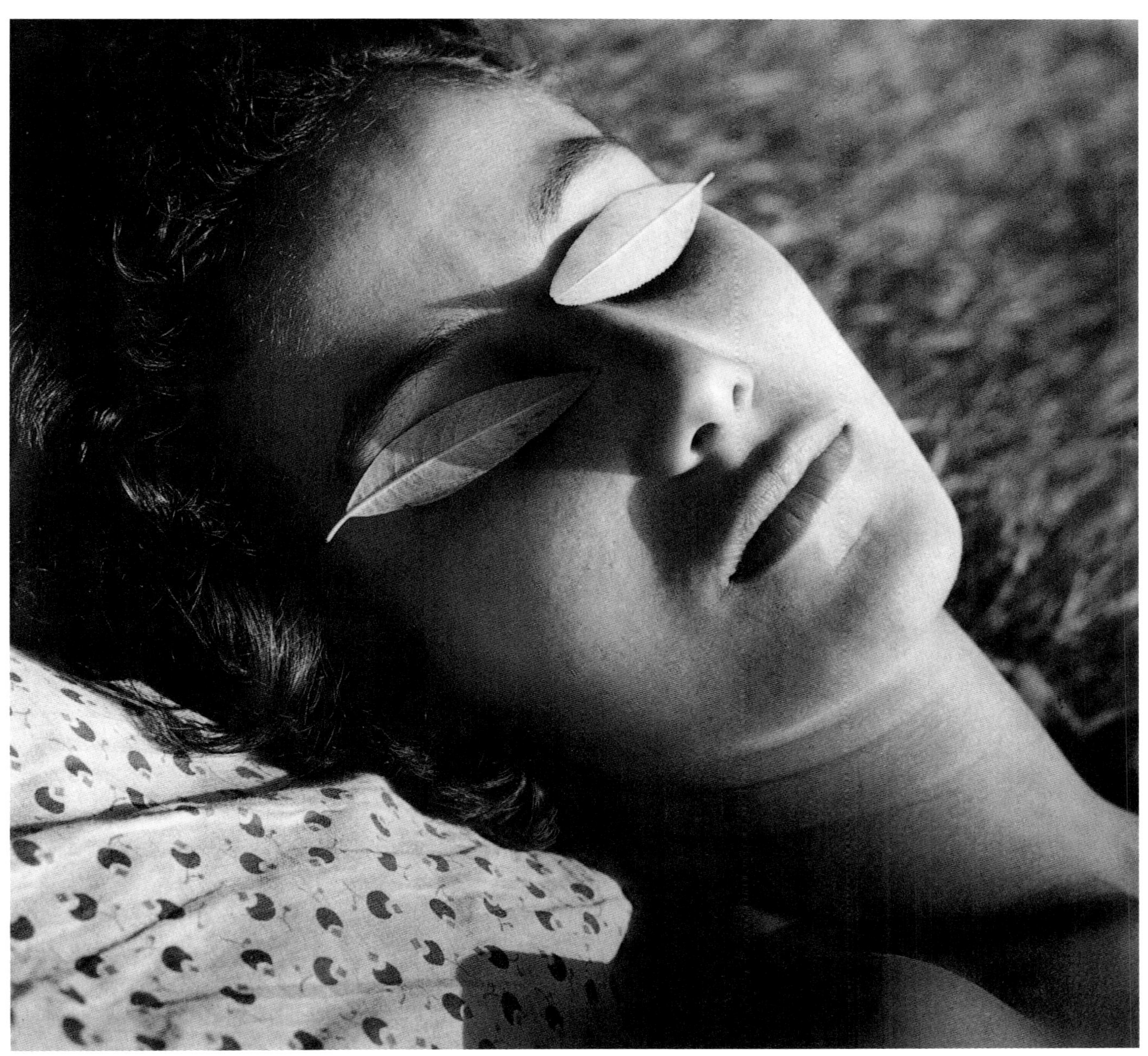

PARIS

1937–1939

Lovers on the Boulevard, 1938

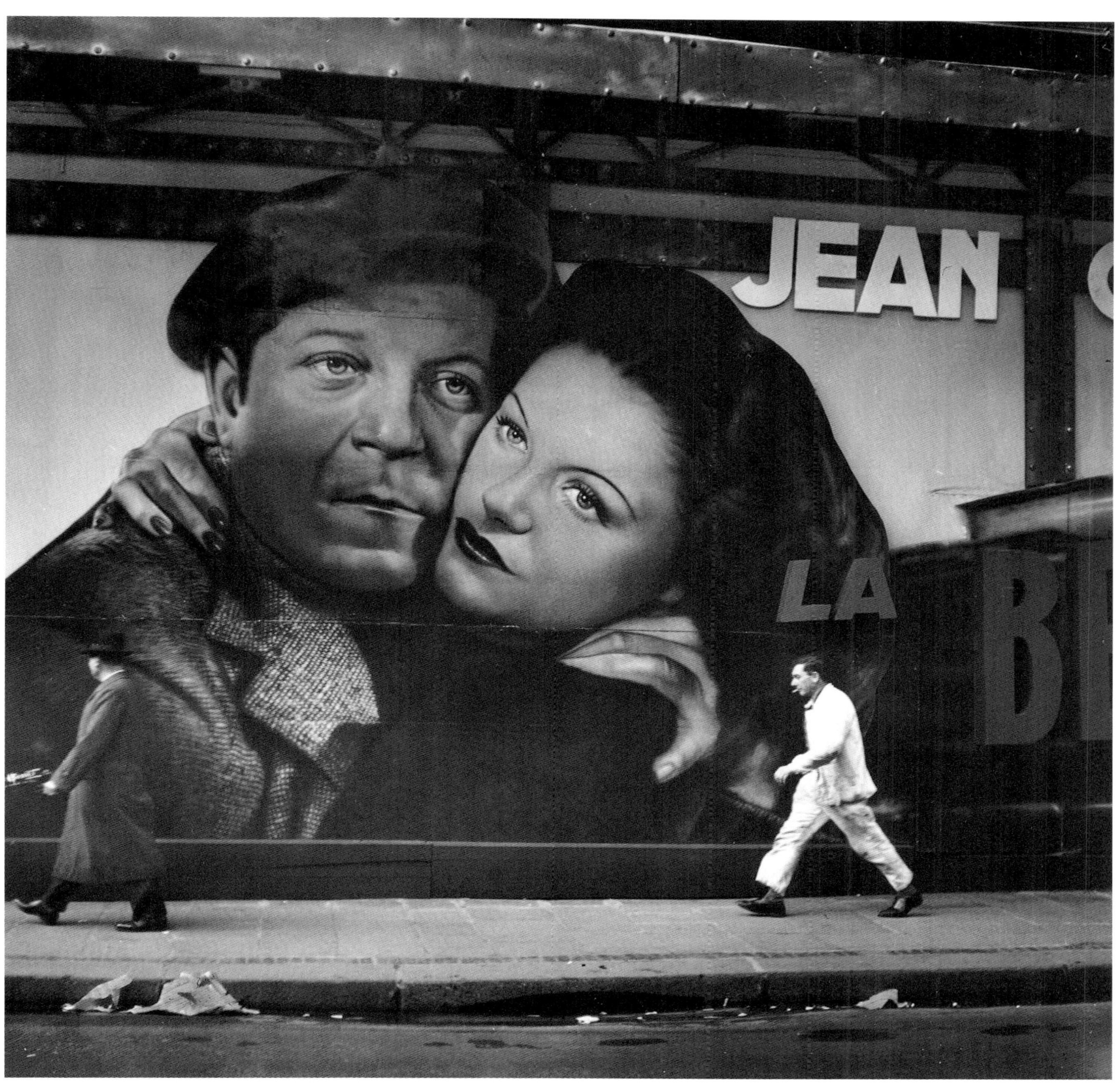

JEAN
LA
B

JAPAN

1940–1960

Akira Kurosawa, Film Director, 1954

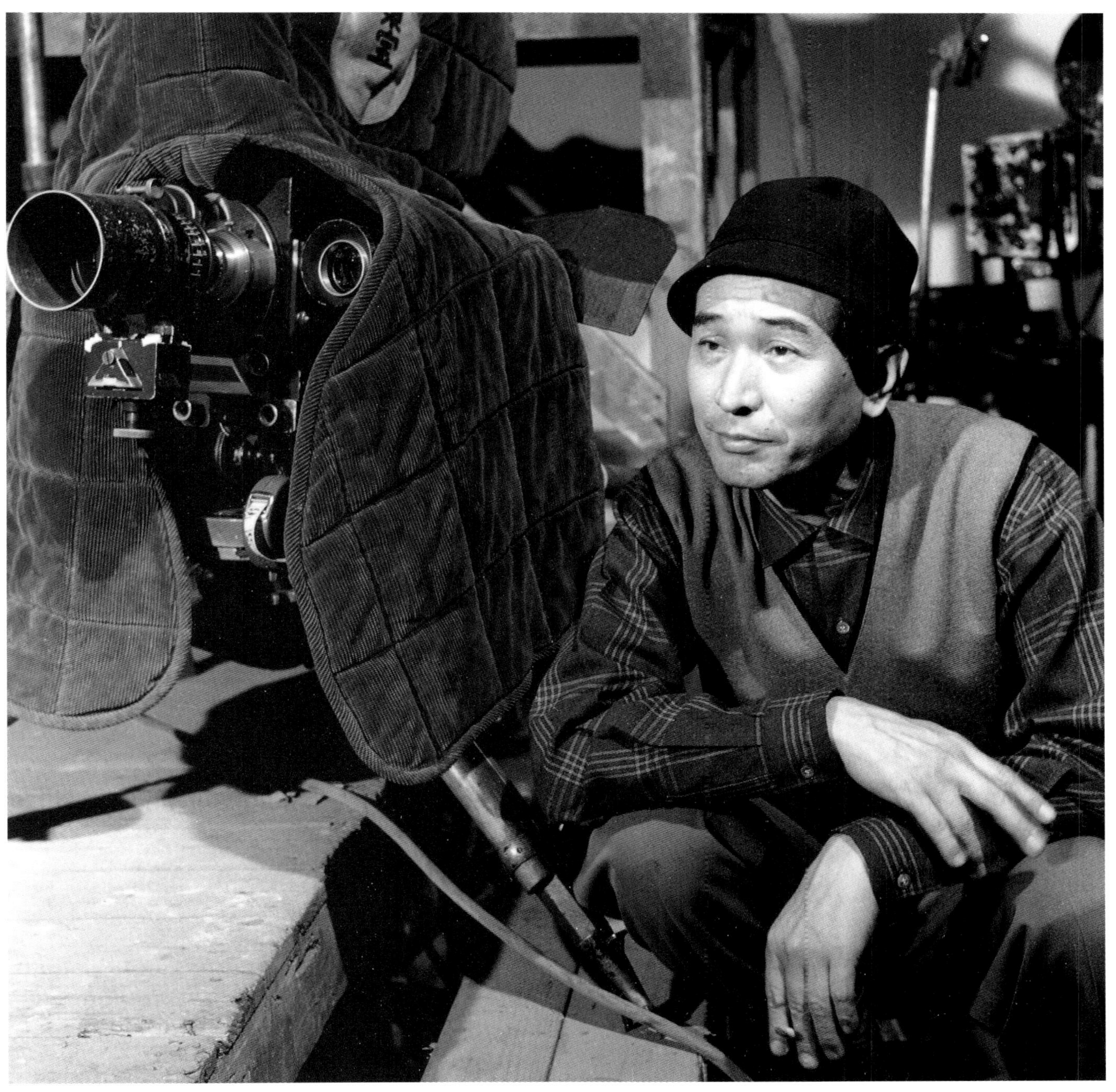

CHICAGO

1956–1959

Freight Terminal, Chicago, 1957

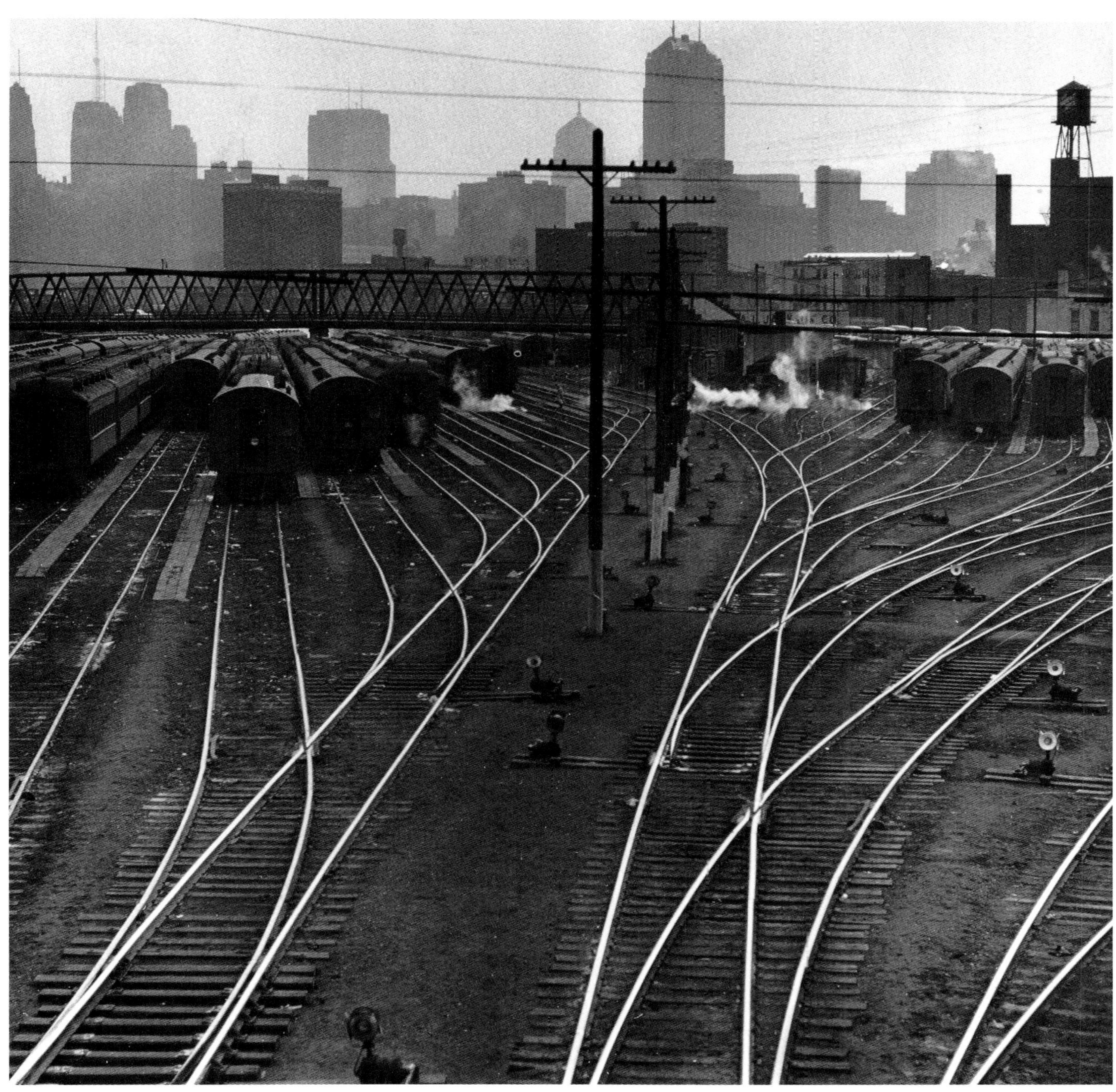

Francis with 'Iolani Luahine at her home in Kona, 1975

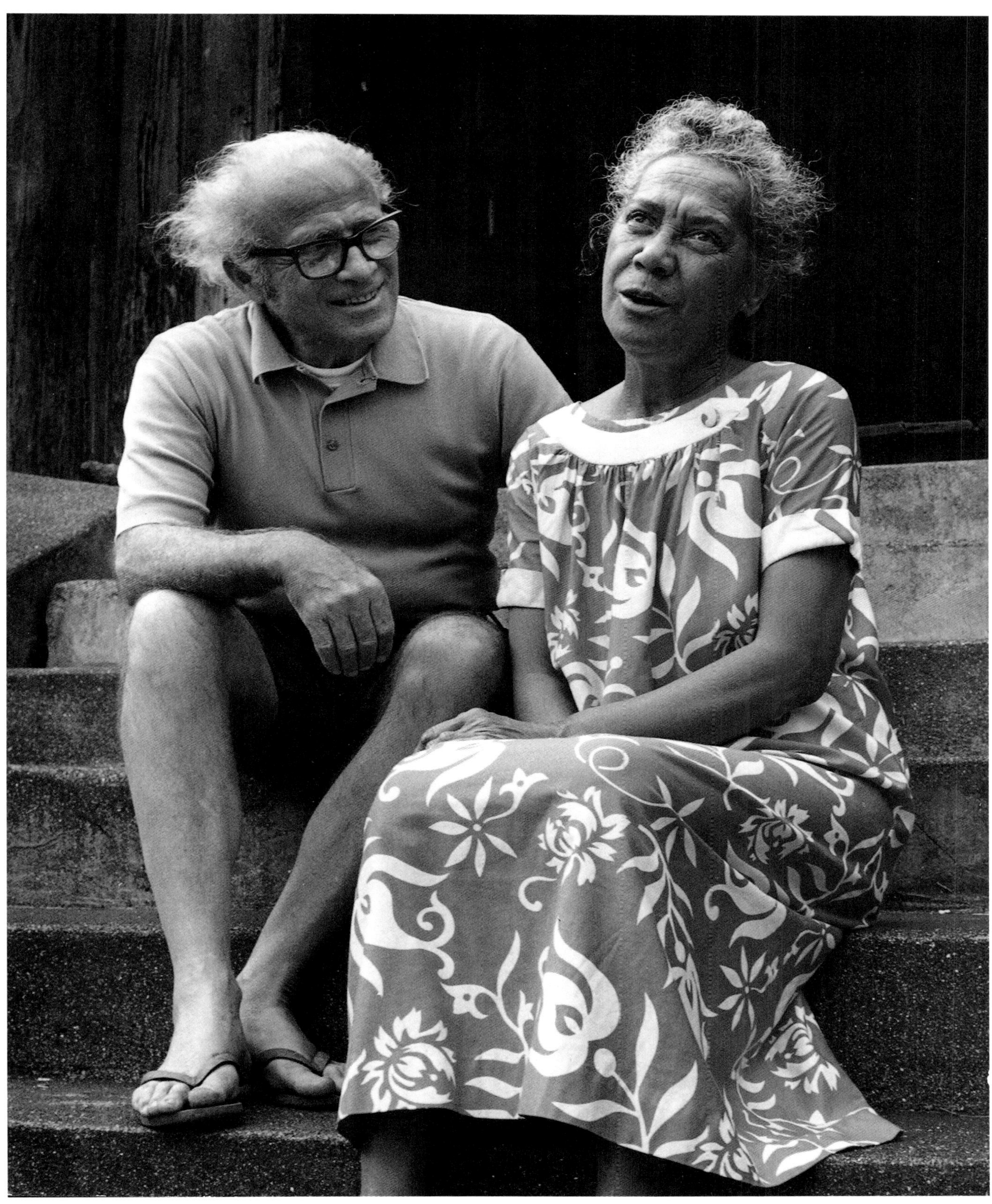

francis

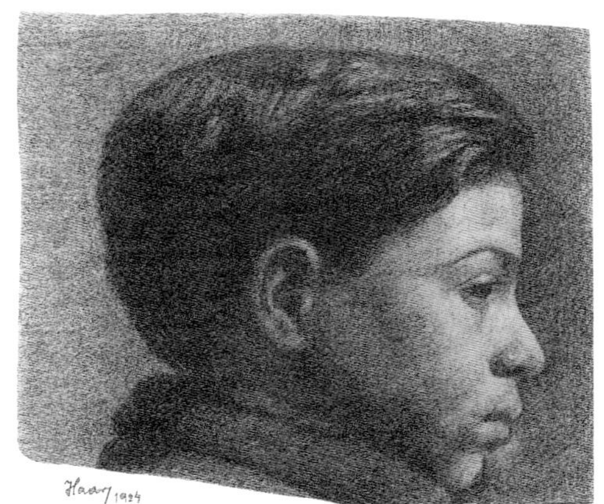

baar

Foreword by James Michener   xvi

Preface and Acknowledgments   xvii

EDITED BY TOM HAAR

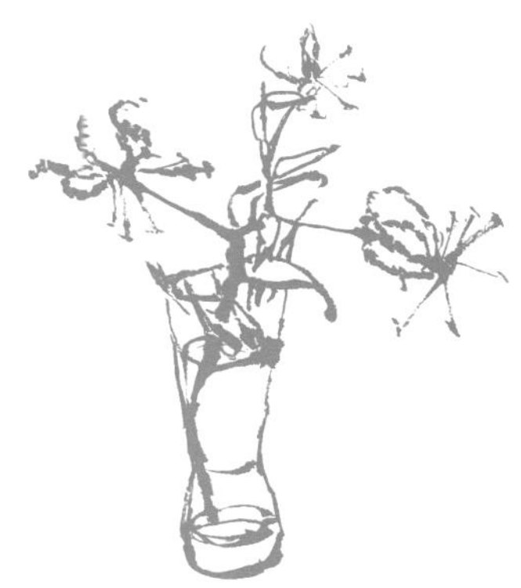

Page xi

Photograph of Francis Haar

and ʻIolani Luahine by

Irene Haar

Page xii

Self-Portrait, 1924

Pencil drawing at age fifteen

Page xiii

One of the last drawings made

by Francis Haar, in 1997

Library of Congress Cataloging-in-Publication Data
Haar, Francis.
  Francis Haar : a lifetime of images / edited by Tom Haar.
    p. cm.
  Includes bibliographical references.
  ISBN 0-8248-2449-0 (cloth : alk. paper)
  1. Photography, Artistic. 2. Haar, Francis. I. Haar, Tom. II. Title.
TR653 .H28 2001
779´.092--dc21   00-050783

A Latitude 20 Book
University of Hawaiʻi Press
Honolulu

Designed and produced by Barbara Pope Book Design.
Composed in Janson, designed by Miklós Kis, and
Univers, designed by Adrian Frutiger.
Printed in Singapore.

For my wife and companion, Irene   FRANCIS HAAR

In loving memory of my parents,
Francis and Irene Haar   TOM HAAR

When I worked in Korea during the war that ravaged the country in the early 1950s, it was my delight to go to Tokyo for the famous R and R, rest and recuperation. A feature of any such stay was a visit to a notable restaurant on a small street off the Ginza, "Irene's Hungaria," a lively spot serving fine cuisine of Central Europe. After a protracted spell of half-frozen GI food in Korea, "Irene's" was a godsend that I frequented as often as my limited funds would allow.

In the course of meeting and talking with Irene, a lively Hungarian woman who spoke enthusiastic English, I heard a good deal about her husband, Francis, who had been, she told us, a well-known photographer in Budapest before the war. Anticipating the upheavals about to engulf Hungary, and eager to experience the heady artistic atmosphere of Paris, husband and wife had made the daring jump to that city, where they established themselves as a well-regarded team.

Curiosity and opportunities to practice photography took them to Japan just before the outbreak of World War II. After establishing themselves in the business community of Japan, they were whisked off to an evacuation camp for foreigners. They spent the war years in extreme deprivation, but when the Americans arrived in 1945, they found themselves surrounded by understanding GIs, who helped them establish the restaurant for Irene and a photography business for Francis.

It was then that I first met the Haars, the wife and then the husband, and I quickly learned that each was an artist, Irene with Hungarian food, Francis with his camera. His photographs were works of stunning beauty, perception, and relevance. He had a sharp eye for meaningful subjects shown in an artful posture, whether that subject was a farm girl or a factory profile. And the fact that he now had a Hungarian-French-Japanese portfolio meant that he was about as international as an artist could be. It was instructive to know him and his pictures.

Years later, to my surprise, I met up with the Haars again. I was working in Honolulu on my exploratory book on Japanese prints when the curator of the art museum there told me, "A famous photographer from Japan has settled here in the Islands, and I think we'll be hiring him to illustrate your book." Expecting to meet some Japanese man gifted with the camera, I was astonished to meet instead my old friend Haar from Tokyo and Budapest. He and his wife had completed their artistic wanderings and come to roost in Hawai'i, their permanent home henceforth.

He did take the pictures relating to my writing on Japanese art. He did establish himself yet again in a new land, his passport being his camera. And he and his delightful wife did became honored citizens of the Islands. It is my warm pleasure to assist in a small way in this tribute to an artist.

James A. Michener
Coral Gables, Florida
June 1, 1989

This book was many years in the making. Francis Haar, my father, originally planned it as a summation of his career as a photographer and documentary film-maker. Illness and old age prevented him from finishing the work. As his son, and having followed in his footsteps becoming a photographer, I assumed the responsibility of completing this, my father's fifteenth book, both as a tribute and to keep his legacy alive in print.

In finalizing this project, I researched many aspects of it and approached the material from several different angles. The photographs alone required considerable attention and have been edited in chronological order. Along the way, some new photographs were added, others were deleted, and several additional ones were selected to illustrate the text. To supplement my father's autobiographical account, I assembled a comprehensive bibliography of his published work and verified the captions and the material in the appendixes.

I am grateful for everyone who contributed to the production of this book, particularly James D. White. He worked extensively editing the manuscript, and he offered the valuable suggestion of incorporating some of Irene Haar's memoirs into the text. Those memoirs were intended as the preface for a book that never came about, a collection of recipes from her restaurant in Japan. Because she did not continue her memoirs after leaving Japan, we could not include her personal recollections about living in Hawai'i—her ambition to continue "Irene's Hungaria" in Hawai'i (she opened "Irene's Hungaria Restaurant" in Kailua), her thirteen years as a dining hall manager for Kamehameha Schools, or her love for creating ceramic folk craft reminiscent of her native Hungary.

This publication would not have been possible without the assistance of Daniel F. S. Lee, president of The Asian/Pacific Foundation of Hawaii, and the benefactors who provided financial assistance that helped bring the book to completion: Mr. and Mrs. Alexander Pickens; Mrs. Catherine Eshbach; Mr. Andras Hautzinger; Mr. Donald Angus; and The Zone XII Photo Group. My sincere appreciation also to Jane Taylor for her scrupulous copy editing, and especially to Barbara Pope for her inspired design.

My father planned to dedicate this book to Irene, his wife and companion of sixty-three years. Having completed the project for him, I have amended my own dedication to accompany his.

Tom Haar
Honolulu, Hawai'i
January 2000

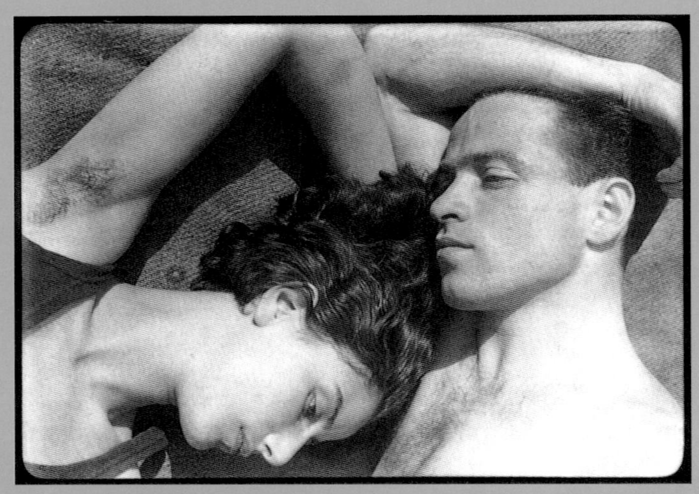

hungary

Recuperating from their labors,
Irene and Francis sunning at
Lake Balaton, 1936

I was born in 1908 in a small town in southeast Hungary, now a part of Romania. When I was two, my family moved to the city of Szekszárd, in central Hungary, where I spent my school years.

From an early age, I was interested in drawing. I remember falling ill during my first winter at elementary school, and the teacher visiting our home to find out the reason for my absence. She was so impressed with the crayon drawings I had done to amuse myself while in bed that she tried to make me the artist of the class when I returned to school.

My father made his living producing embroideries, such as piping and other decorative work, for military uniforms and for women's dresses. His work was so highly regarded that in the 1900 World's Fair in Paris, the government used his work to represent Hungarian handicrafts. He was also an amateur photographer. He had a large wooden 8 × 10 box camera mounted on a tripod, which he used mainly to take glass plate pictures of our family. I remember he used to do the developing himself in our basement.

Vác, a town 30 km north of Budapest, 1918. I remember the end of the war. It was frightening. From our window, I could see our neighbors' sons coming home, the ones who did come home. Some were limping, some did not have arms or legs. What made me really scared was a neighbor's son who ran around like a wild animal, shooting his gun into the air.

There were all sorts of political happenings, which we children did not understand. At times the government called themselves Communists, then another party came to power. Revenge was in the air. People were hanged, in public, in our favorite park.

*It seems now that the whole town was in a whirl, disorganized, terrified. We tried to live apart from political changes, and stay within the family.**

When the time came for me to decide which field of work I should enter, I wanted to pursue my interest in art and enter an art school, but my mother was against it. "You will always be hungry as an artist," she warned, advising me

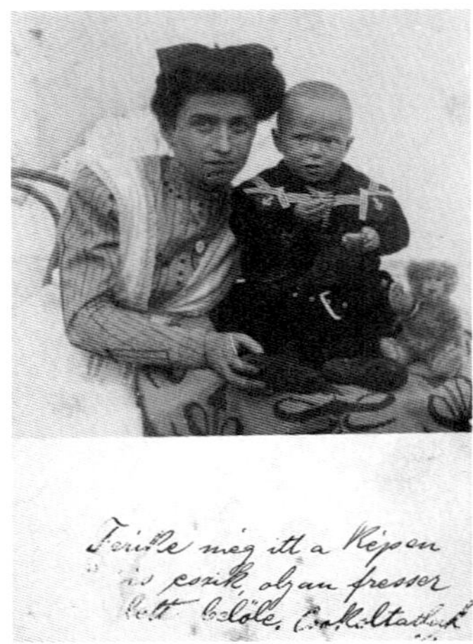

Haár Ferenc (Francis) with his mother, Adél, 1909

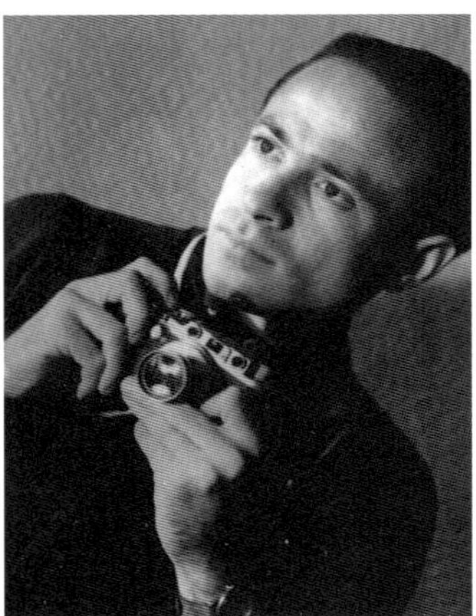

Francis (seated) at the National Academy of Industrial Arts, Budapest (1924–1928)

Photography evolves from an avocation to a vocation in the early 1930s.

instead to go to a business school and become a bank employee. Nevertheless, I decided to take the entrance examination for the National Academy of Industrial Arts in Budapest. I was overjoyed to pass all the tests and begin my studies in interior and architectural design.

I did well in my college, and after graduation, in 1928, one of my professors gave me a letter of recommendation to work in the office of a prominent architect in Budapest. My job was to do the architectural renderings, or the details of a project. Early assignments that I remember ranged from making the plans for a hospital to designing a chapel, a project in which I was responsible for the massive front door, the benches, and even the altar.

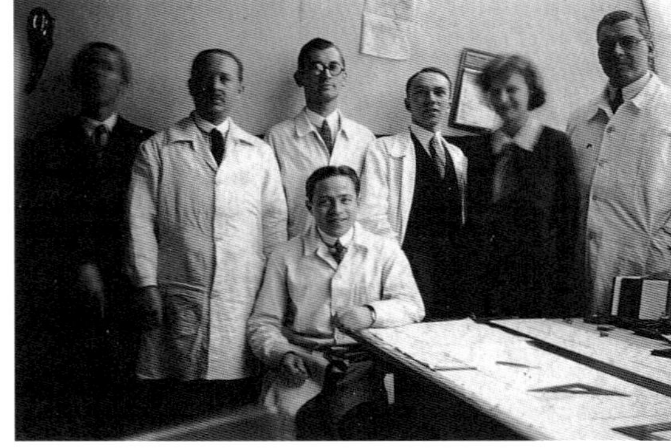

One day, a former classmate from art school invited me to an evening performance by a group of young avant-garde artists and intellectuals known as Munka Kör (Work Circle). The program consisted of folk songs, a violin solo, modern dance, and a recital of poetry. I found it fascinating and was stimulated by the discussions among the artists, architects, journalists, musicians, and college students that followed. Several young painters from the Academy of Fine Arts who were active in the group later became world-renowned artists. I learned that the members met regularly for discussions on modern art and other contemporary issues. After a couple of weeks, I was so excited by their activities that I too became a member of the circle. My first interest was in folk songs, and I used to sing with the folk group.

It was during this period of mixing with other artists that I became interested in photography. I purchased my first camera in 1929 and concentrated initially

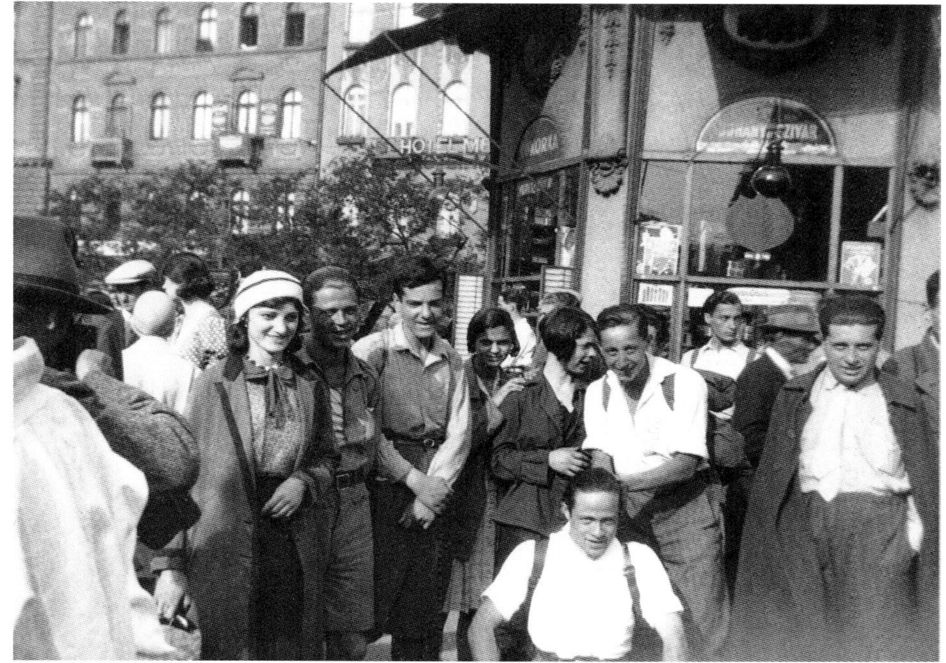

Group photo with other Munka Kör members in Blaha Lujza Square, Budapest, around 1930. Francis Haar is squatting in the middle.

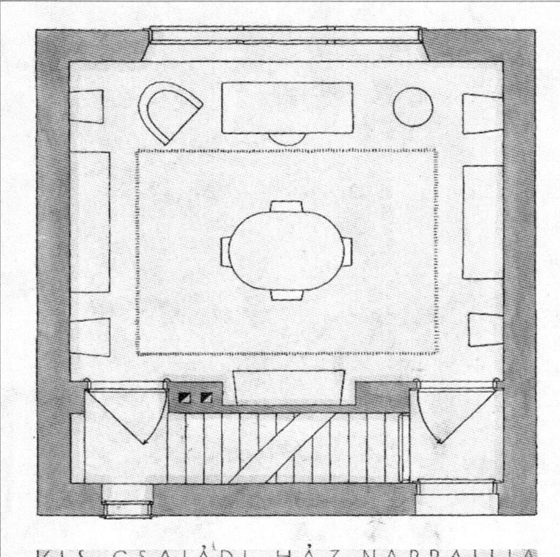

KIS CSALÁDI HÁZ NAPPALIJA
FALAK FEHÉRRE MESZELVE,
AJTÓK, ABLAKOK ZÖLDRE MÁ
ZOLVA, BÚTOROK DIÓFÁBOL
FURNIROZVA AMERIKAI
TÖLGYFAPADLÓVAL ÜLÖ
BÚTOROK KÉK RIPSZ HU
ZATTAL. LÉPTÉK 1:50 TERV.
HAAR FERENC 3. B.T. 1926

An example of Francis' work from school, 1926

on the buildings that were being designed at the office, photographing the construction sites and so on. Not long afterward, during my third year with the architectural firm, there was a shortage of work and several of us were dismissed. While I was able to find occasional work in architectural design, all my spare time was spent experimenting with images. I became more and more engrossed with my photographic work, having purchased a better camera, a 9×12 Voigt-lander. With my background as an architectural designer, I knew how to photograph buildings from the most advantageous angle, and soon I was working for other architects—this time as a photographer. The work was a great pleasure to me. I really enjoyed the feeling of being involved from right at the beginning all the way to the end, from the taking of the picture through the developing, print-ing, enlarging, and mounting.

I began to show my pictures around and met a writer who was planning a book on the traditional architecture of Budapest. For those not familiar with that ancient city, until 1872, when bridges first spanned the Danube, Budapest was split into two parts. The district called "Pest" (p. 35) is flat and is the govern-mental and business center of the city, but "Buda" is situated on several wooded hills that descend to the banks of the Danube (p. 34). The Royal Palace is located in Buda, along with many beautiful old buildings and cathedrals. These were to be the focus of the book.

We discussed the project and agreed I should do the photographic work. *Budapest*, my first professional assignment, came out in 1933 and was very successful.

As I became more involved with the artists' group Munka Kör I began to meet others who were captivated by photography. I proposed that we present a collection of our work in a group exhibit. Together with Lajos Kassák, the leader of Munka Kör, we selected the thirty best photographs for the exhibit. A writer as well as a modern painter, Kassák had great insight into contemporary art, liked what he saw, and decided to publish our pictures. This book, for which Kassák wrote the foreword, was titled *A Mi Életünkből* (From Our Lives).

On the opening day of the group exhibit, a friend and fellow artist, Ernö Shubert, invited his girlfriend, Relli, to the show. She came from Vác, a small town outside Budapest, and brought along her younger sister, Irene. I walked Irene around the exhibit and was immediately attracted to this vivacious young girl of eighteen. Her questions and sensitive comments impressed me. After she returned home, I wrote asking when I might see her again. In response, she wrote that Relli would soon marry my friend Shubert and they would live in Budapest, where she planned to visit them often. I was very happy to learn this.

In the summer, our group had a favorite spot on the shore of the Danube. It was located about halfway to the town where Ernö Shubert and the girls lived.

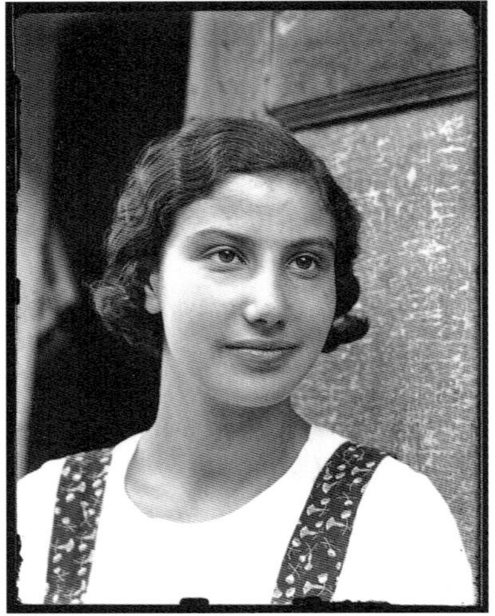

Irene at eighteen, 1930

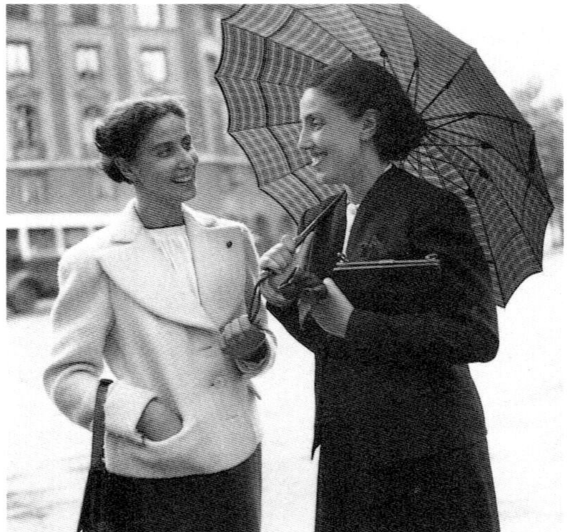

Irene (left) and her sister Relli

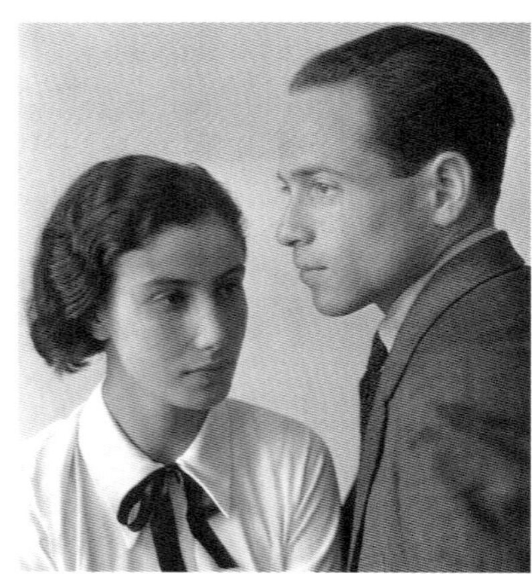

Studio portrait of Francis and Irene taken by their friend Lajos Lengyel

They often went boating on the weekends, somehow managing to drift down to our little beach. In this way, Irene and I could meet and get to know each other.

Francis was drafted into the army in June 1931 and was sent to Györ [120 km west of Budapest]. During his two years of training, we corresponded often and also met a couple of times when I visited my relatives nearby.

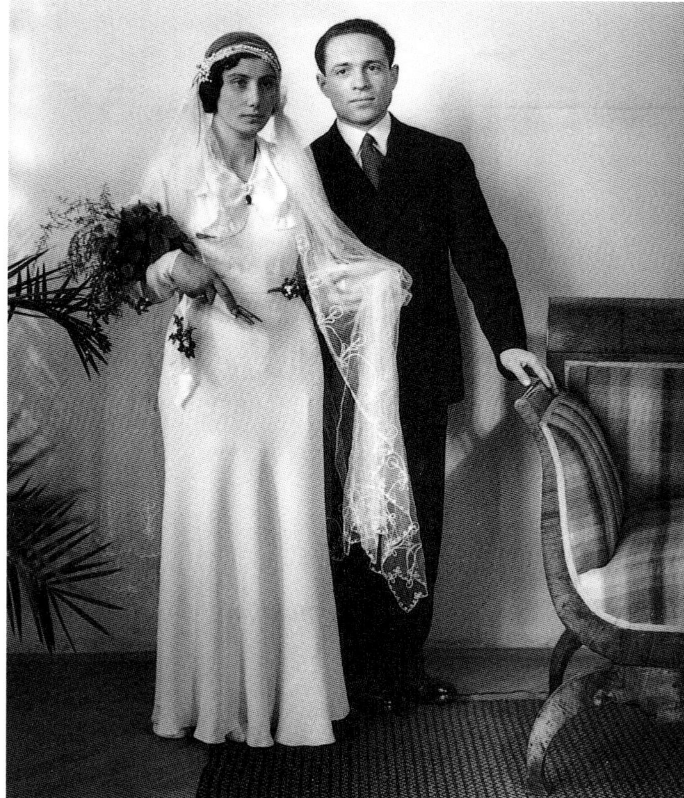

Wedding day, 1934

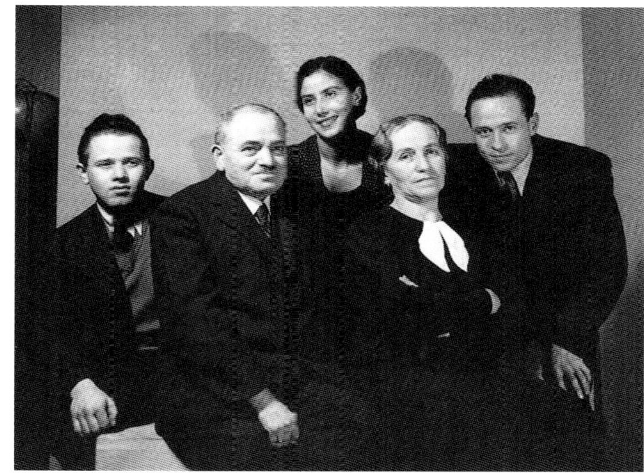

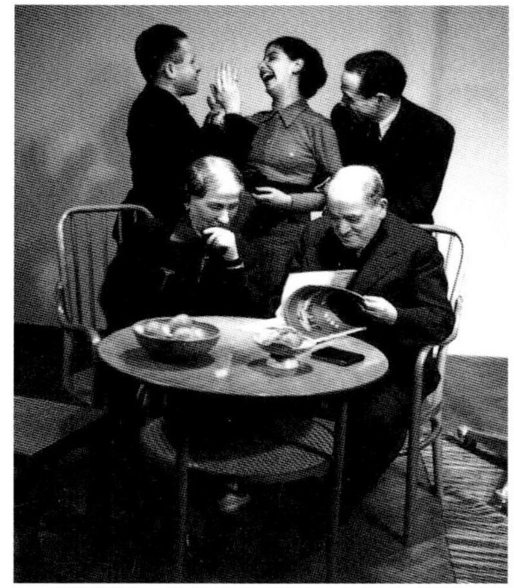

Family portraits (above and top right) with Francis' brother Istvan and their parents, Arnold and Adél, before Francis and Irene left for Paris, in the fall of 1937

Our friendship, which began with a simple exchange of letters, quickly developed into a serious love affair. As it turned out, another close friend, a graphic designer named Lajos Lengyel, was attracted to a third sister in the family, and within a relatively short period, three friends married three girls from the same family.

Francis took many photographs of me. I was so happy and proud to be his model. The pictures were published in newspapers and magazines. One of them, called "Sunbathing," became famous. It was just my head, with two leaves covering my eyes—that's what I used to do when I was sunbathing. Later, in 1940, it appeared as the cover photo for U.S. Camera.

Irene and I were married in 1934. We rented a small, one-room apartment in downtown Pest, where I managed to do my darkroom work in the bathroom. Our first year of married life was full of hardship, but we were devoted to each other and believed our love and idealism were enough to overcome any difficulty. Irene became my first assistant. We jumped at every opportunity to earn money, including entering a poster contest to promote tourism. To our great joy and excitement, we won the third prize of five hundred *pengo* [about $100, roughly equivalent to $1,000 today], which seemed like a fortune in those days.

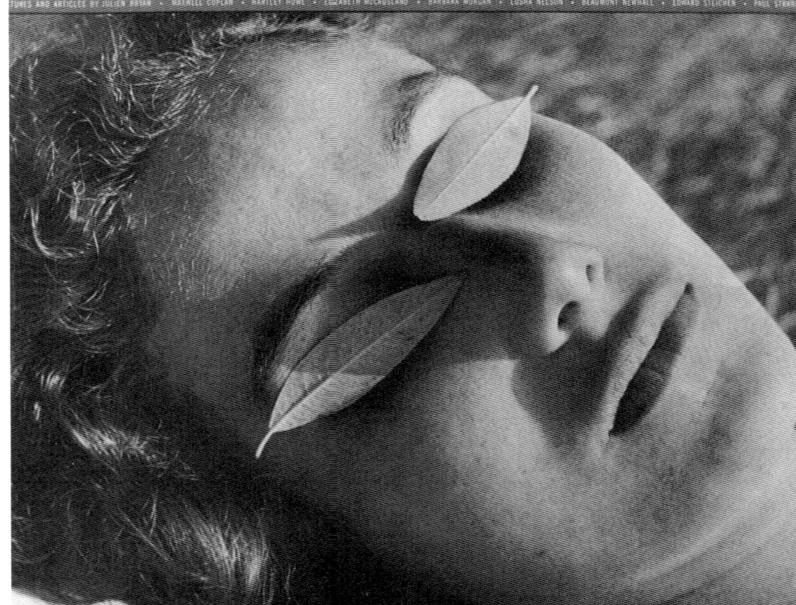

Irene Sunbathing, 1936
One of Francis Haar's best-known images, this picture of his wife sunbathing with leaves covering her eyes was taken at Lake Balaton in Hungary. It appeared on the cover of U.S. Camera magazine in 1940.

▶

Chocolate, 1936, and Tobacco, 1936
Commercial still-life photography illustrating Hungarian graphic arts and packaging

View of Pest, 1936
At the outset of his career as a professional photographer, Francis won first prize in a national photo contest for this shot taken from the tower of the basilica in Pest.

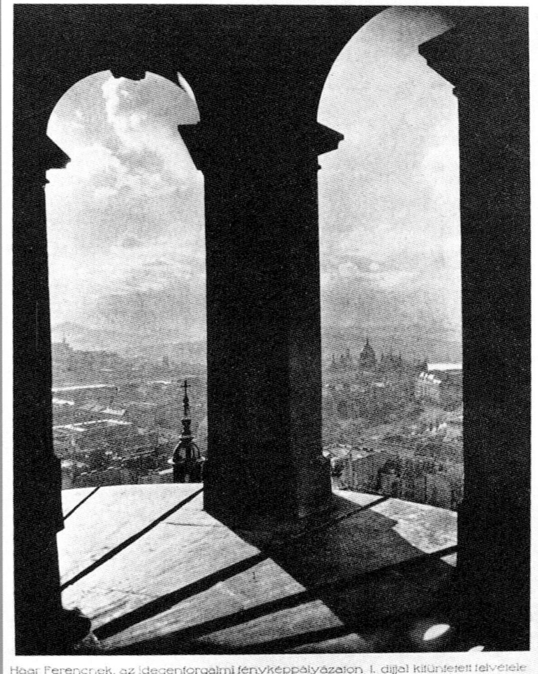

Near the end of our first year together, a prominent architect named Lajos Kozma called to tell me about an elderly lady friend of his, Olga Mate. She was a well-known portrait photographer who was planning to retire and was looking for a young photographer to take over her studio; Kozma had recommended me. I needed no further encouragement and visited her the very next day, portfolio in hand.

Her beautiful, large studio was located on the top floor of an imposing building in the center of the city, an excellent location. She liked my work, and when I told her I was a National Academy graduate, she agreed in principle that I was the right person to take over her studio. Because I was not a licensed photographer, which used to be a professional requirement in Hungary, she agreed to employ me as an apprentice for a year until I could pass the examination.

During my apprenticeship, I worked hard on portrait and advertising assignments and also entered two national photo contests. Both photos, one a view of the Danube and the other a bird's-eye view of Pest, were awarded first prize. At the end of the year, I took the exam. It was a rigorous two-day affair, an ordeal I suspect is rare nowadays. For the practical part of the exam, I had to pose a model, set the lighting, expose and develop the negative, then retouch the face and finally make an enlargement. The theoretical test was even more grueling, as I had to answer questions about optical science, about all the different kinds of cameras, shutters, and lenses, and about photo chemistry. Fortunately, I was well prepared and passed, becoming a Master of Photography and a member of the Hungarian Professional Photographer's Society. Most important, the certificate permitted me to operate the studio.

It also allowed me to enter a major portrait photography contest. I decided to submit an unretouched portrait of a peasant woman, her face heavily lined from age (p. 13). I fully expected my photograph to be rejected by the conservative panel of judges, who in those days were accustomed to viewing work where the wrinkles had been removed by retouching the negative. To my great surprise, my more realistic style was accepted, and I was awarded the bronze medal.

Soon after I began working as a professional photographer, I received a series of government tourist promotion assignments, which helped establish my name. One was to photograph the annual yacht races on beautiful Lake Balaton. I was also asked to depict the Hortobágy, the great plain of northwestern Hungary (pp. 20–25), and the villages of Kisber and Bábolna, where the best horses in Hungary were bred (pp. 18–19)

Some of Hungary's leading art directors began to take note of my work. One of them, Charles Rosner, was also a correspondent for the prestigious British art magazine *Studio*, for which he put together a photo essay on my work. Following the publication of this article, he asked me to shoot the work of leading Hungarian graphic designers to illustrate his article about Hungarian graphic arts and packaging. Commercial still-life photography was a new field for me, and my approach therefore was uninhibited and experimental, which produced some interesting

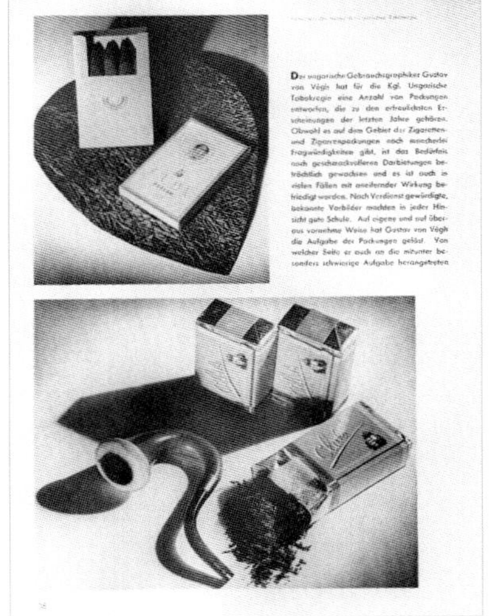

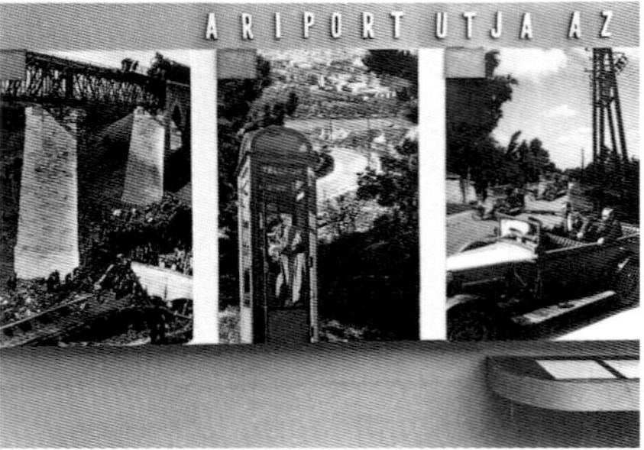
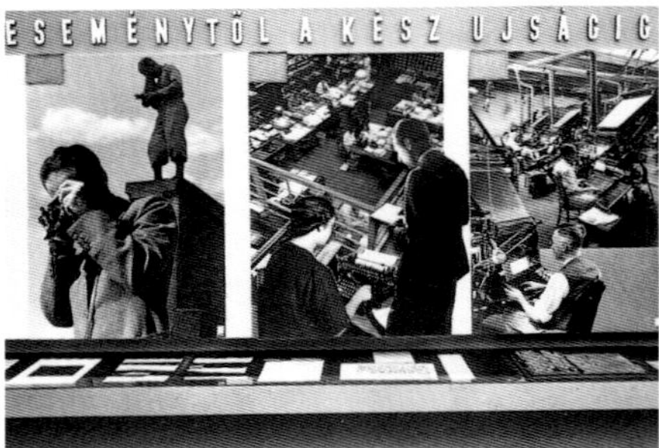
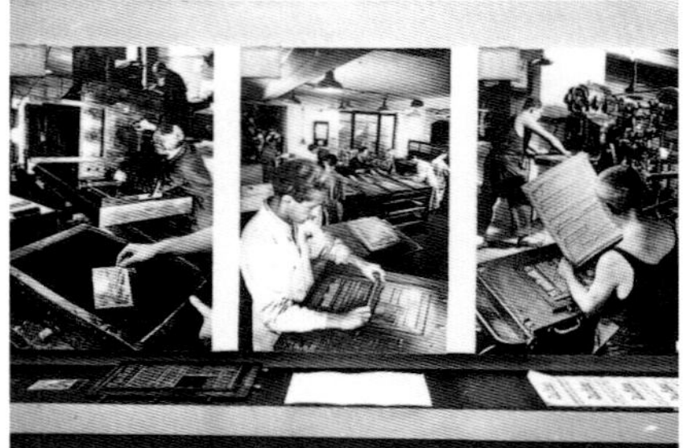
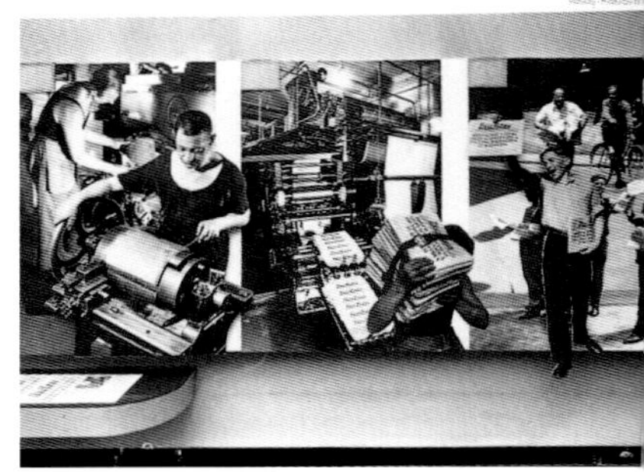

National Printing Exhibit, 1936

Four giant panels were prepared

by the Haars for a major exhibition.

results. The illustrated article was published in two London magazines, *Commercial Art* and *Art and Industry*. Irene and I soon learned that the Victoria and Albert Museum wanted to purchase two of the photographs for their permanent collection. My career was on the move.

My next project was for a National Printing Exhibit, designed to present all the different printing processes in one of the largest exhibit halls in Budapest. I won this major assignment in the face of stiff competition. I was awed by the scale of the work. It required me to photograph huge papermaking, typesetting, and printing machines. Then I enlarged the negatives to mural-size prints, some as large as 3×6 feet, and made composite images.

Irene and I worked for six full months to produce all the pictures needed for the exhibit. As the day of the opening drew closer we were working around the clock to meet the deadline. While one of us rested a few hours the other washed the oversized pictures in the bathtub. The exhibit was a great success, but we were completely exhausted. We went to Lake Balaton for a week to recuperate.

When we returned, the Foreign Ministry notified me that they were preparing to participate in the 1937 Paris World's Fair and wanted to order mural-size enlargements of two of my prize-winning photographs for the Hungarian Pavilion. This was no problem for us following our experience with the National Printing Exhibit. After delivering the pictures, we decided to go to Paris ourselves, to see our work exhibited there.

What a wonderful trip! We took the train and stopped at Venice, Ventimillia, Monte Carlo, and Marseille before reaching Paris. We saw the vast blue beautiful ocean for the first time in our lives.

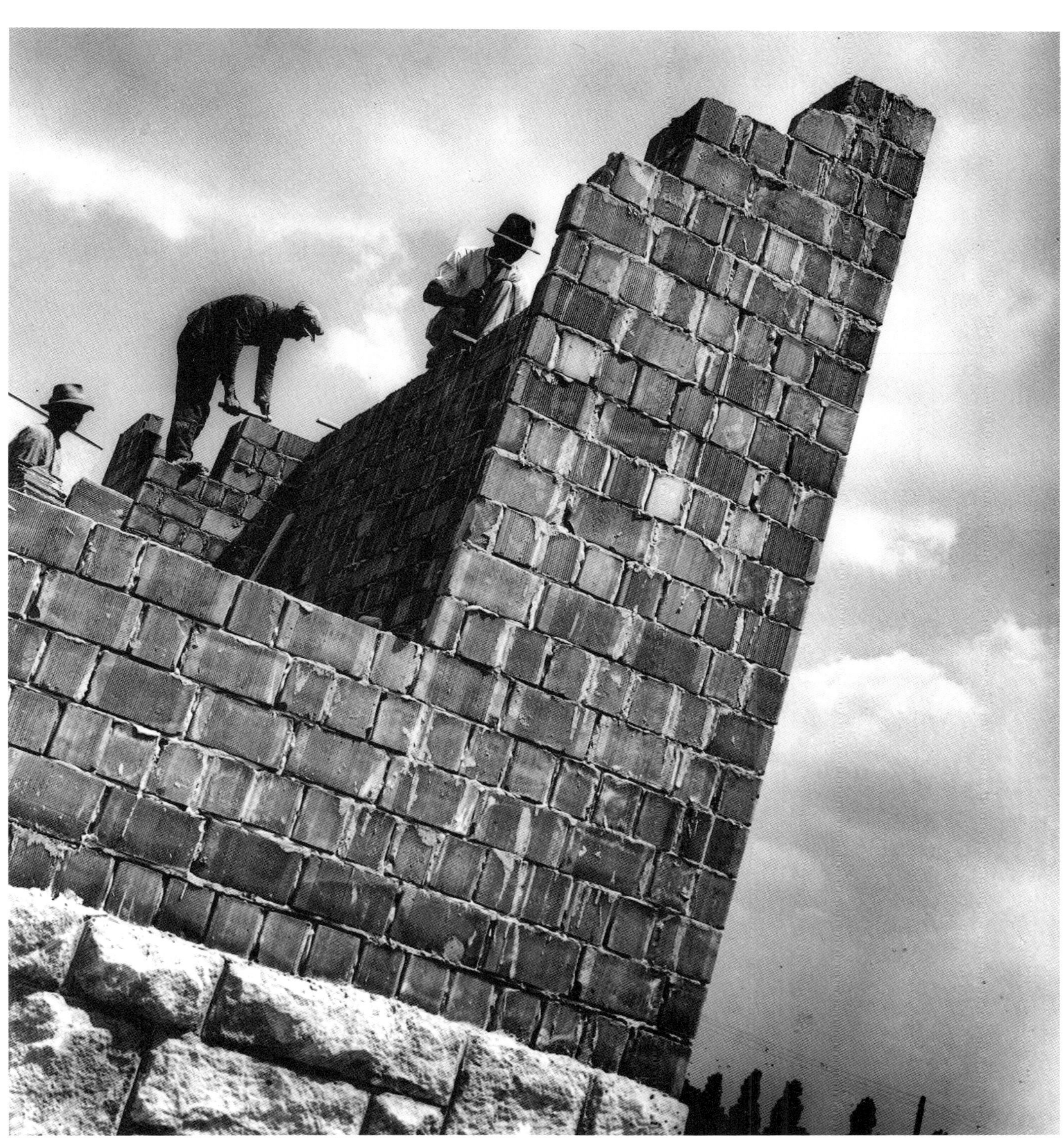

Bricklayers, 1930
One of my earlier photographs,
this was taken while I was
working as an architectural
designer.

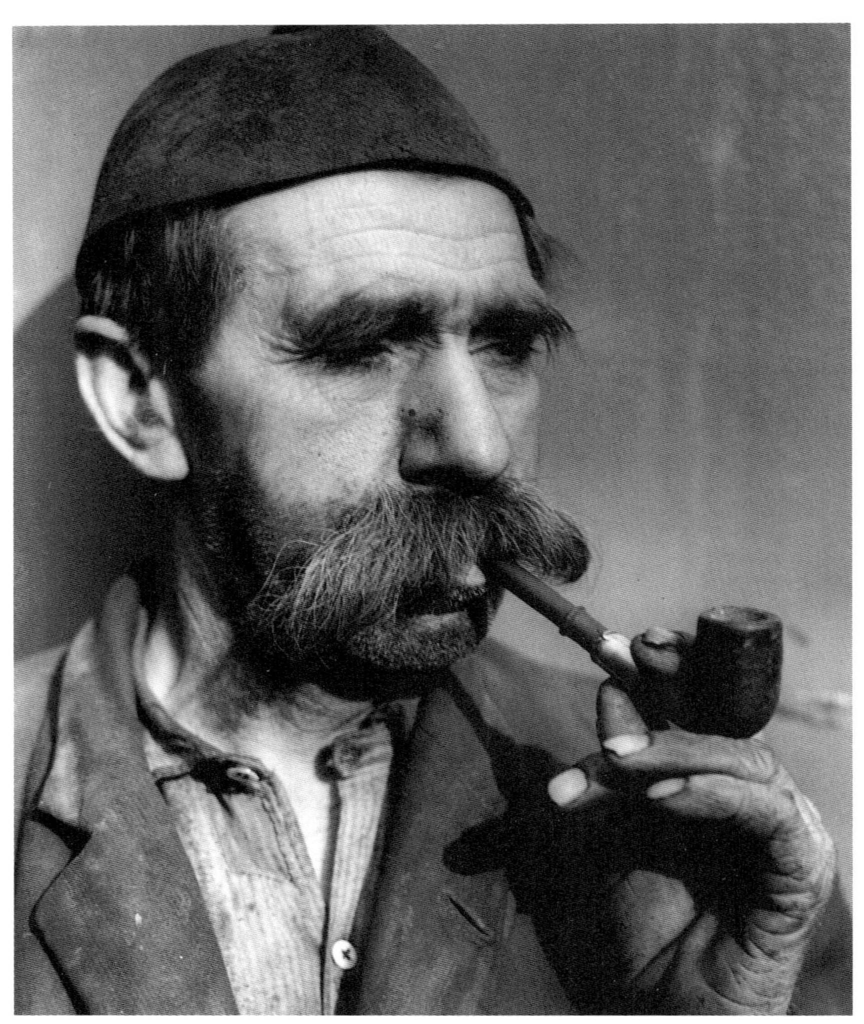

Foundry Worker, 1933
Sporting a bushy moustache,
the fashion of the times, a
worker in heavy industry is
captured in a contemplative
mood.

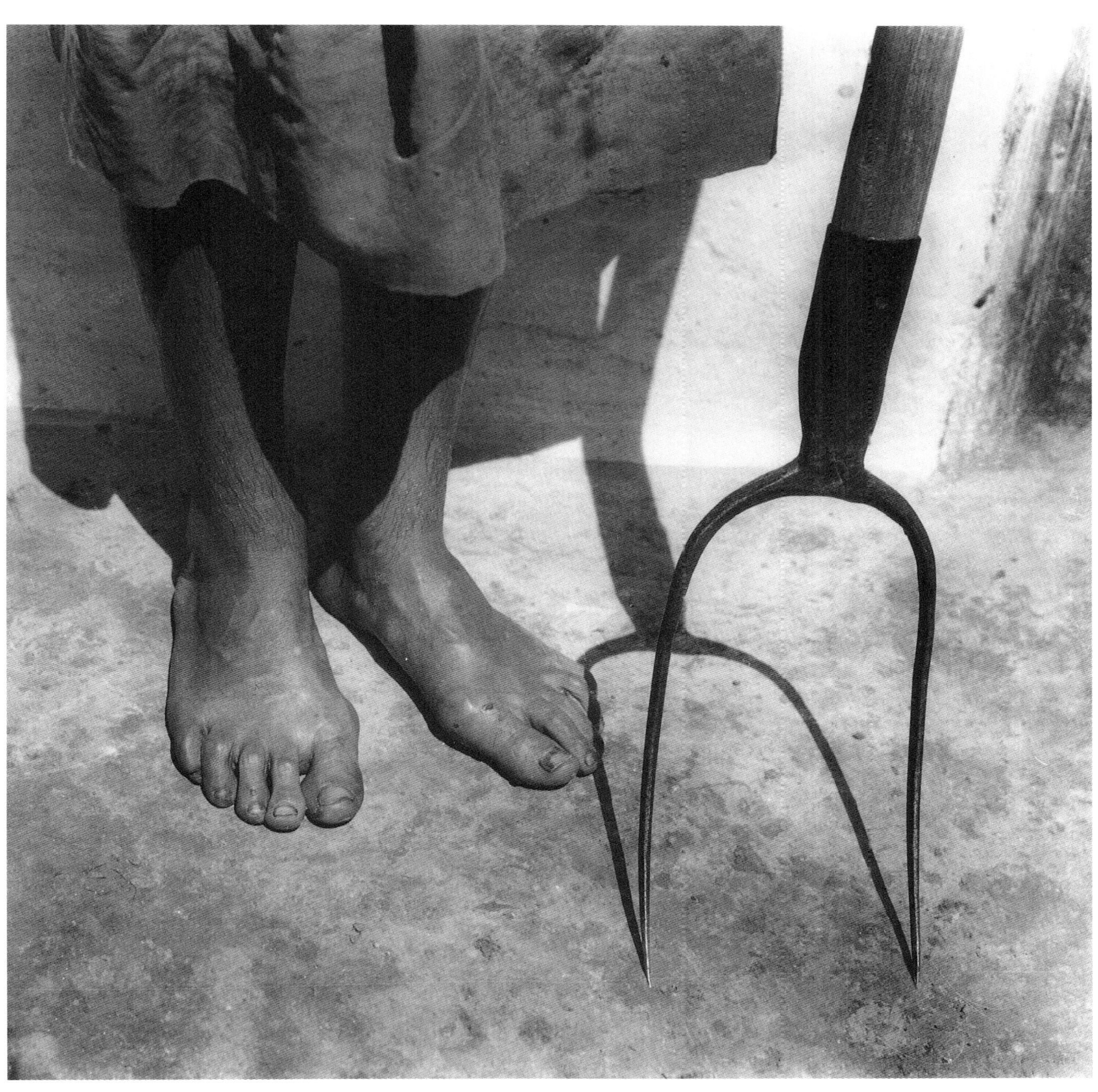

Field Worker, 1931

During my travels around the
Hungarian countryside, I took
many pictures that captured the
harsh reality of peasant life.

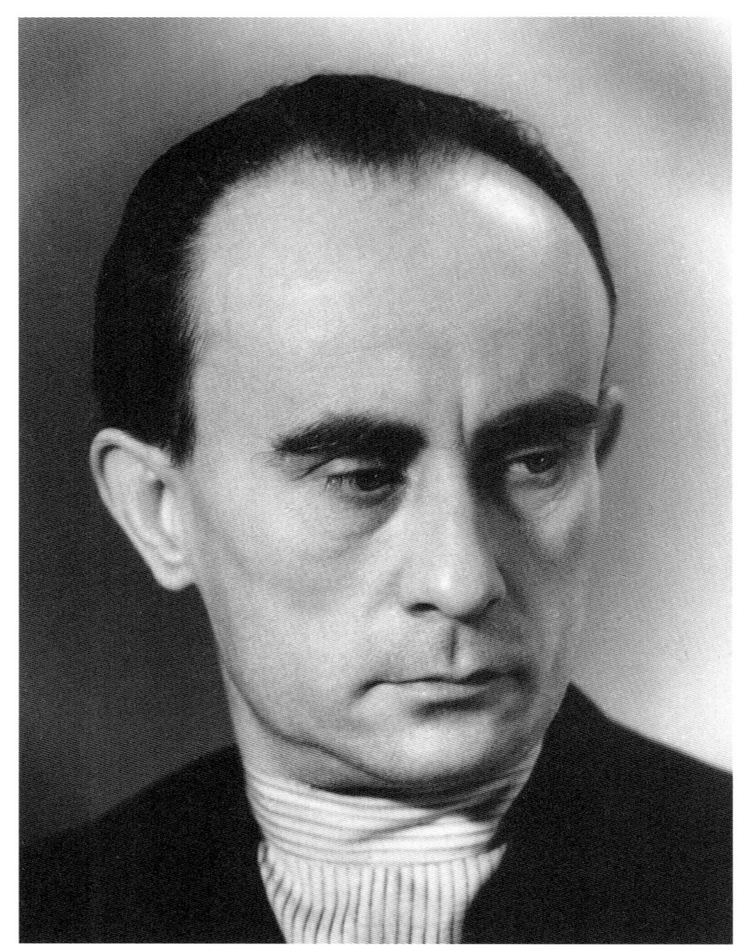

Lajos Kassák, 1936
An influential writer and painter,
Kassák organized the cultural
circle Munka Kör.

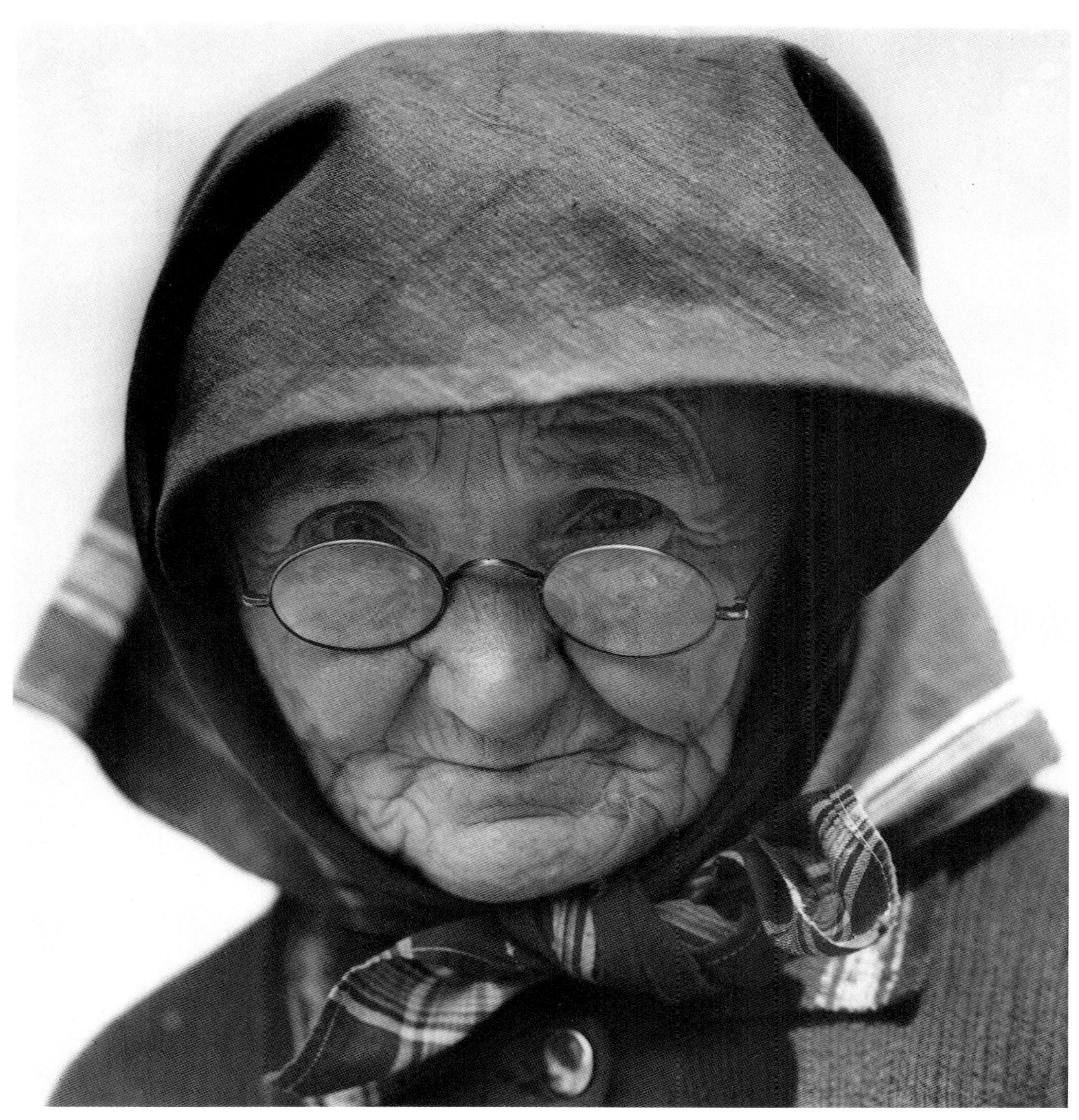

Village Grandmother, 1935

*In the 1930s, portraits were
often retouched, but for
this prize-winning photo,
I preferred the natural look.*

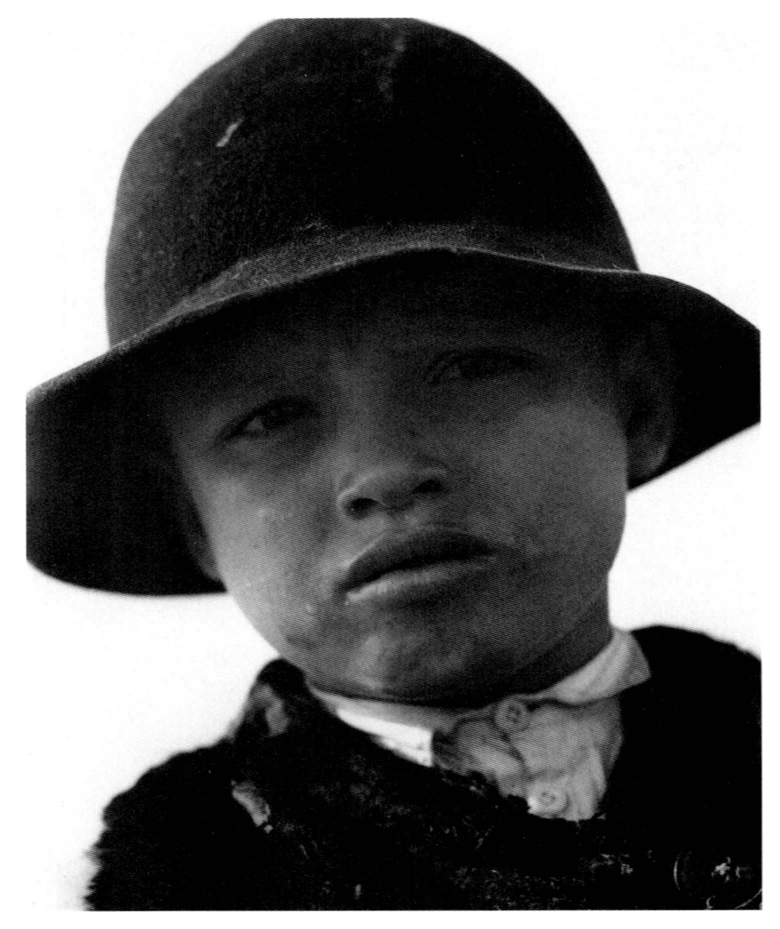

Peasant Boy, 1931

I met this boy when I was walking near Lake Balaton. As I started to talk to him I was impressed by the strong expression in his eyes.

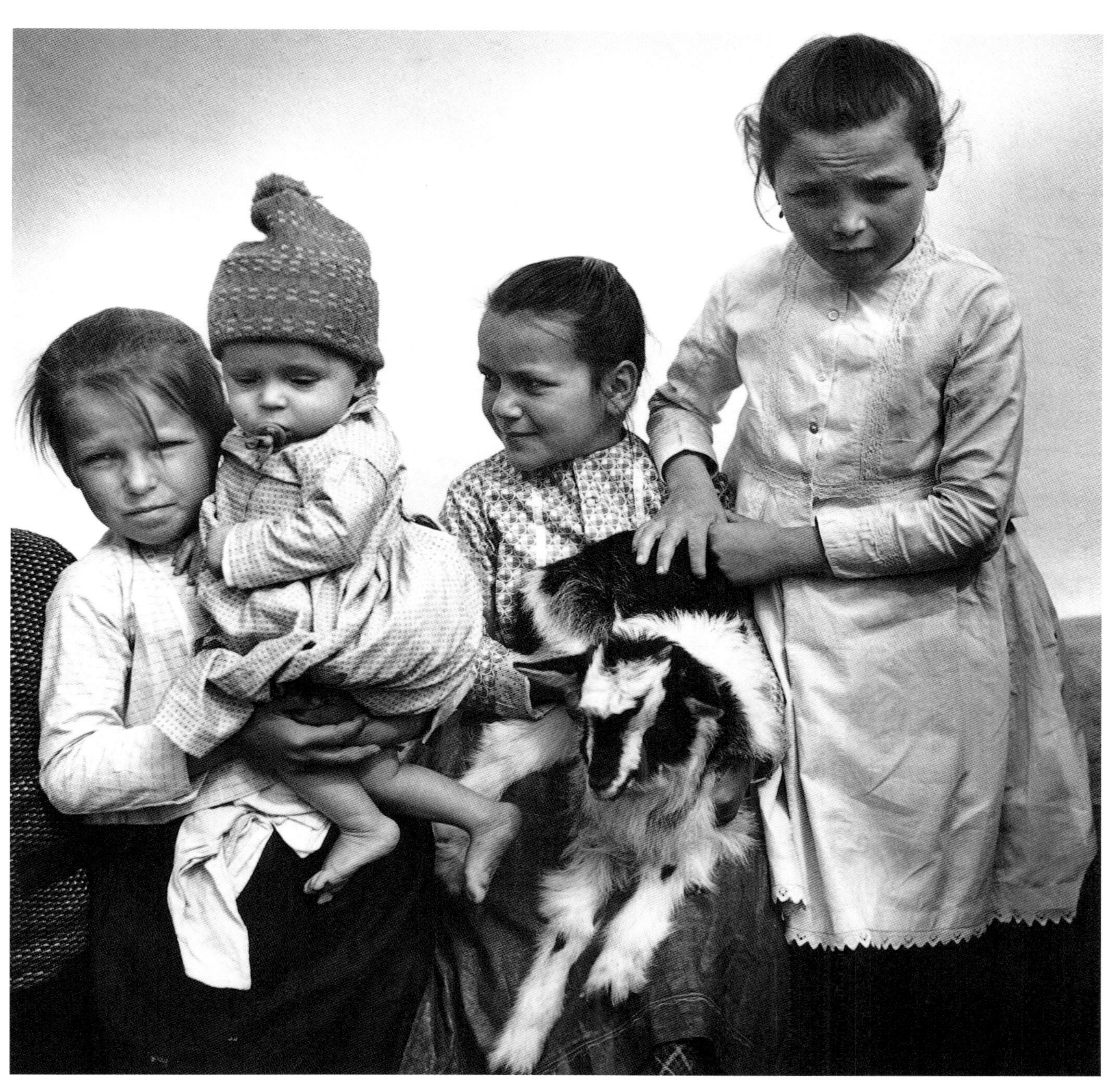

Children in Pilis, 1931
This group of village children
posed for me with their
pet goat.

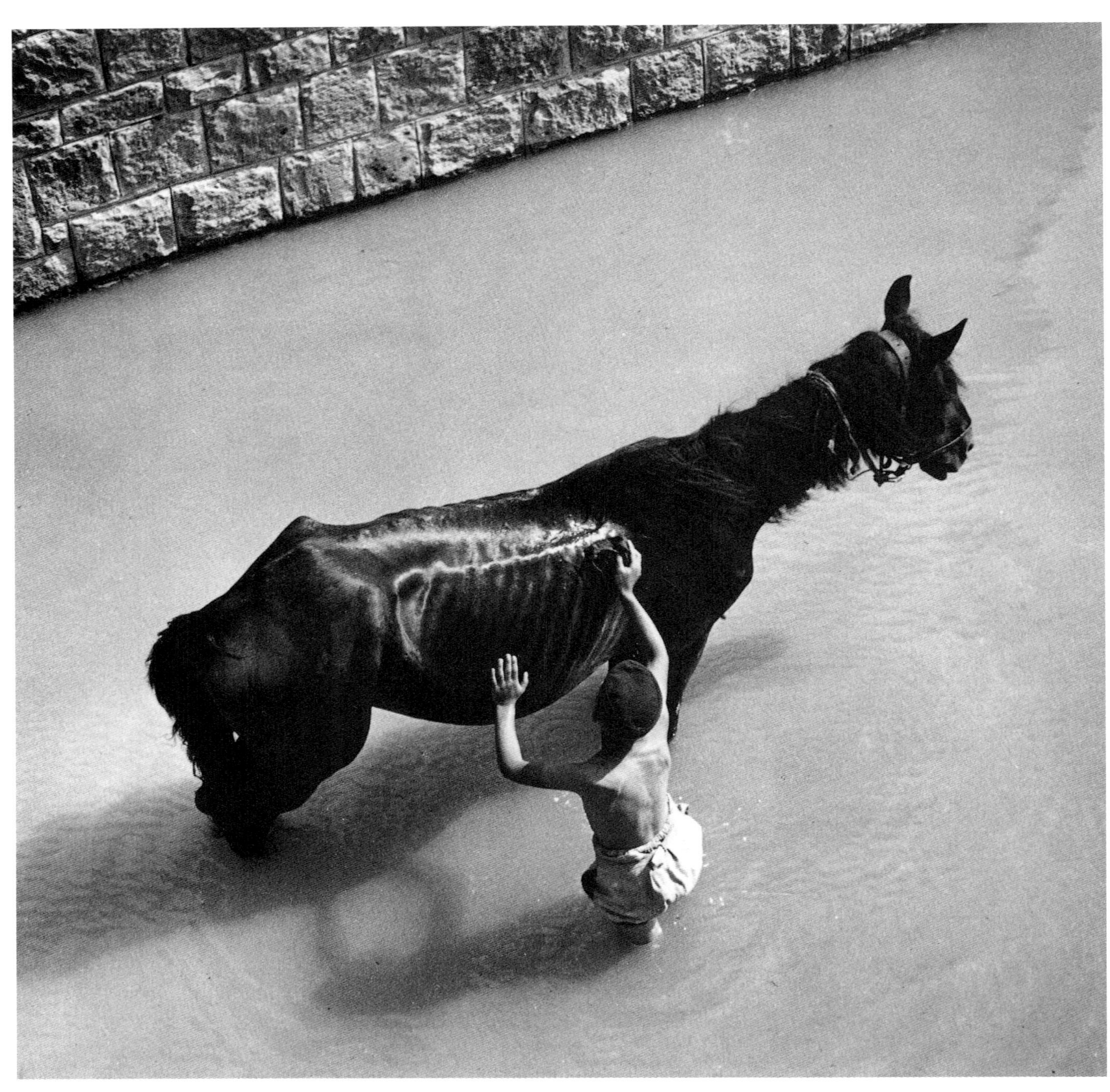

Washing the Horse, 1934
The economic hard times of
the mid-thirties in Europe are
captured in this photo of a
boy washing an old horse.

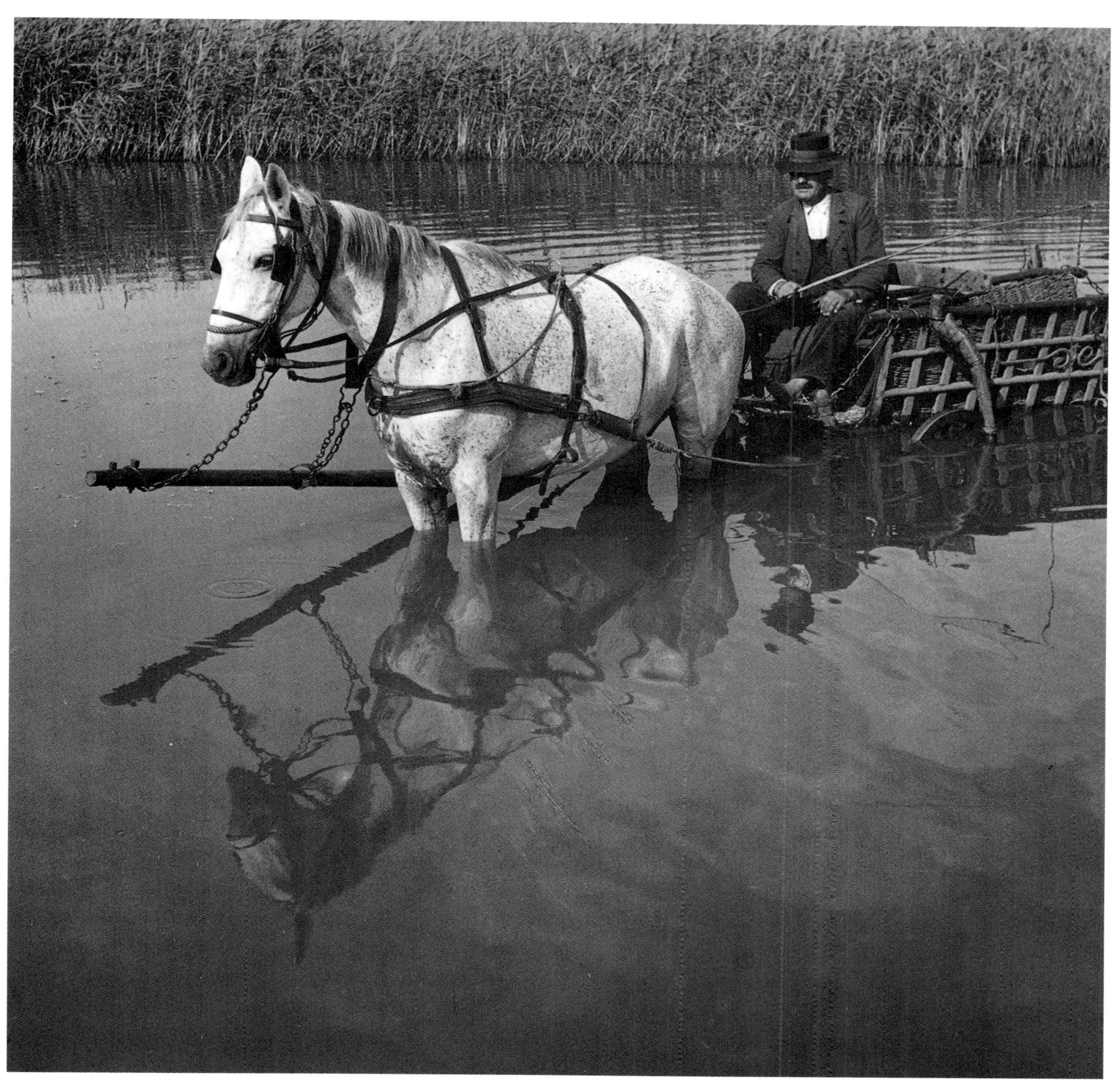

Cooling Off, 1934

*A considerate farmer lets his
horse enjoy the cool of a river
on a hot summer day.*

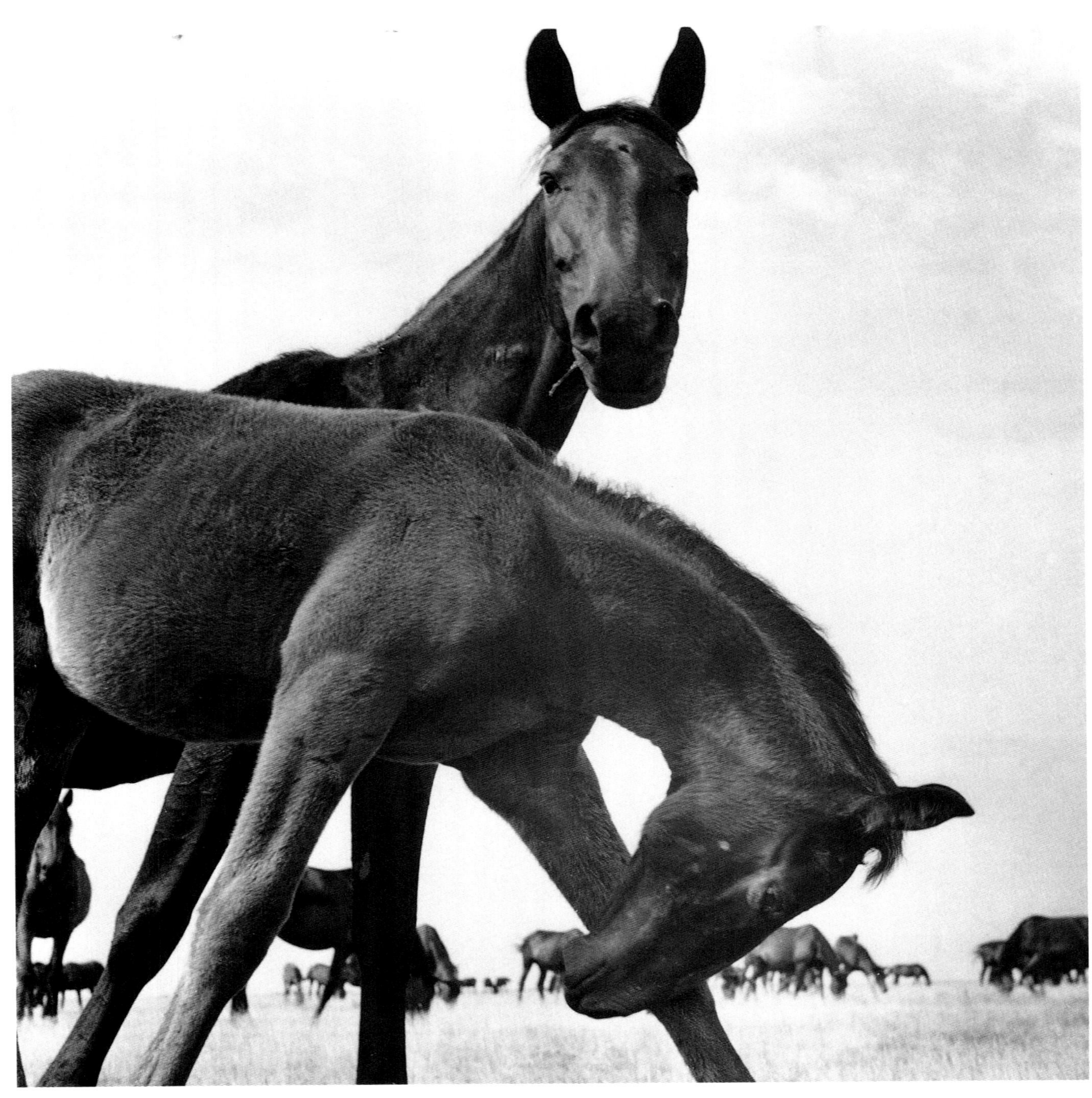

Colts at Hortobágy, 1935
One of my first assignments
as a licensed professional
photographer was to document
the life of the Hortobágy, where
the best horses in Hungary
were raised.

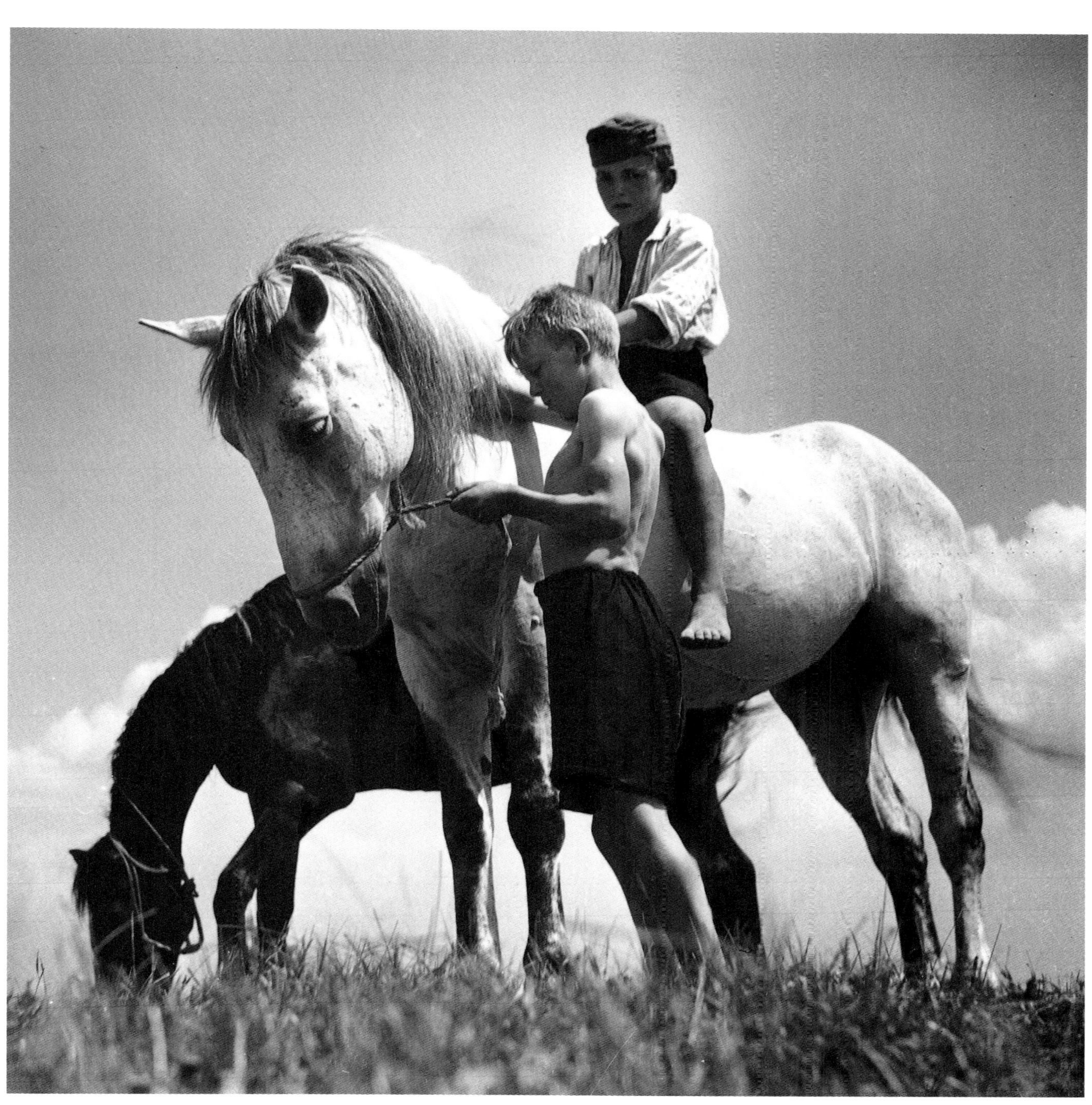

Boys with Horses, 1935

I found this idyllic scene of two
boys and their horses near a
small village.

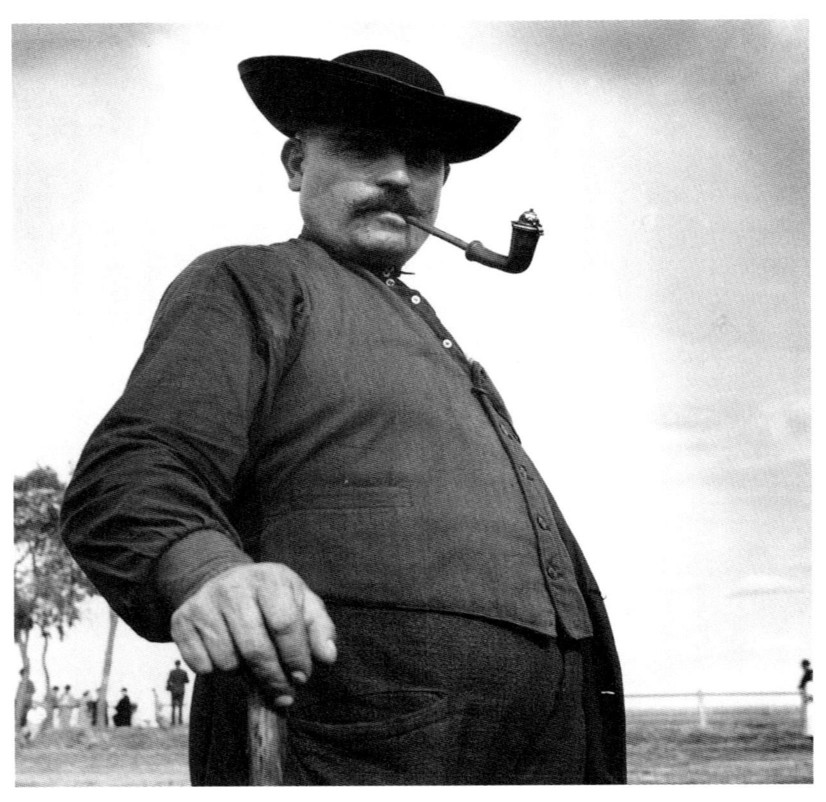

The Landlord, 1935

*A village landlord with traditional
headgear was out supervising
the workers on his farm.*

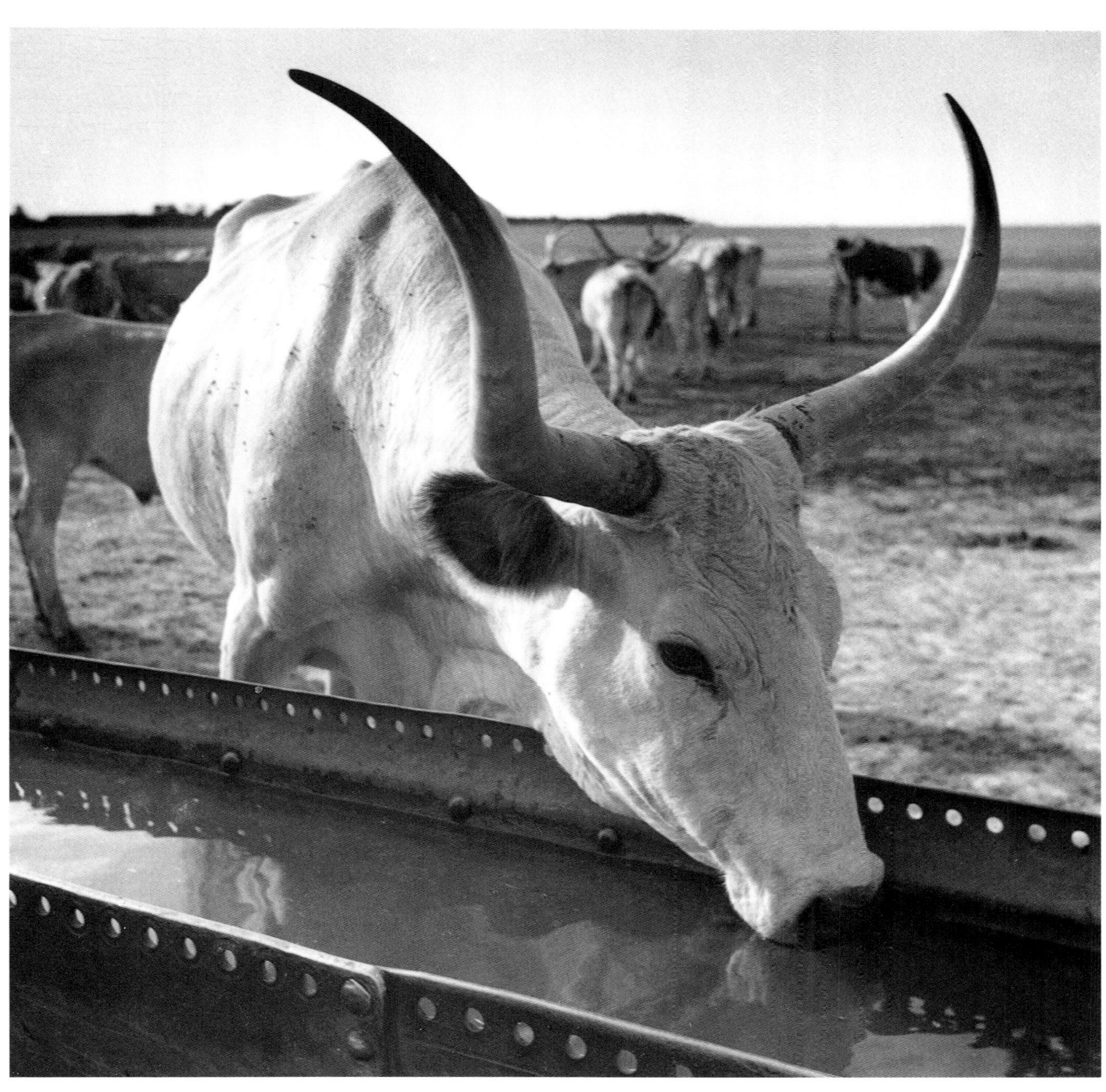

Hungarian Longhorn, 1935

Hungarian Longhorns roam
the wide Hortobágy plain
all year-round.

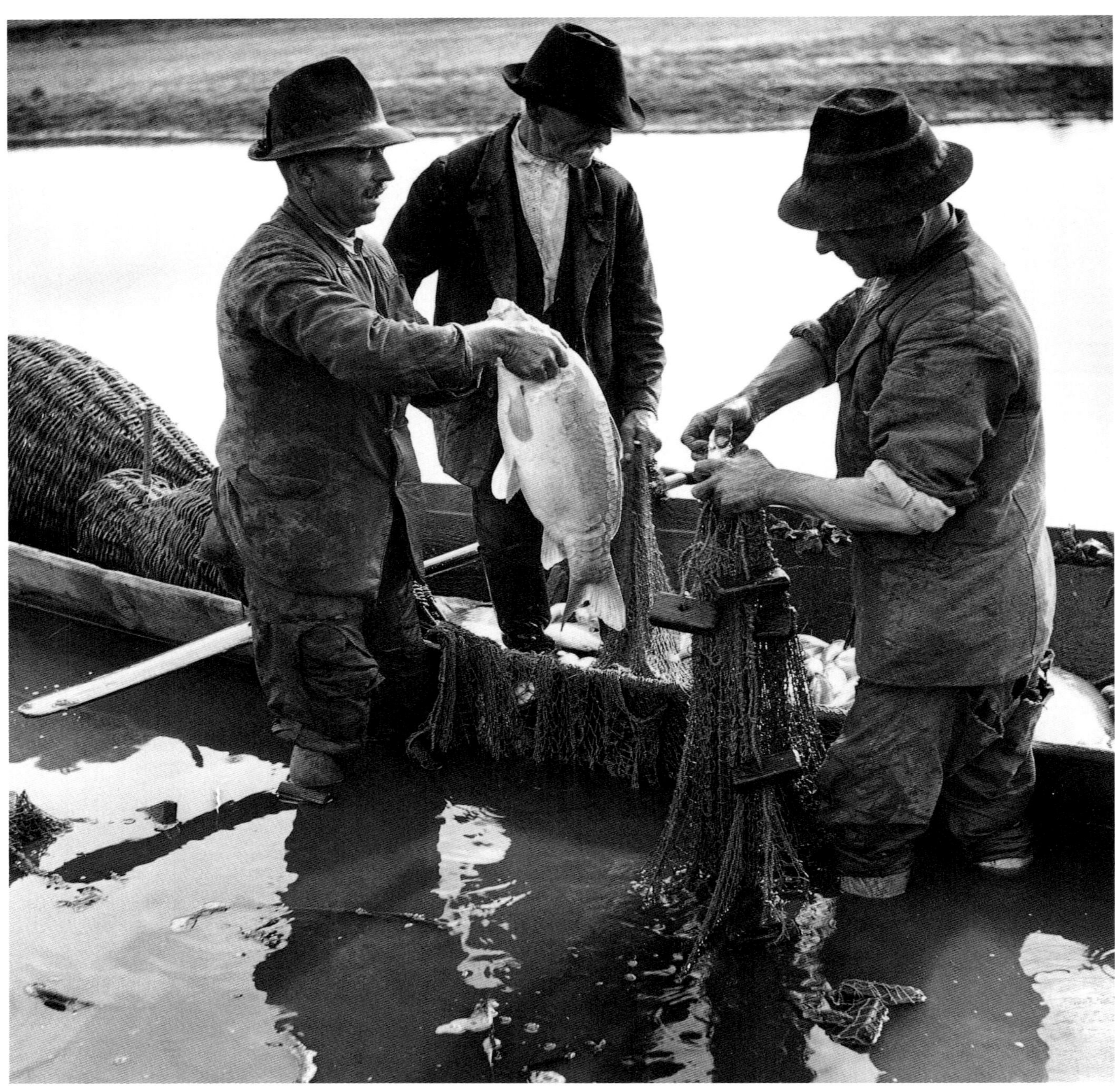

Carp Fishing, 1935

A river in Hortobágy yields

a healthy catch.

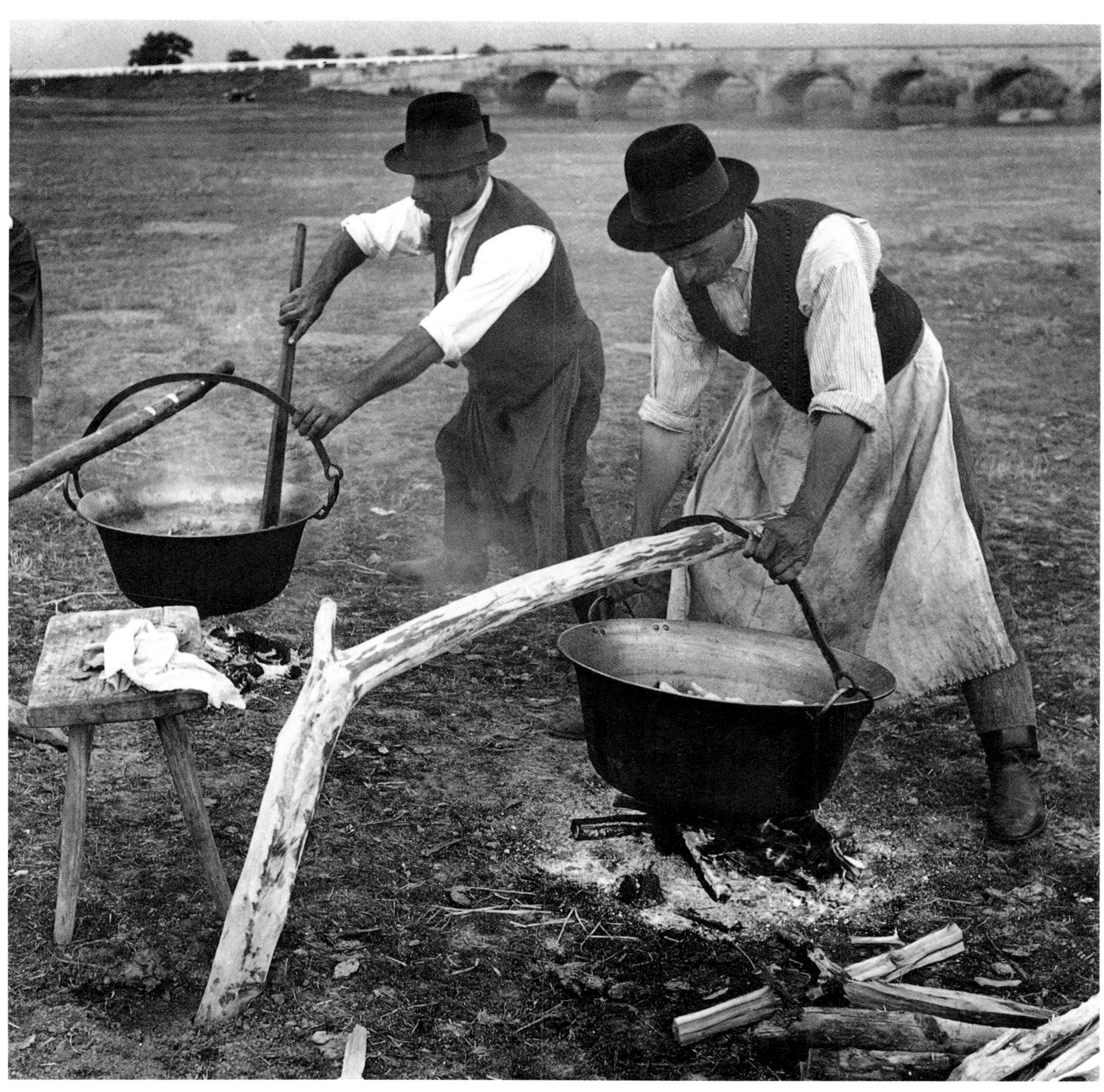

*Herdsmen Cooking Gulyás
(Goulash), 1935*
*In those days, men kept their hats
on even when preparing the evening
meal. The famous Hortobágy Nine-
Arch Bridge is in the background.*

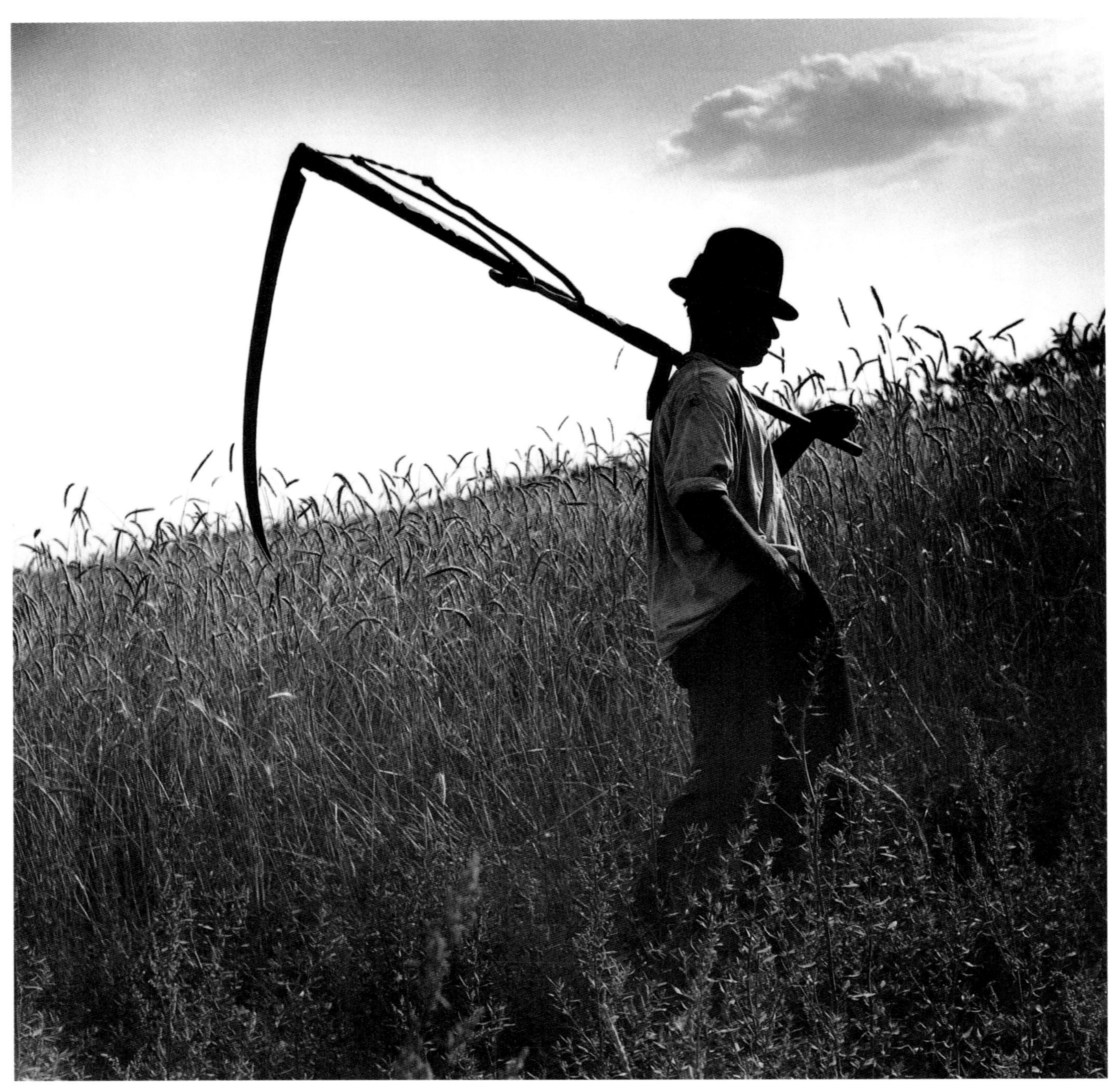

The End of the Day, 1935
A field hand returns home
with his sickle after a day
in the field. All farm work
was done with hand tools
at this time.

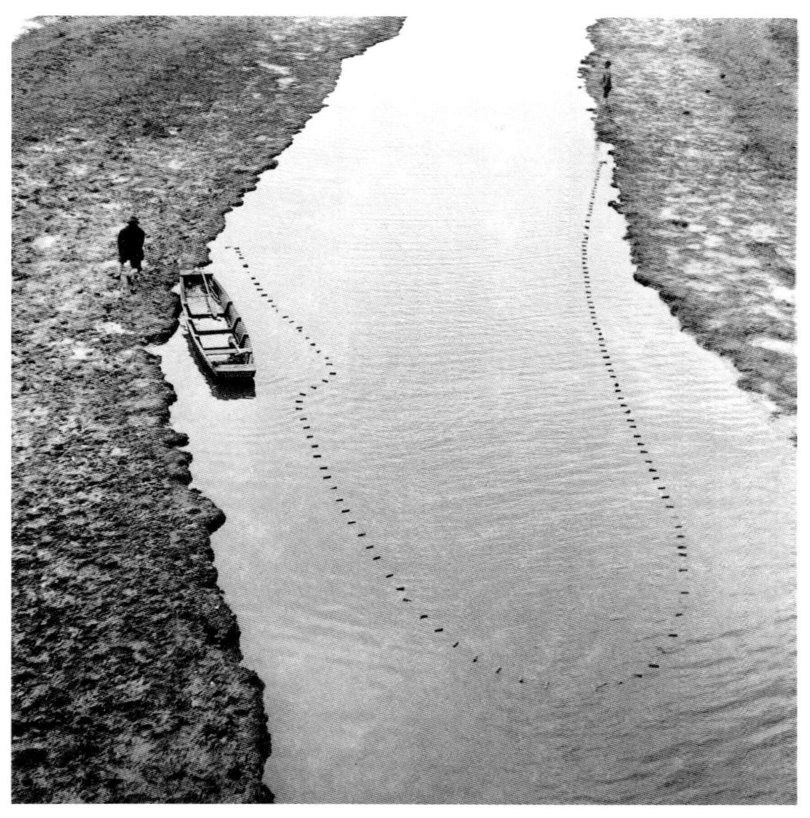

River Fishing, Hortobágy, 1935

A fisherman checks his net.

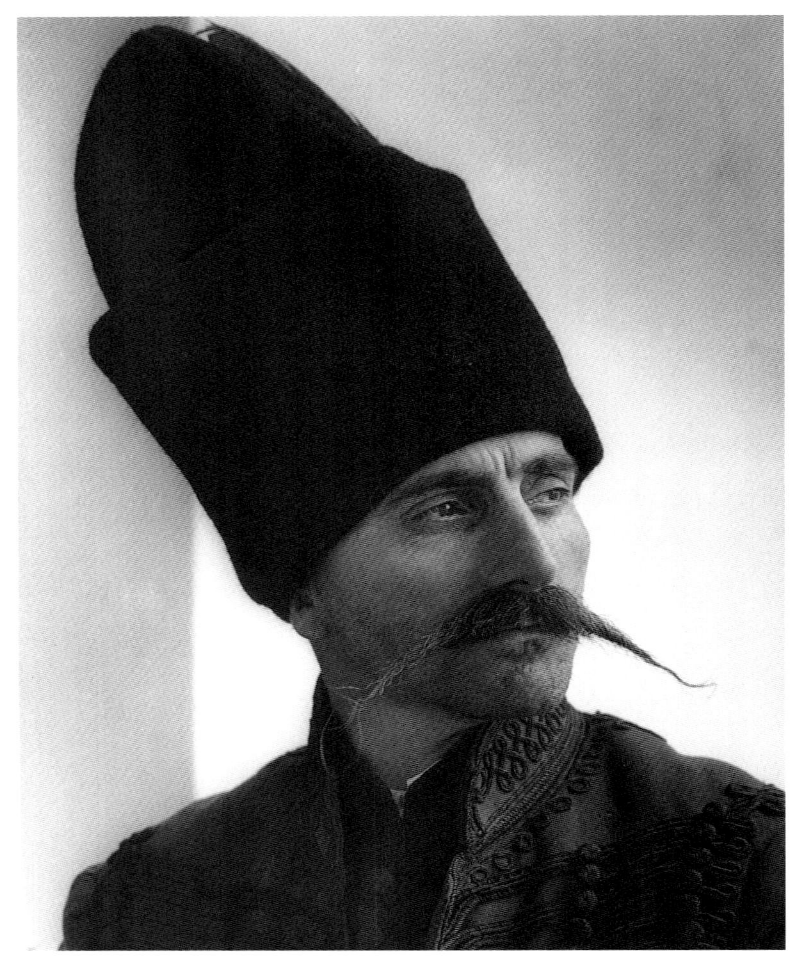

Man in Hun Suveg Hat, 1936
I asked the custodian of a
restored Hungarian village in
Halas to pose for me. I was
as much impressed by the
swirling moustaches of my
model as by the braiding
on his jacket.

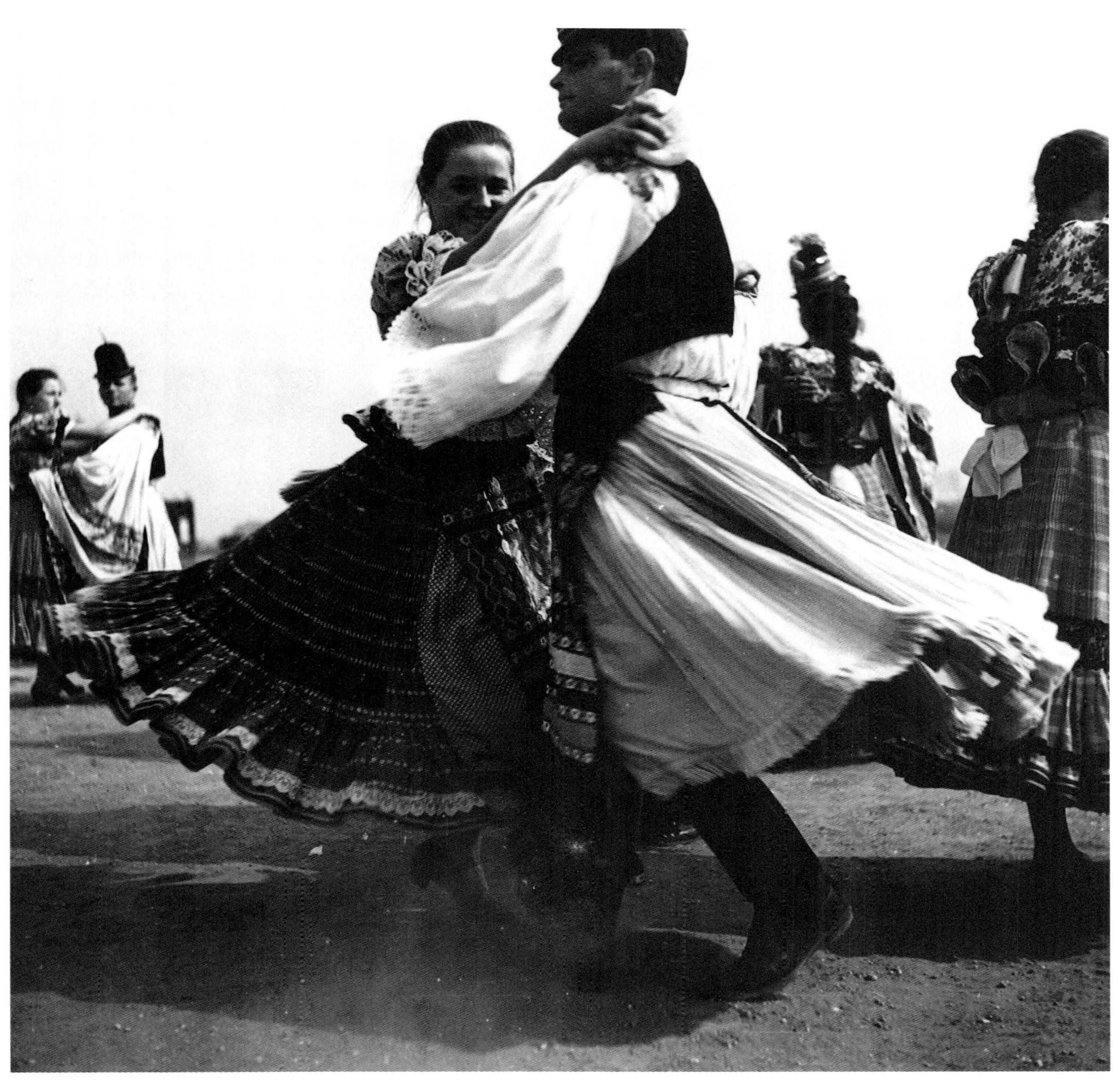

Csardas, 1936

*Csardas, the famous Hungarian
folk dance, is being performed
by the Gyöngös Bokreta
Dancers, members of a touring
professional dance troupe.*

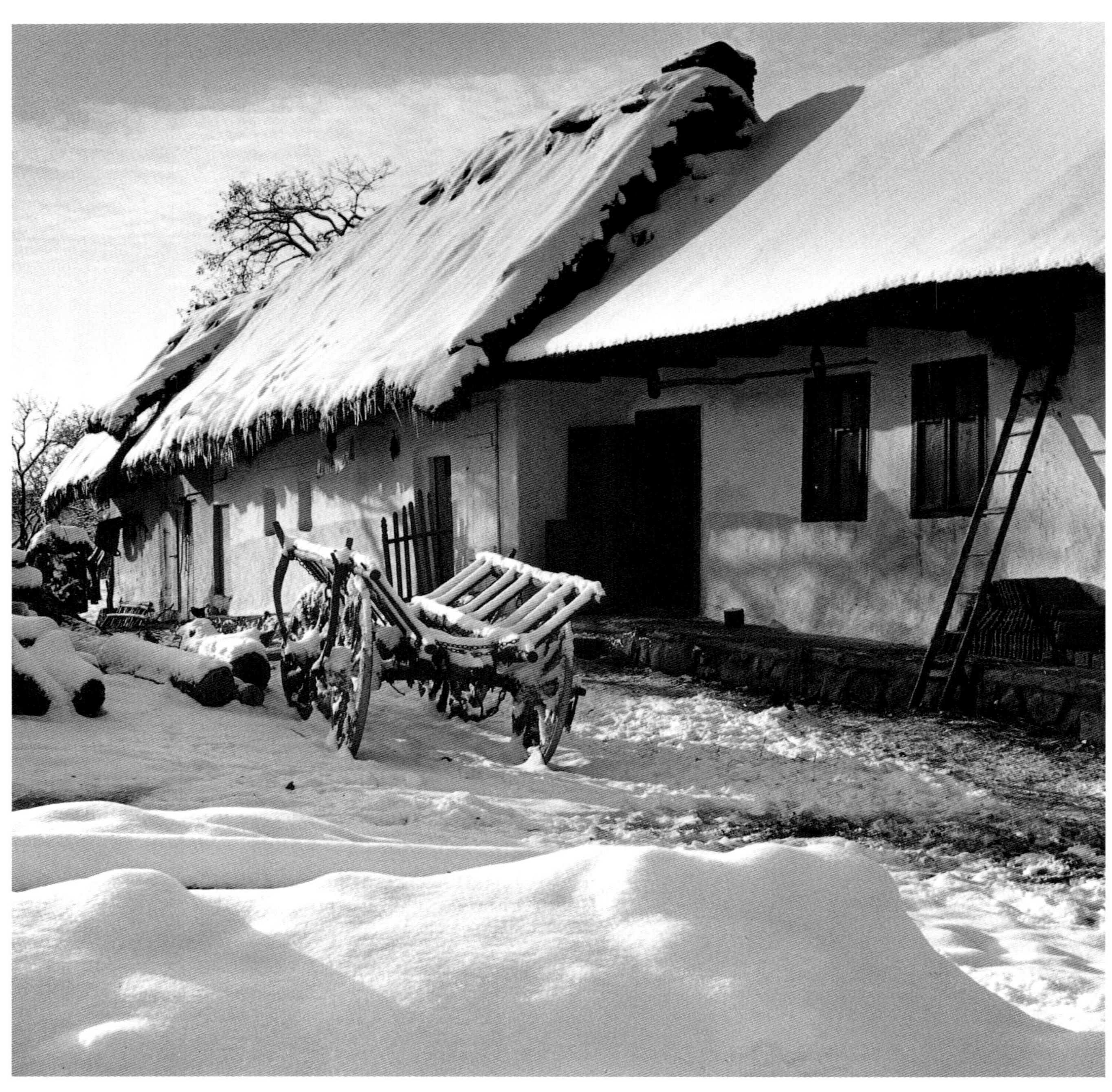

Winter in the Village, 1935
Icicles dangle from a thatched-
roof farmhouse as a horse-
drawn wagon rests in the snow.

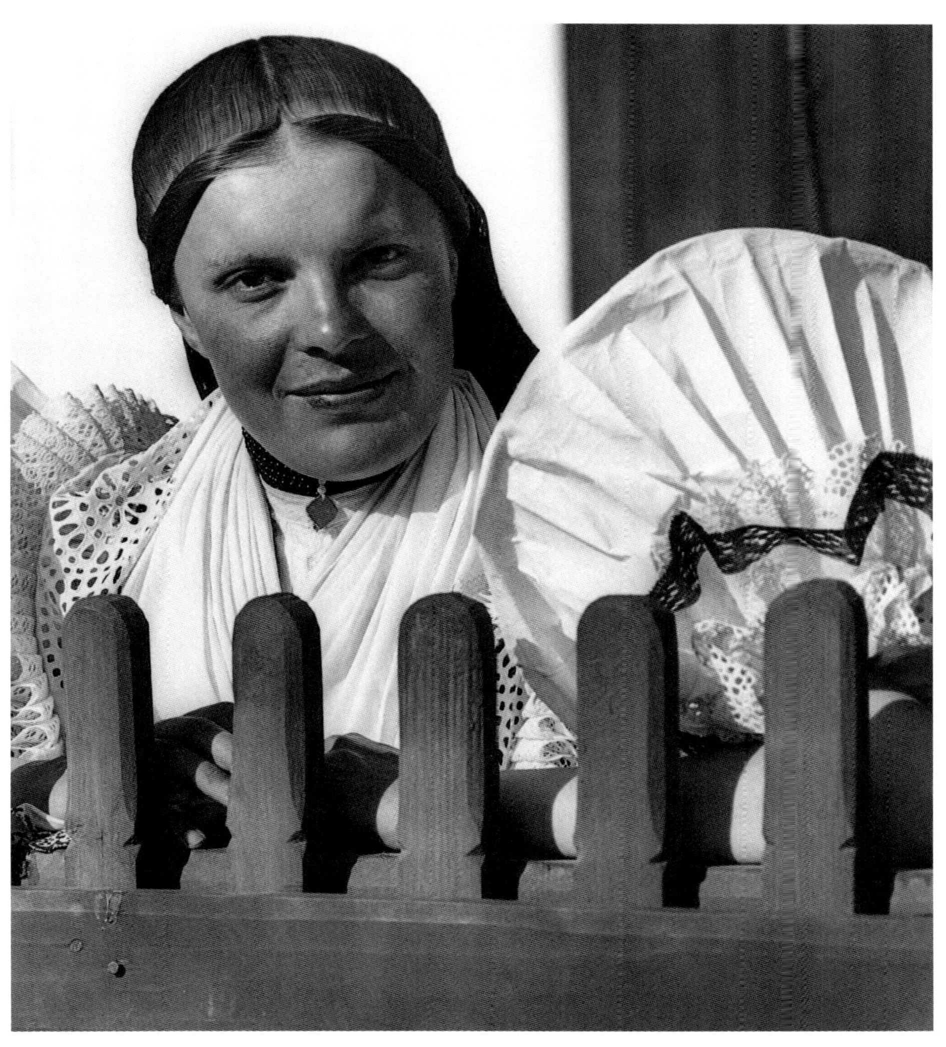

Local Girl from Boldog, 1936
Traditional costumes and hair-
dos varied according to the
region. This girl was from
Boldog, a small town east
of Budapest.

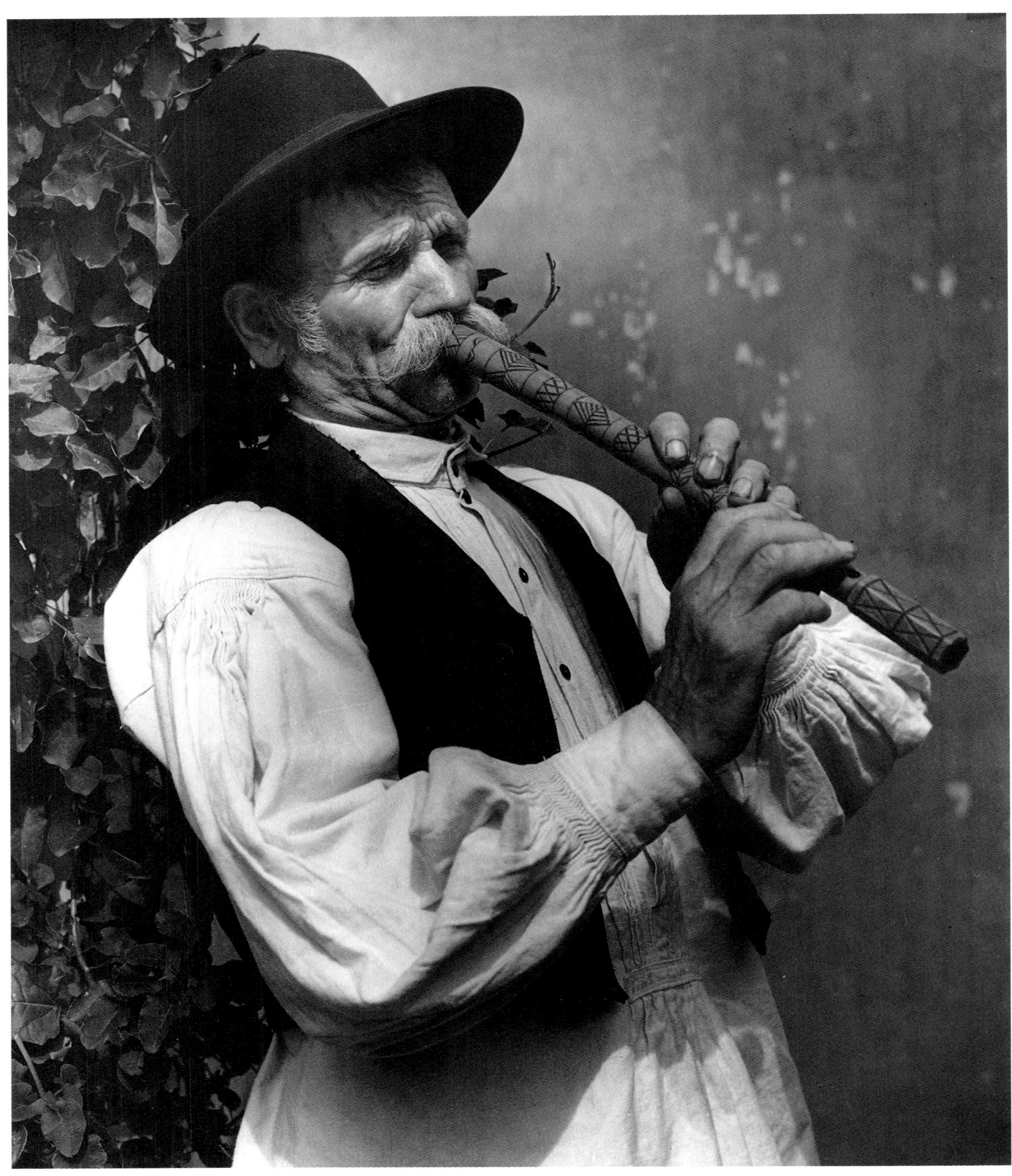

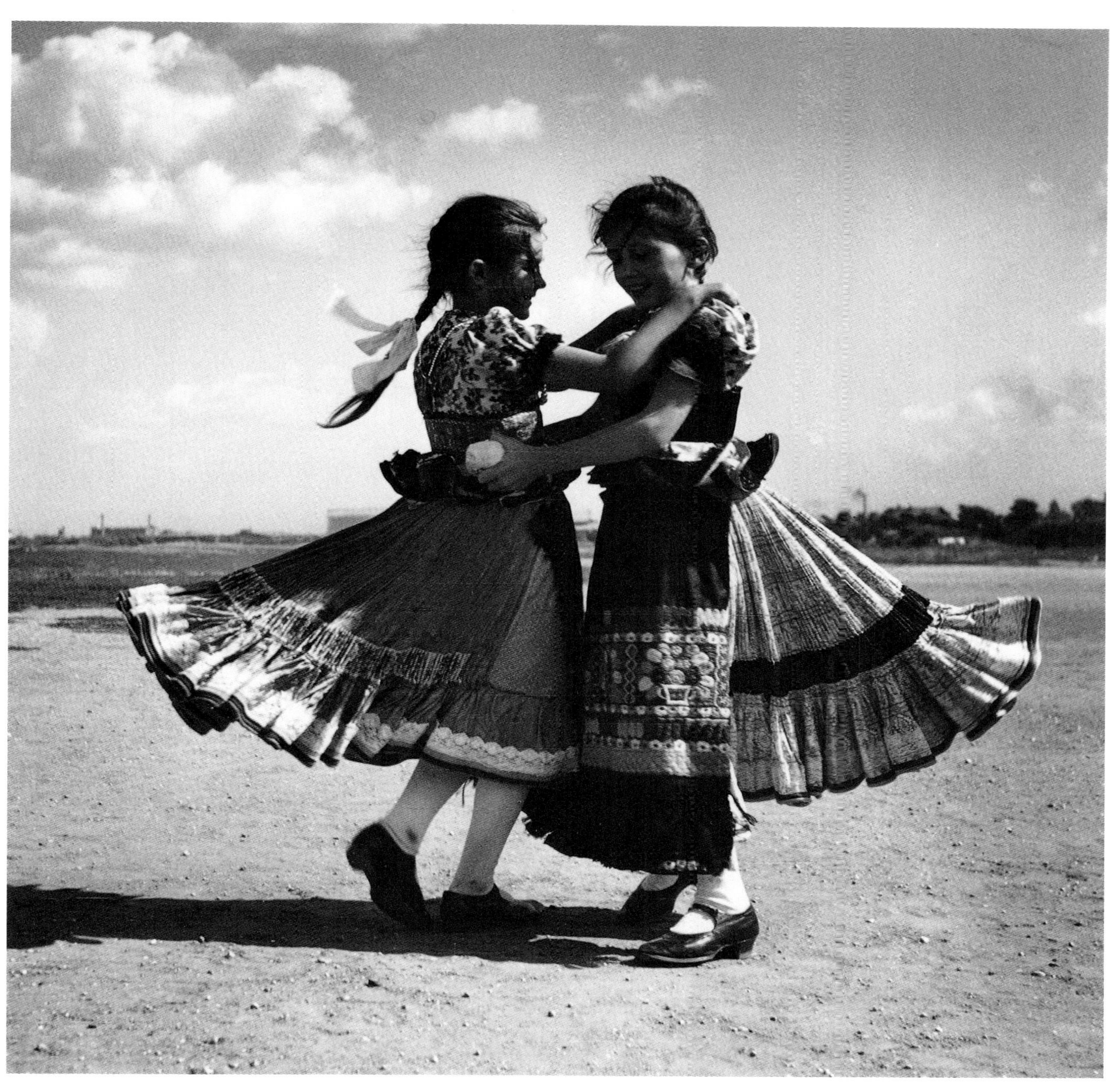

◄

The Flute Player, 1936
The flute the herdsman is
playing is itself a piece of folk
art, carved by his own hand.

Young Csardas Dancers, 1936
Budding performers are
dancing the csardas in the
town of Mezőkövesd.

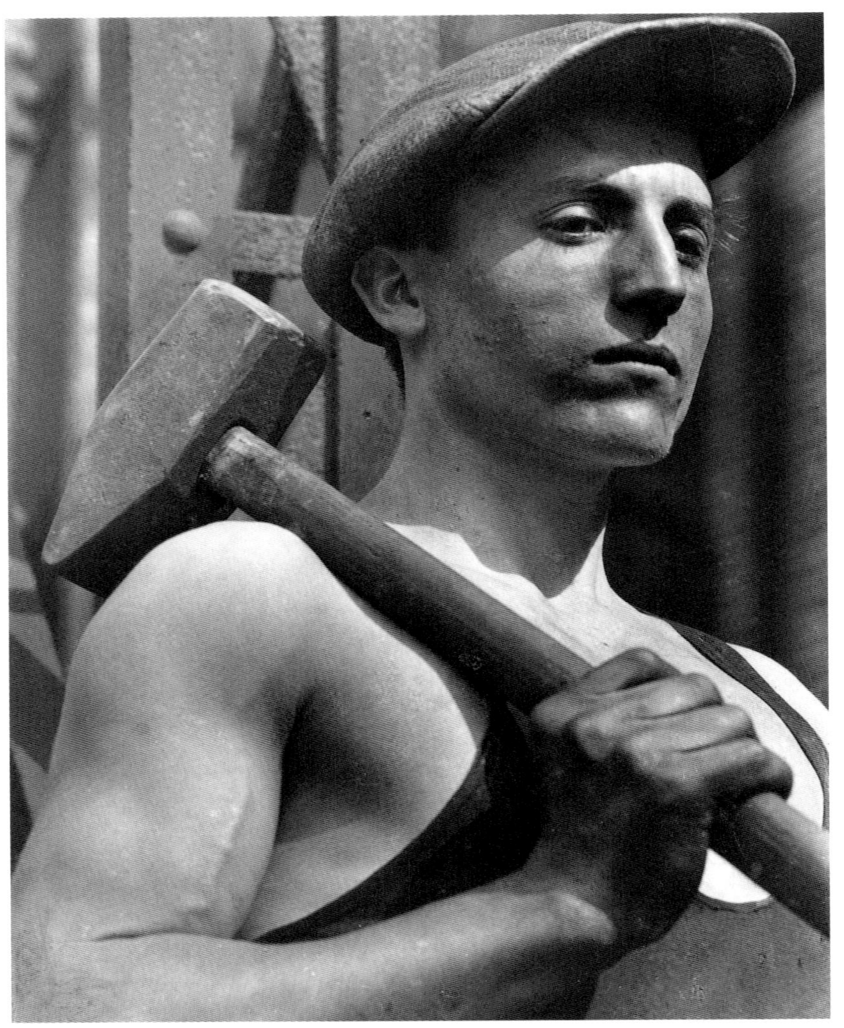

Iron Worker, 1936

Shot in classic social realist
style, this photo was part of
an assignment on the steel
industry.

The King Stephan Monument, 1936

King Stephan was the first
King of Hungary, crowned by
the Pope in the year 1000 and
later canonized for bringing
Christianity to Hungary.

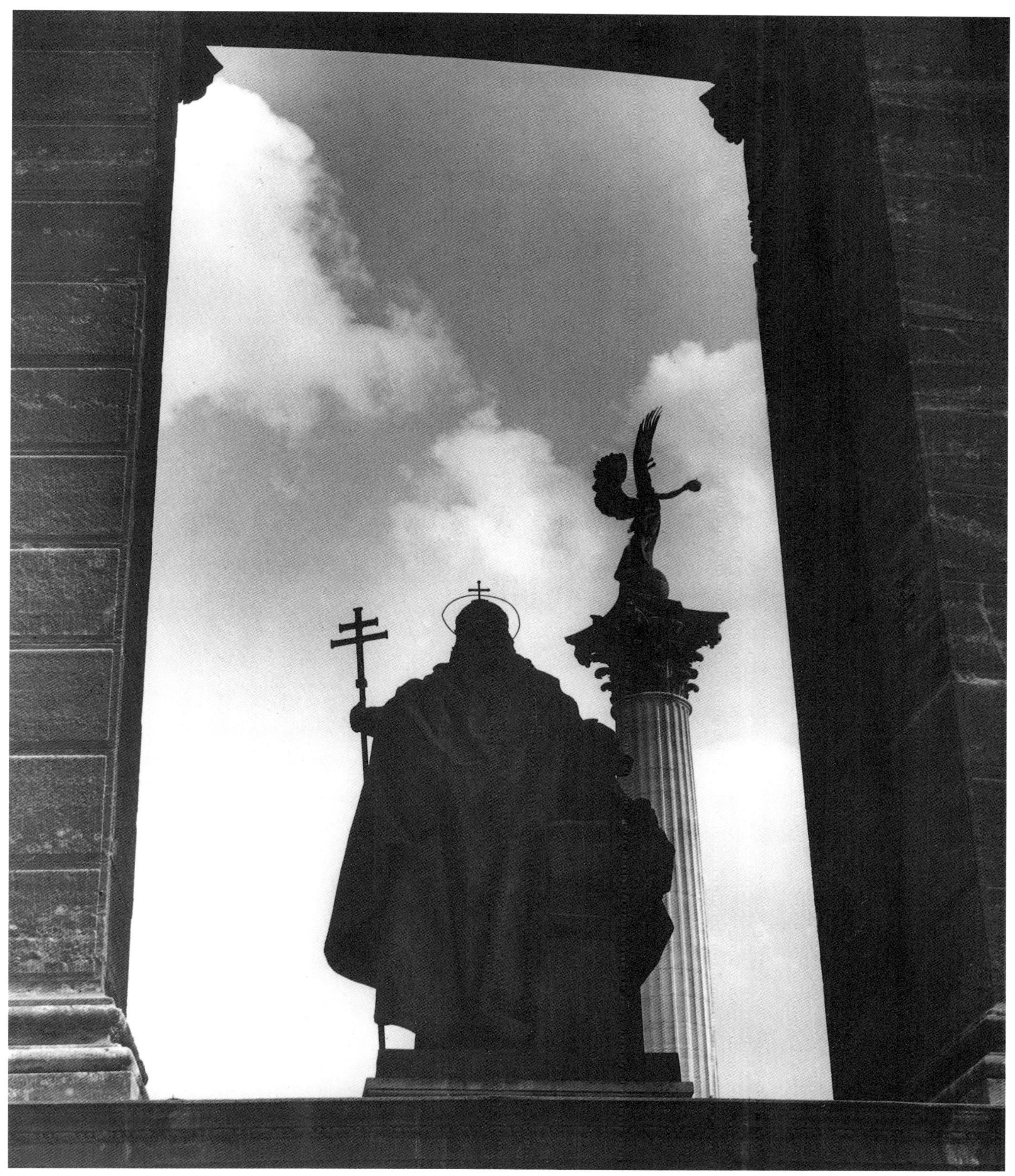

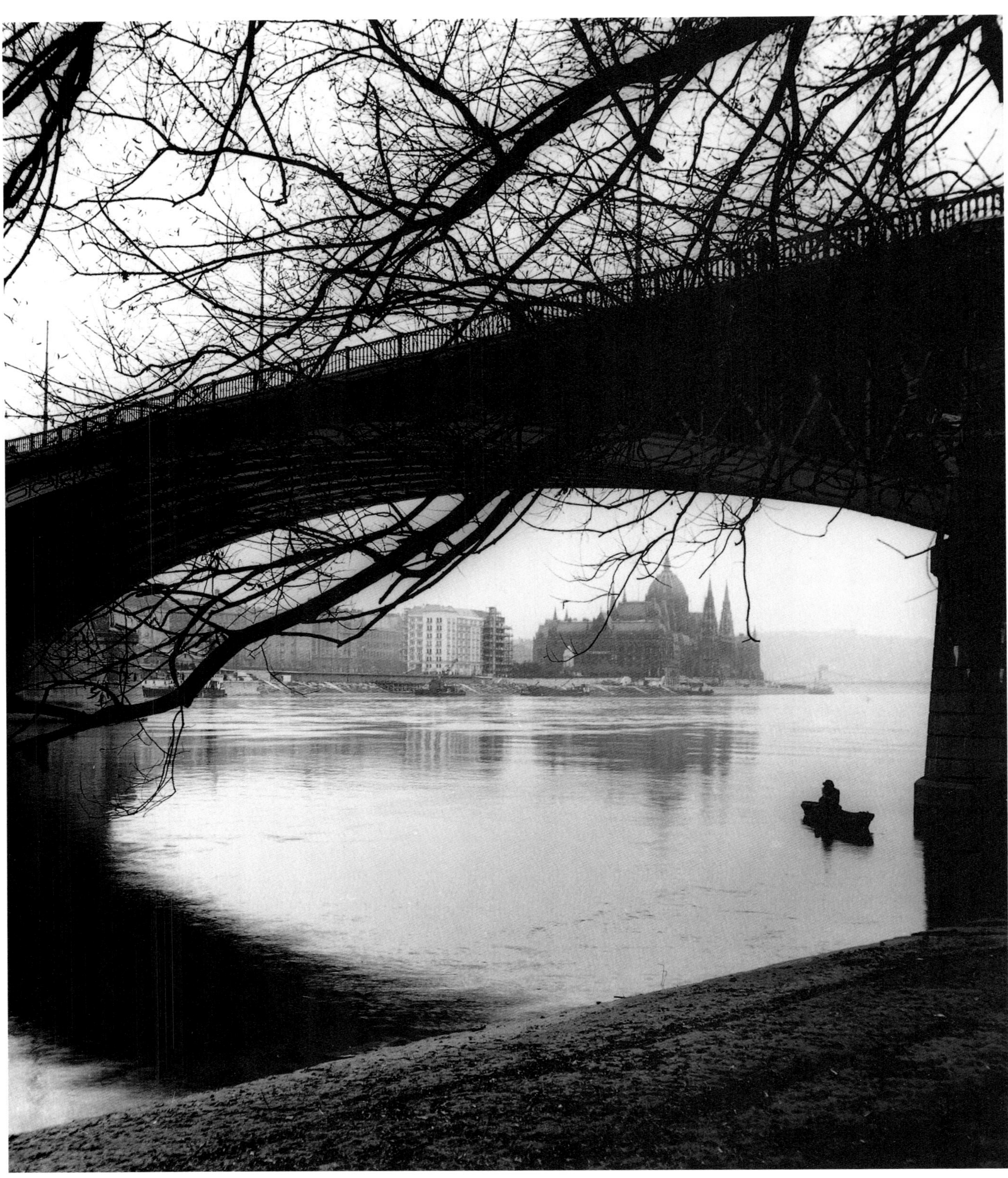

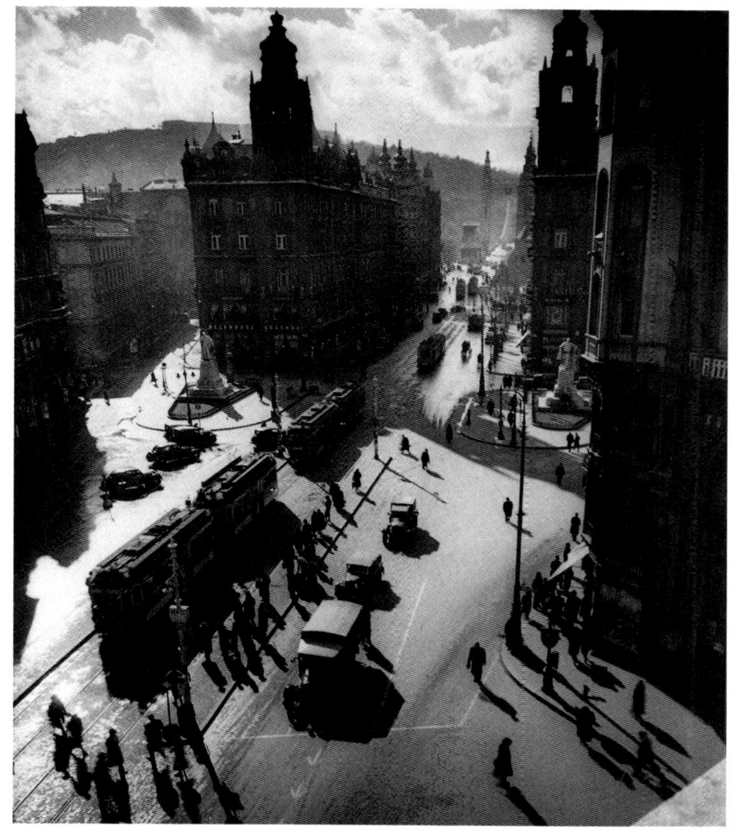

The Parliament Building and
the Margit Bridge, 1936
On the opposite shore of the
Danube, the old Parliament
Building is framed by one of
the seven bridges that cross
the river in Budapest.

Aponyi Place, Budapest, 1936
In the center of Budapest,
streetcars were the main
mode of public transportation
in the 1930s.

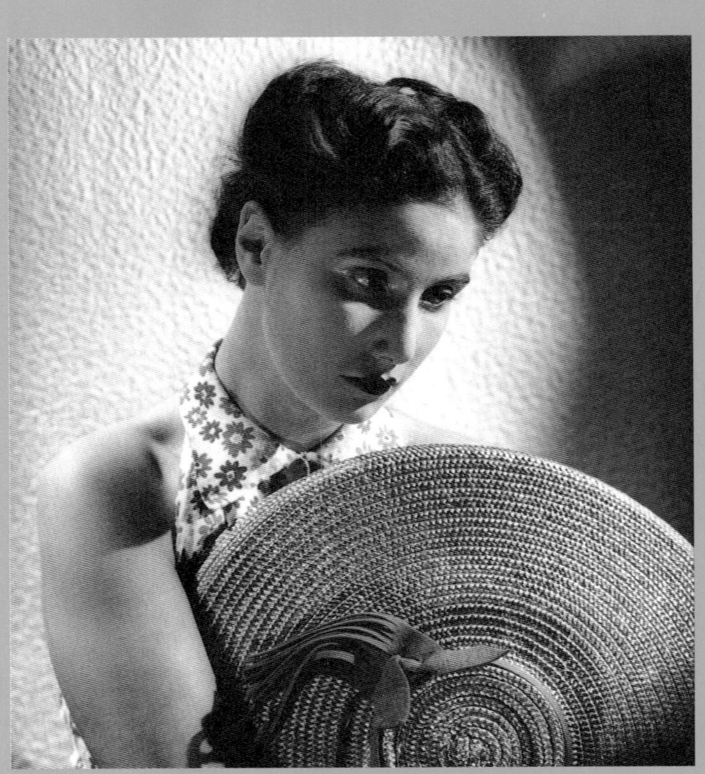

paris

We arrived in Paris in September 1937 and found a simple apartment, or *pension*, in the Latin Quarter, up winding stairs to the sixth floor. Around the corner was the Boulevard St Michel (p. 46), and nearby were Montmartre, the Pantheon, the Jardin du Luxembourg, and all those cafés. We stayed for only a week but loved every moment of it.

As we visited the different pavilions of the World's Fair we felt the whole world was opening up to us. We admired the architectural simplicity of the Japanese pavilion, which contrasted with the monumental styles of the American and Russian pavilions. For me, the Japanese pavilion was a kind of ideal of what modern architecture and modern design should be.

Paris was the center of the art world at this time. We saw fine gallery exhibits of Braque, Cassandre, and Matisse. One day as we were sitting on the terrace of the Café Dome I recognized Pablo Picasso at a neighboring table with his friends. Paris was a wonderful experience for us, and we felt an irresistible desire to live in this community. We returned to Budapest to finish up our assignments, and made preparations to move to Paris as quickly as possible.

The day before we boarded the train, I decided on a whim to track down the address of a high-school classmate, Francis Gergely, who had moved to Paris years before. It was a fateful decision.

Shortly after we arrived in Paris, I contacted Gergely, hoping he could help us out. Sure enough, he gave us valuable advice for setting ourselves up in Paris. We had hoped to find a studio in the center of the city, preferably in the area round the Avenue de l'Opéra, where the fine dressmaking studios were located, but the rents there were prohibitively expensive. Then, Gergely heard about a studio that had gone bankrupt. The price was reasonable, it had living accommodations above the shop, and we quickly moved in. Luck was with us.

We were fortunate to make other friends, such as a publisher from Hungary who introduced me to the art director of *Vogue*. The art director looked at my portfolio, which was made up largely of horses and cows from the Hortobágy, and bare-footed peasants—not the best selection for a high-fashion magazine.

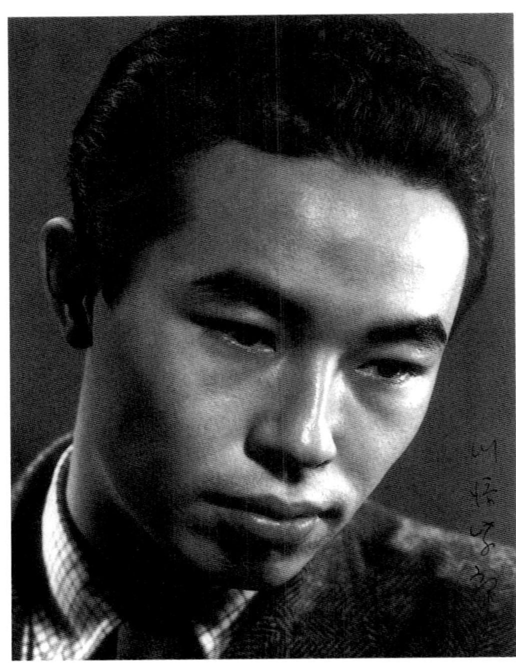

Hiroshi Kawazoe, 1938

Kawazoe, captured here in one of Francis' studio portraits, was to play a key role in his life.

He told me he couldn't see anything special in my photos, and he knew of at least ten other photographers in Paris who could do the same level of work. Oddly enough, his comment encouraged me. I thought, if he's ranking me up there with the top ten photographers in Paris, the center of the art world, then I can't be doing too badly.

To my surprise, *Vogue* called me back two weeks later for a test shoot. The large, well-equipped studio, located on the Champs-Elysées, looked to me more like a film studio, with its large lighting equipment and huge studio cameras. My model was a Czechoslovakian dancer, and we had difficulty communicating because of my limited French. After struggling for almost an hour, I felt I had the poses I wanted. Next day, I made some prints and anxiously awaited the verdict on my work. A few days later, I was notified that one of my pictures was accepted for publication in the magazine *Jardin des Modes*, a subsidiary of *Vogue*. Despite this promising start, breaking into commercial photography was difficult.

Once our studio at 35 Avenue de l'Opéra was ready, I began doing portrait photography. One day, while visiting our friend Gergely, who worked as secretary for a Japanese film importer, I invited his boss, Hiroshi Kawazoe, to come for a portrait. I had met him earlier and wanted to photograph him because I liked his intelligent, handsome face.

Kawazoe came to the studio a few days later, and I succeeded in making a few good pictures of him. He was so pleased with the results that he began sending all his Japanese friends to our studio. In this way, we had opportunities to photograph Japanese officials, architects, painters, and dancers who happened to be visiting Paris.

Paris was an exciting and beautiful city, full of color and flavor. Most of all, it was the center of the world for art and artists. So much history was alive there—the lovely Quartier Latin, the beautiful Avenues, famous museums, the opera houses and cathedrals. With the help of a good friend, we opened a photo studio right on the Avenue de l'Opéra. We were introduced to a Japanese film importer, Hiroshi Kawazoe, and his lovely and talented wife, Chieko Hara, who had recently won the Grand Prix at the International Chopin Piano Concours in Warsaw. We became friends instantly. They would tell us about Japan and its culture, so different, picturesque, and exotic to us. We went to see movies about Japan at the Cinéma Ursuline, as well as tasting their cuisine in a Japanese restaurant. We were served by kimono-clad Japanese ladies, so polite and so graceful, making our meals all the more enjoyable. Japan seemed like a place we could only dream about. Our interest in visiting the Orient grew steadily.

Our days in Paris were full, as we were lucky to make some good friends there, including some who went on to make names for themselves, such as painter Victor Vasarely, sculptor Josef Csaky, and photographer Brassai.

In the autumn of 1939, the danger of war became apparent when Hitler invaded Czechoslovakia and Poland (pp. 54, 55). I went to City Hall because I had decided to volunteer for the French Army, but my *carte d'identité* had expired and I was not accepted. The next day, Kawazoe came to our studio with his wife, Chieko Hara, a prominent concert pianist whom I had also photographed (p. 51). They were returning home because of the political situation and asked if we would be interested in going with them. He was inviting us, he said, because he wanted me to teach modern photography and because he thought my work would be much appreciated in Japan. We certainly didn't want to go back to Hungary—it was already occupied by the Nazis. Given the appeal of the invitation and the precariousness of our continued residency in Paris, we happily accepted. Mr. Kawazoe promised to arrange an official invitation. It arrived three weeks later from the Kokusai Bunka Shinkokai, the International Cultural Society of Japan.

When World War II started, in 1939, all foreign nationals living in Paris were ordered to leave, and new cartes d'identité [permits to stay] as well as renewals were not issued. We tried to reach America by contacting my uncle, who lived in Cleveland, Ohio, at the time, but we never heard from him. Without a sponsor, there was no chance of getting an immigration permit. Anyway, sponsorship took time, and time we did not have.

We felt desperate and stranded, not knowing which way to go nor what to do. But luck was with us. Hiroshi Kawazoe, who admired Francis' work, asked if we would like to go to Japan with him in order for Francis to introduce Hungary through his artistic photography. The Far East was a dreamworld for a photographer, and we quickly agreed.

It is interesting how fate rules our lives. If I hadn't thought of getting the Paris address of my former classmate, Gergely, I would never have met Kawazoe and probably never would have gone to Japan. The rest of my life would have turned out quite differently.

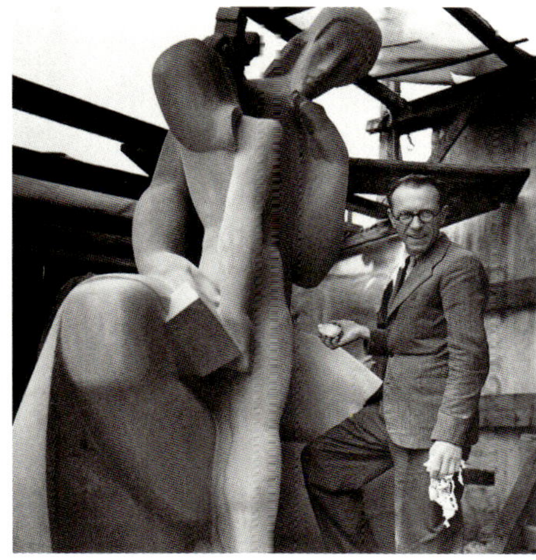

Sculptor Joseph Csaky, 1938

One of the Hungarian expatriate artists Francis befriended in Paris

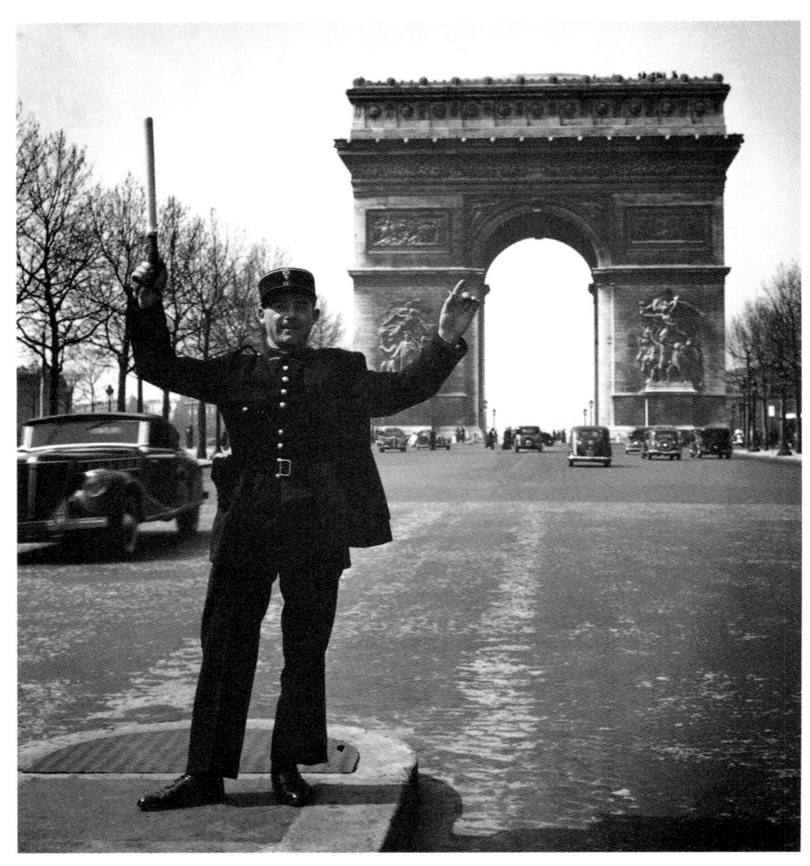

Arc de Triomphe, 1938

A policeman directs traffic

on the Champs-Elysées.

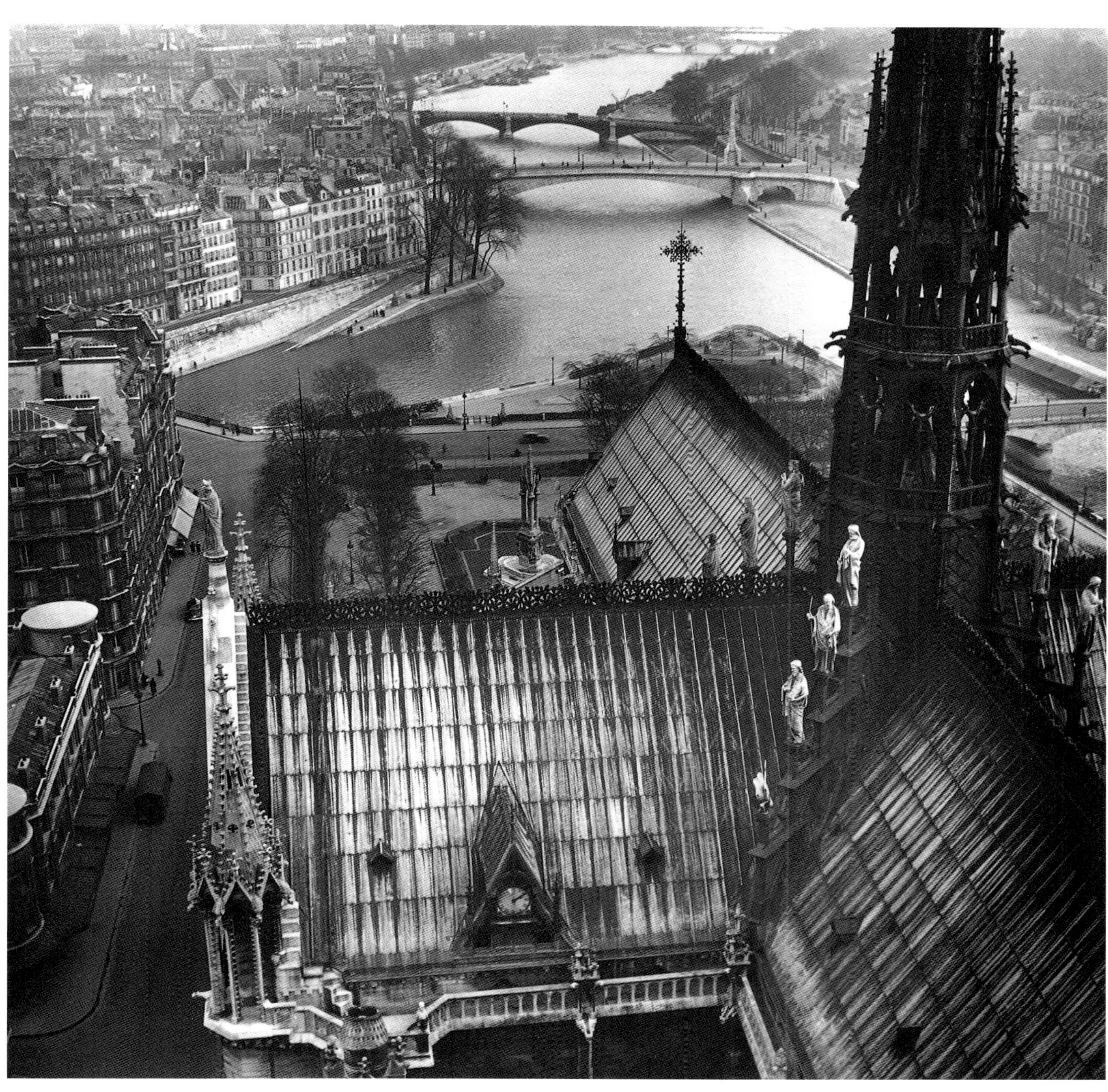

Notre Dame Rooftop, 1937

With my interest in architecture,
I always looked for unusual
angles to photograph from.

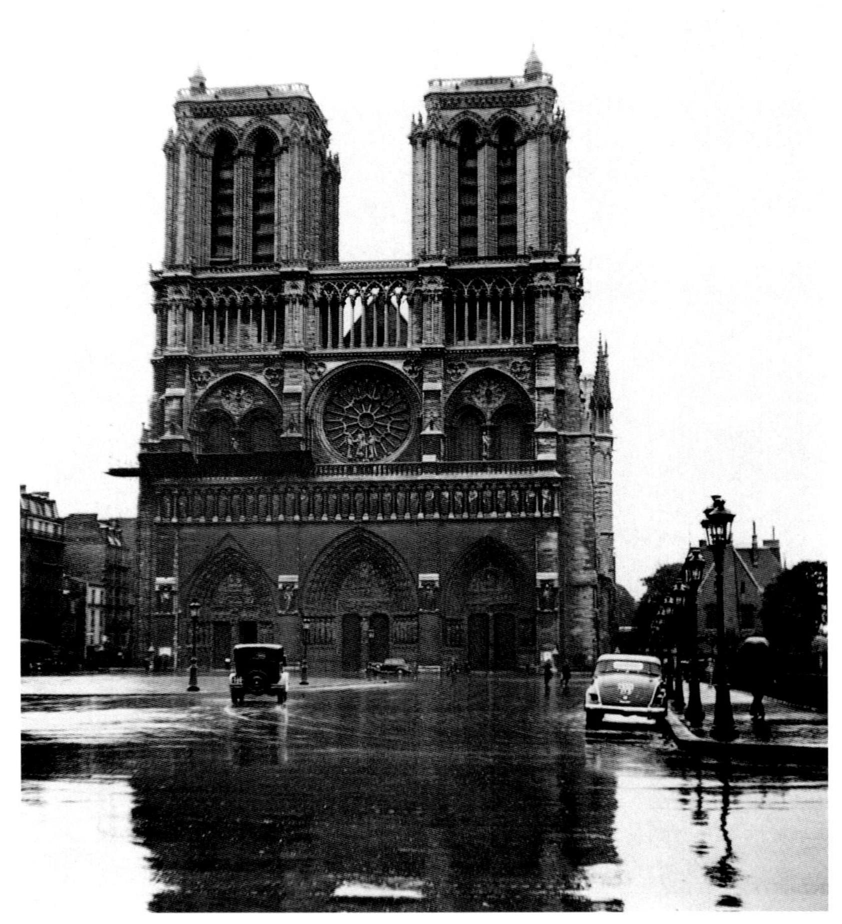

Notre Dame in the Rain, 1937

This photo of the famed

cathedral was taken during

our first visit to Paris.

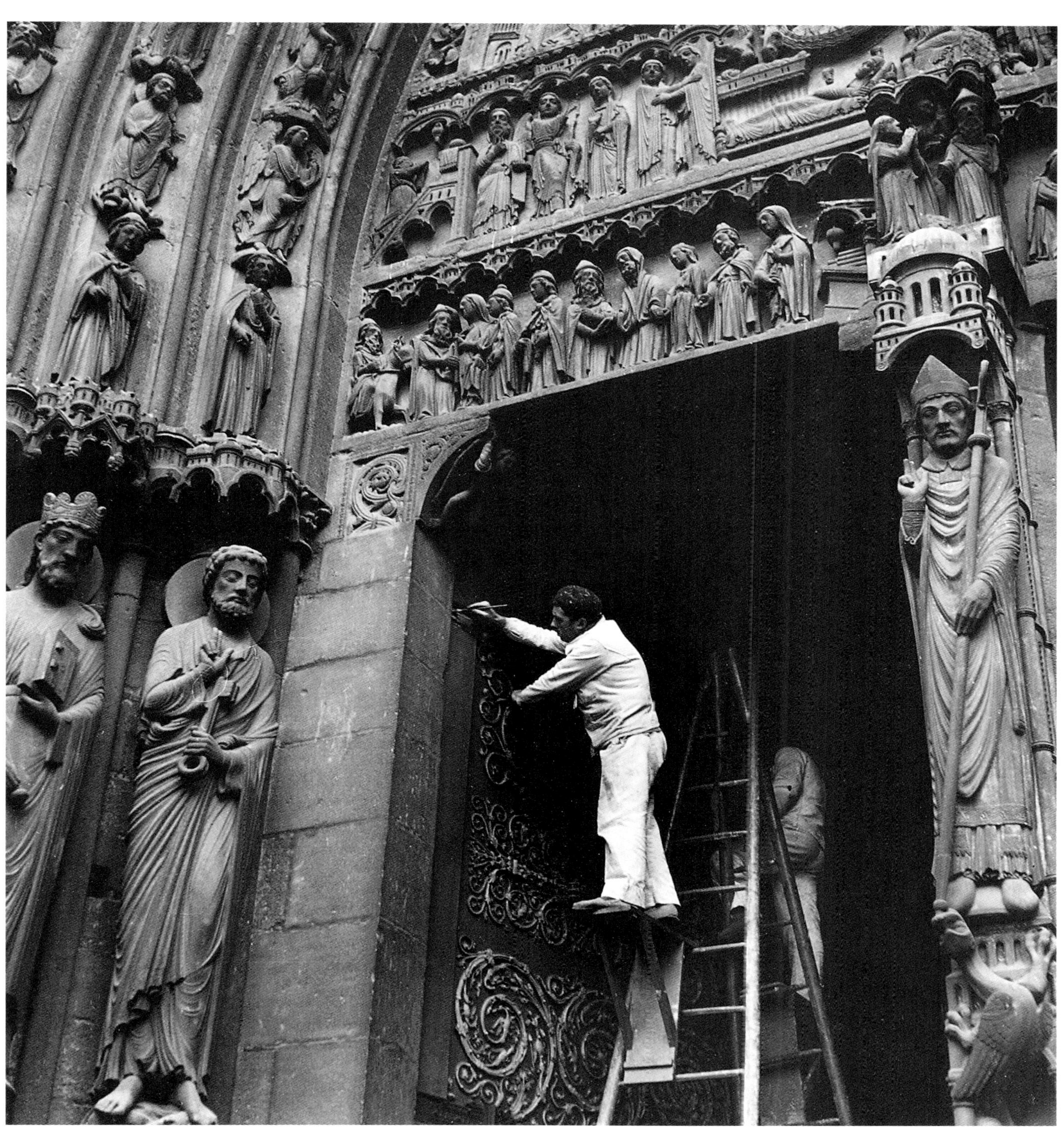

Restorers, 1937

*Restoration work was
under way on the doors
of Notre Dame.*

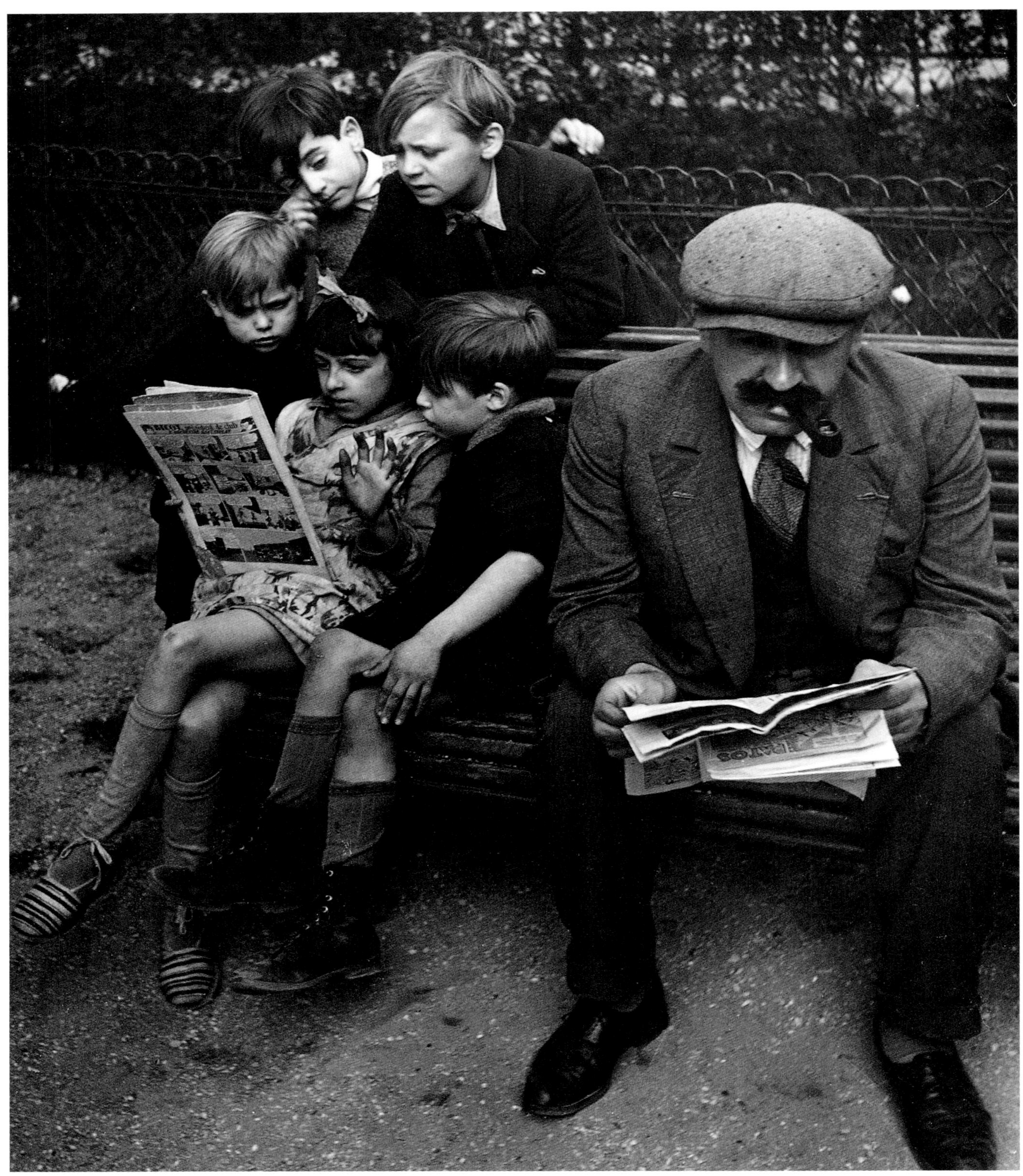

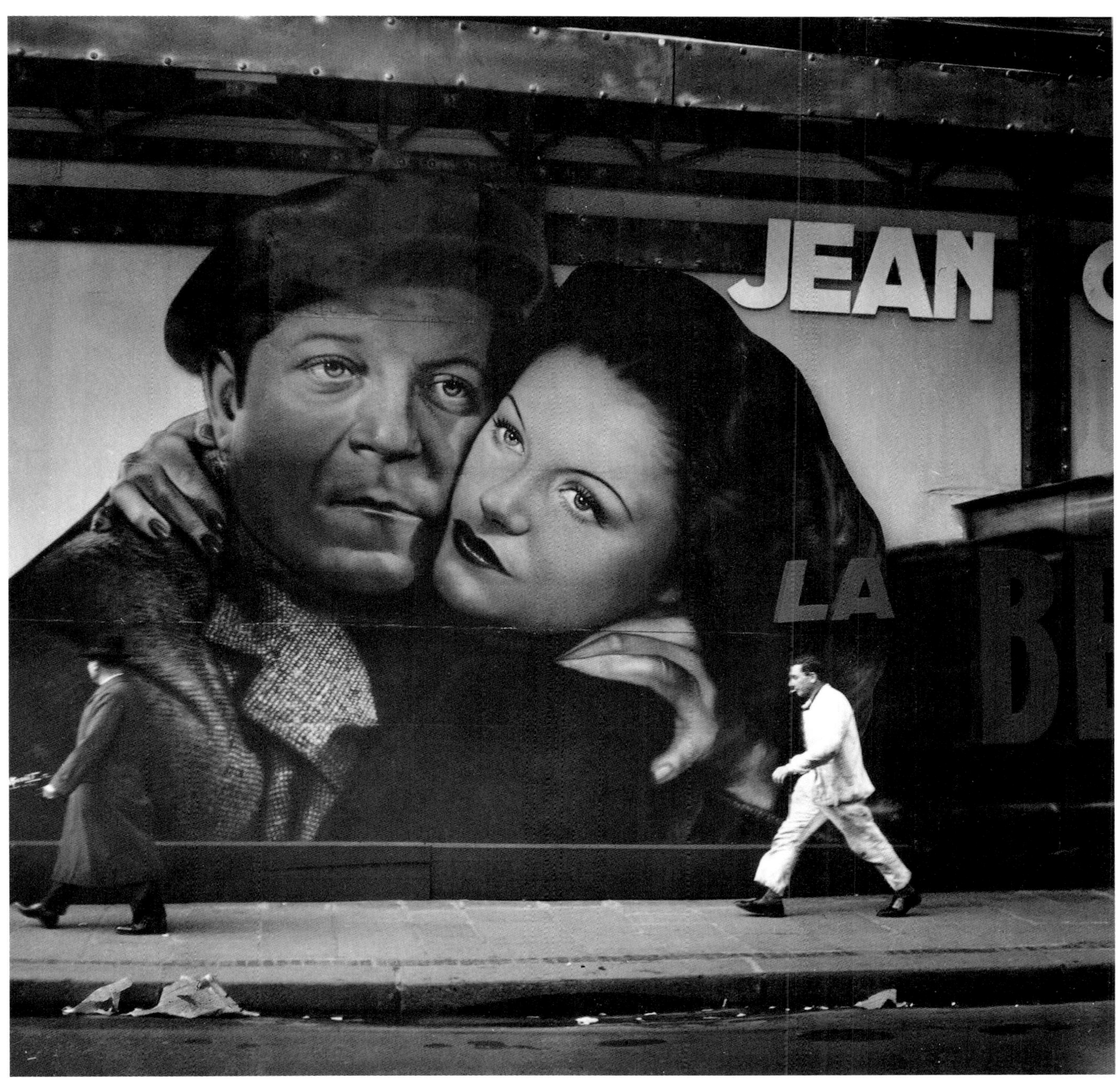

Fascinating Reading, 1938

For children and adults alike,

reading was an absorbing

experience.

Lovers on the Boulevard, 1938

In the City of Love, a huge

poster advertising "La Bête

Humaine," with Jean Gabin

and Simone Simon, dwarfs

pedestrians hurrying by.

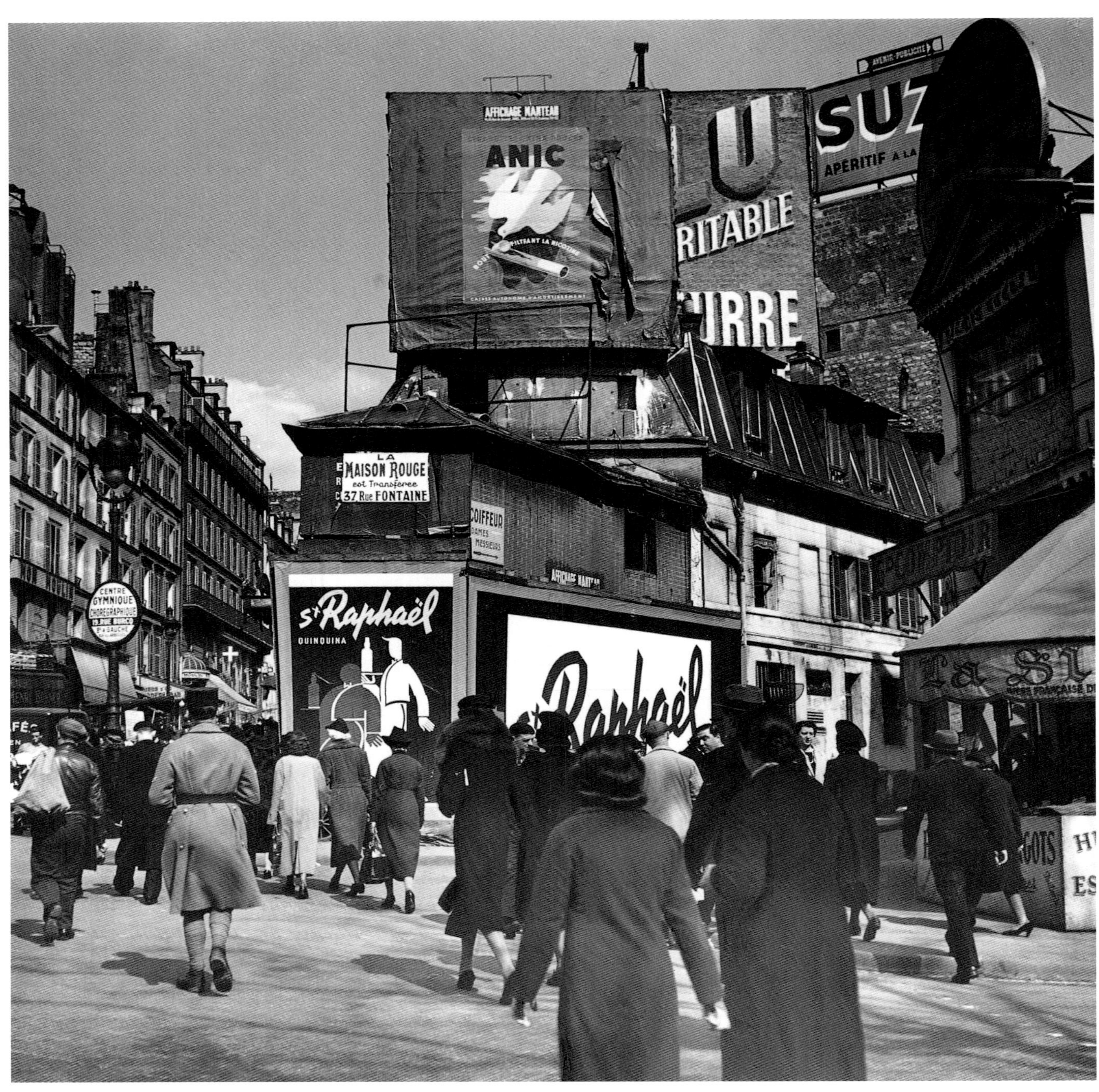

Boulevard St Michel, 1937
We stayed in the Latin Quarter
during our first visit to Paris.

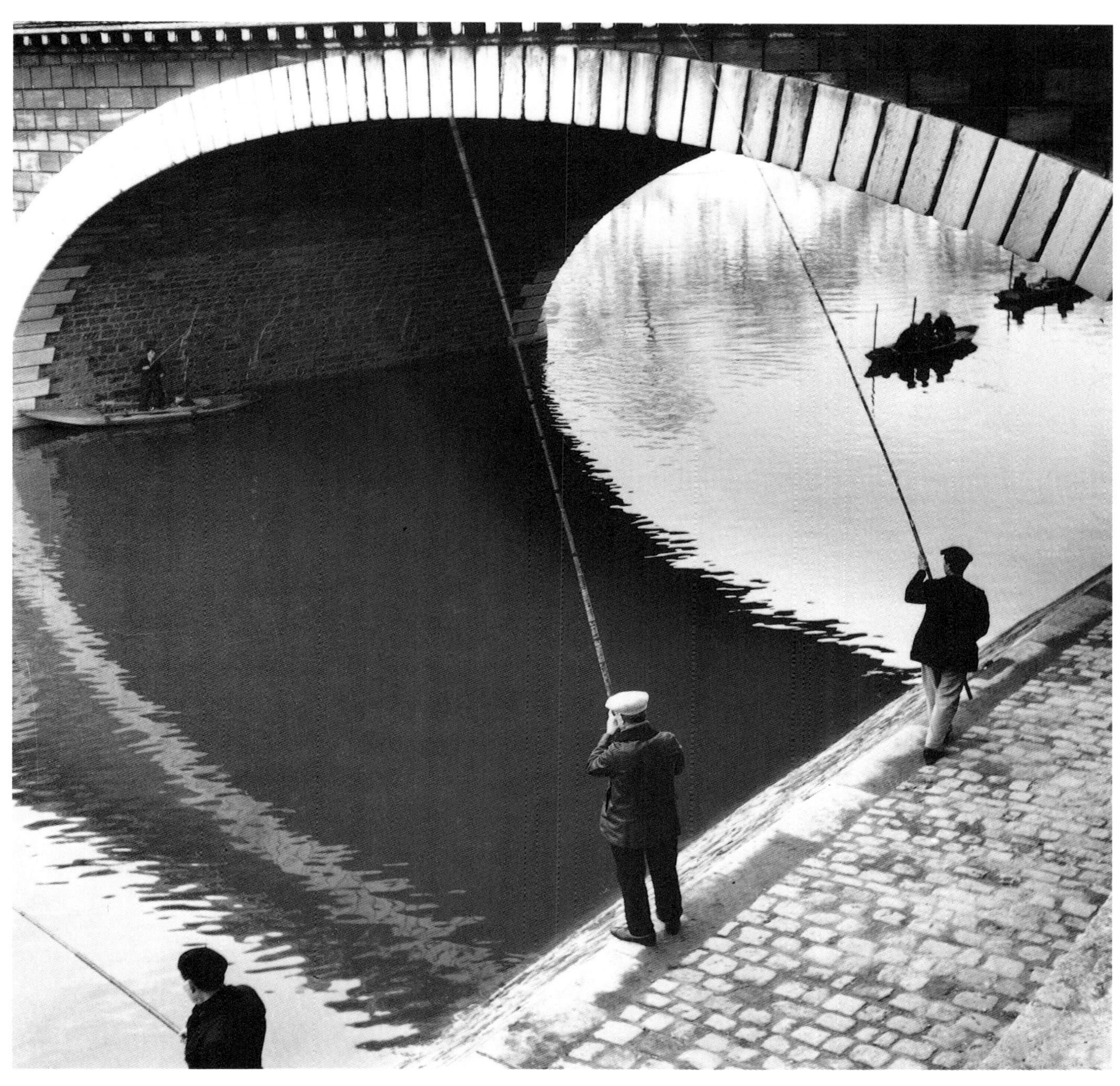

Fishermen on the Seine, 1938

The banks of the Seine are
not only for lovers.

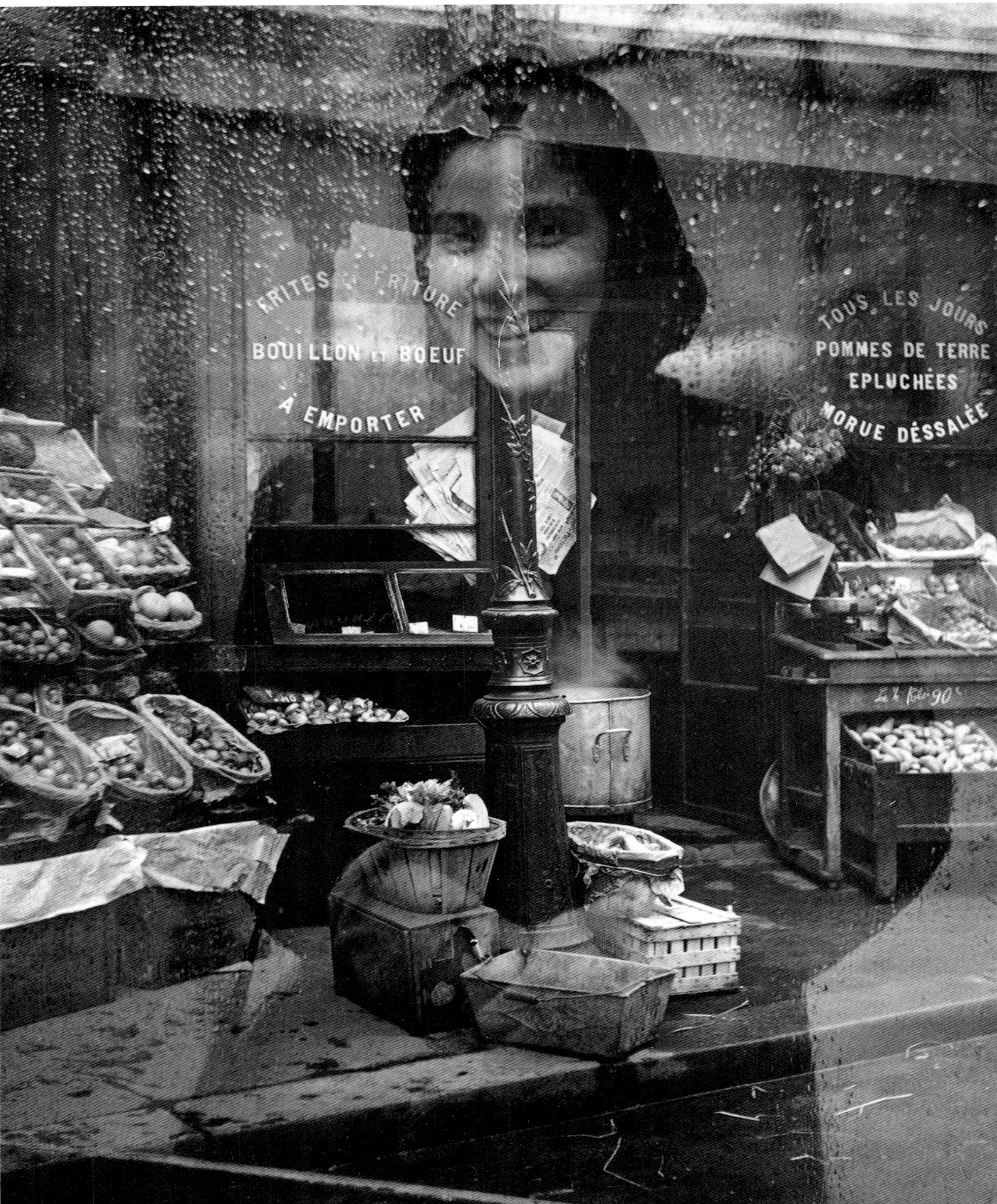
FRITES & FRITURE
BOUILLON et BOEUF
À EMPORTER
TOUS LES JOURS
POMMES DE TERRE
EPLUCHÉES
MORUE DÉSSALÉE

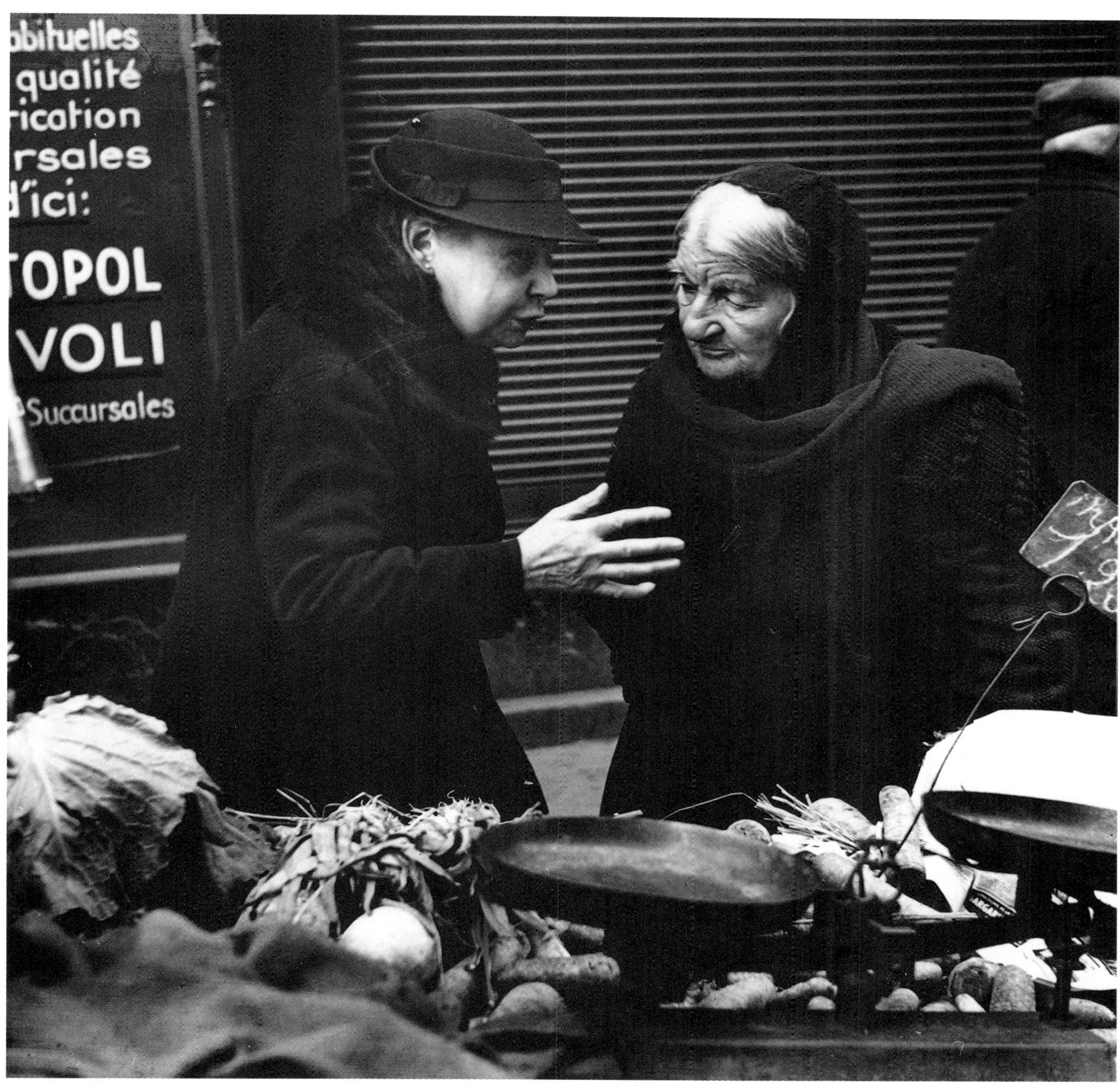

◄

Window-Shopping, 1938
This double print was made to
show how much Irene enjoyed
shopping at the corner market
in Paris.

Marketplace Gossip, 1933
Two old friends stop for a chat.

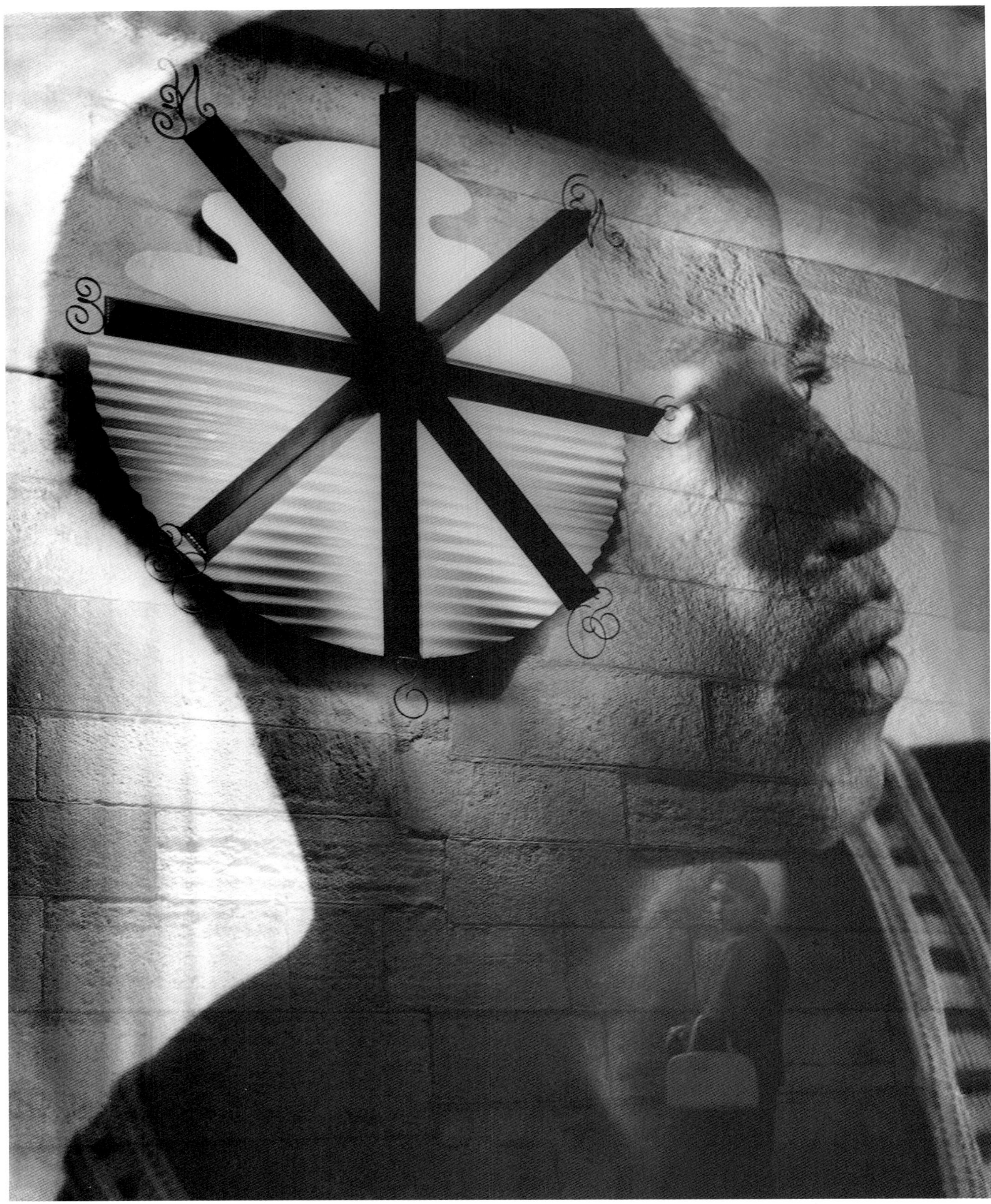

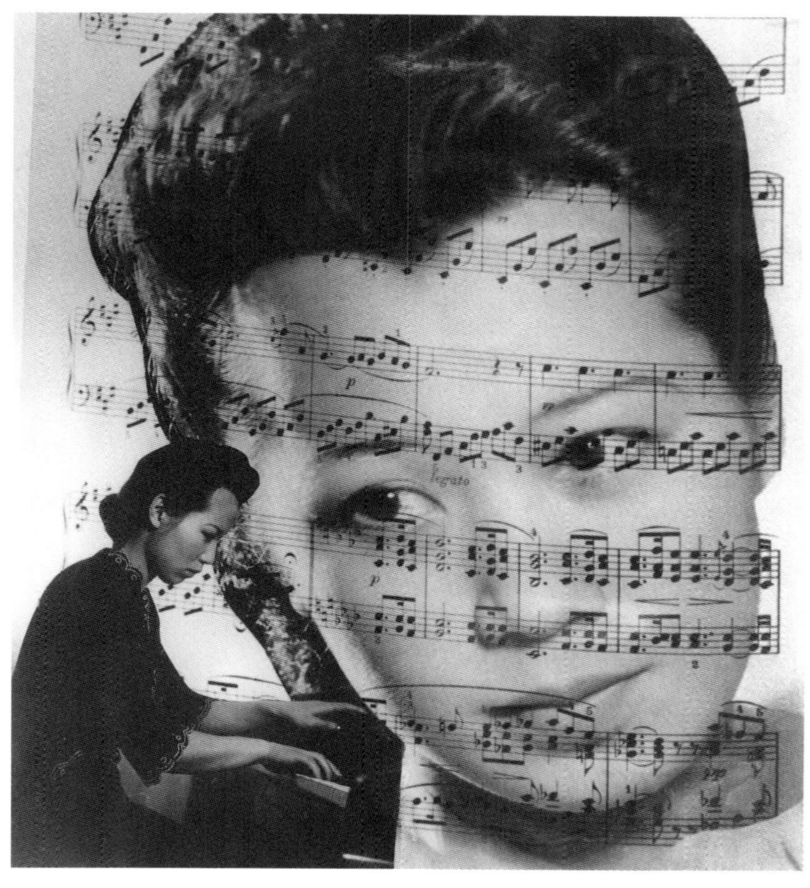

◄

Latin Quarter Montage, 1938
The image of a nightclub entertainer from the Latin Quarter
was superimposed on a shot
of a neon sign to create this
photomontage.

Chieko Hara Montage, 1938
I tried experimenting with multiple imagery of Chieko Hara,
who at the age of nineteen had
just won the renowned Chopin
Piano Concours in Warsaw.

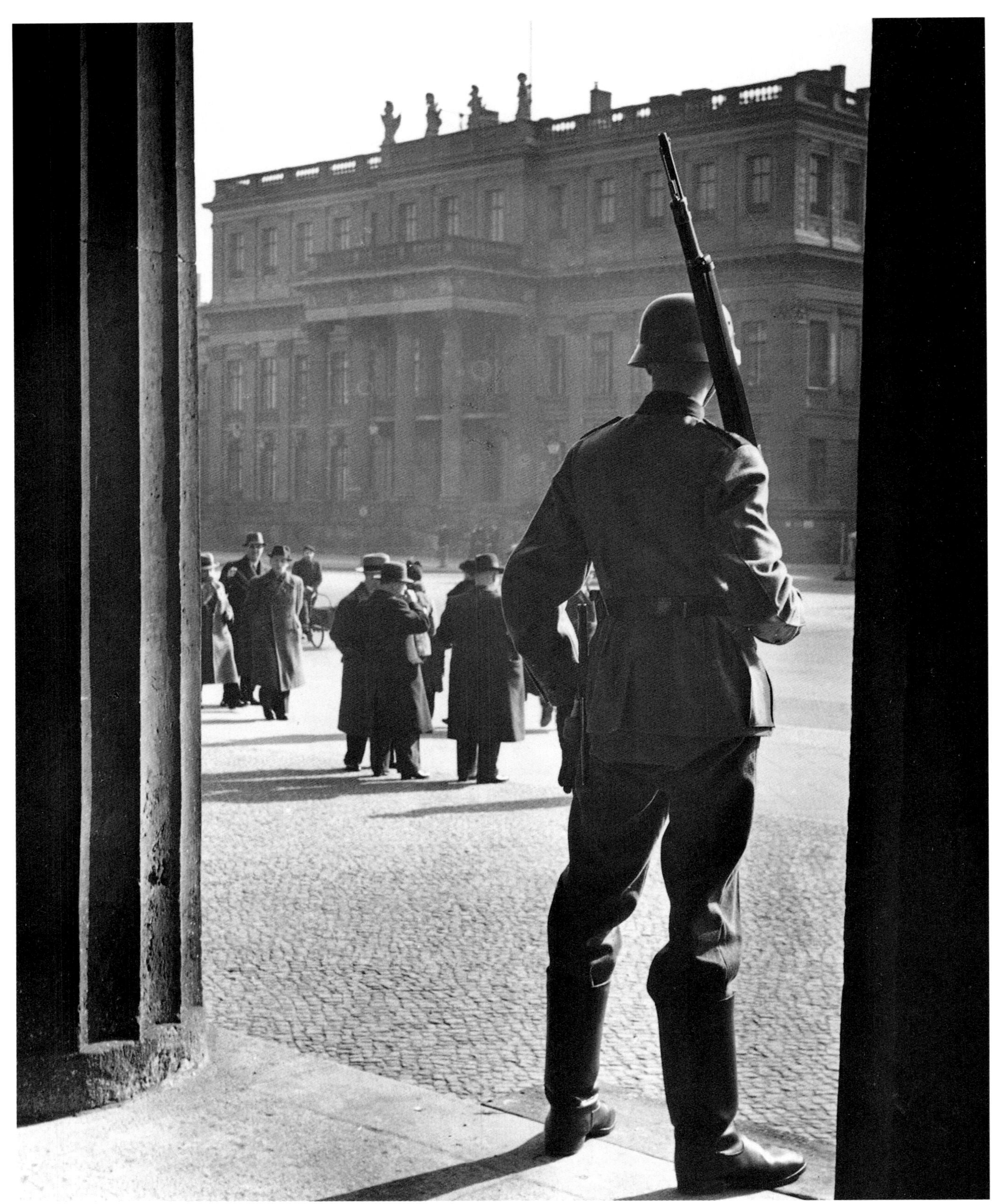

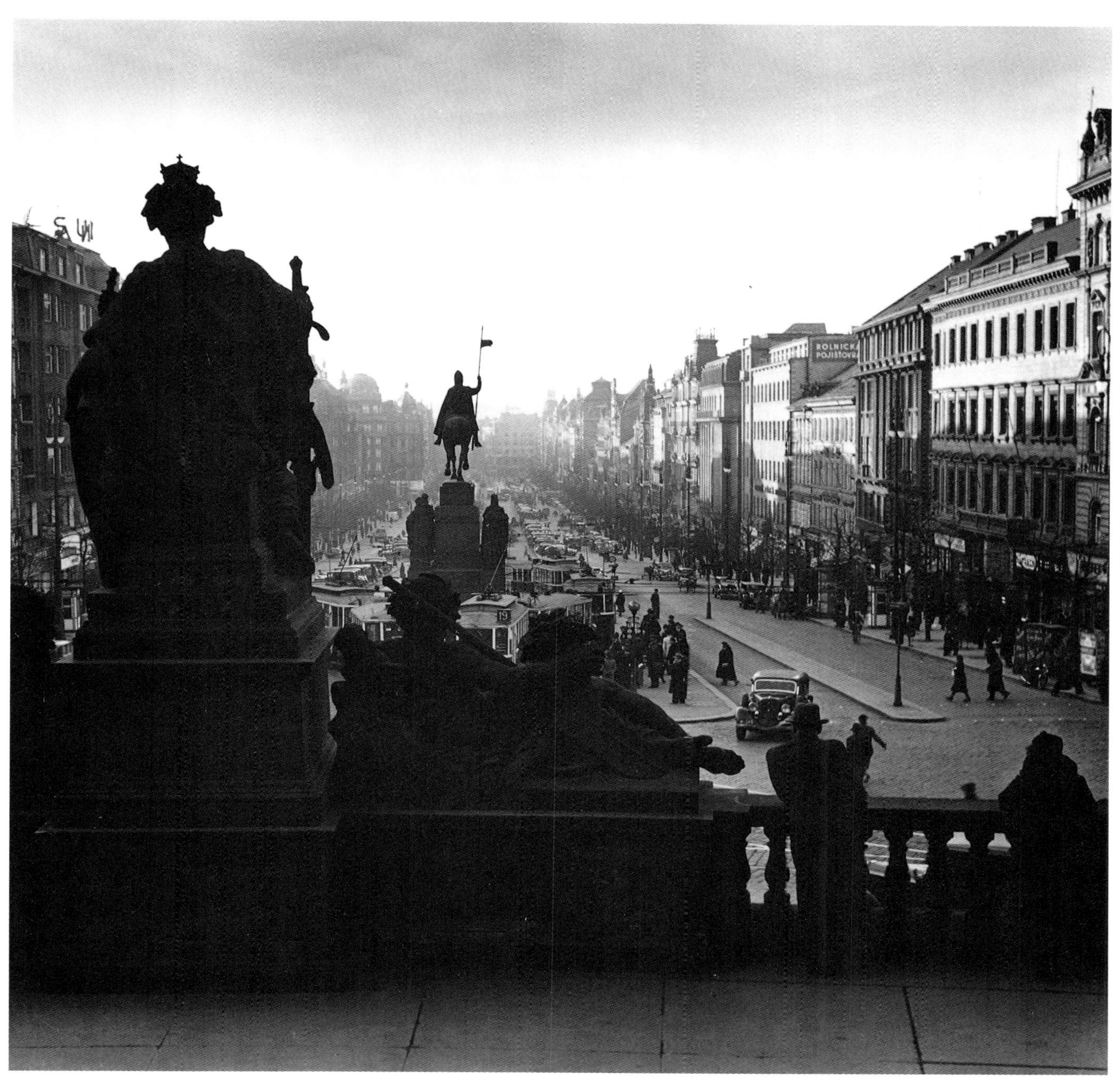

Berlin, 1938

With trepidation, I captured the
bold pose of a German soldier
during a brief visit to Berlin.

Prague, 1938

This historic city reminded
me strongly of Budapest.

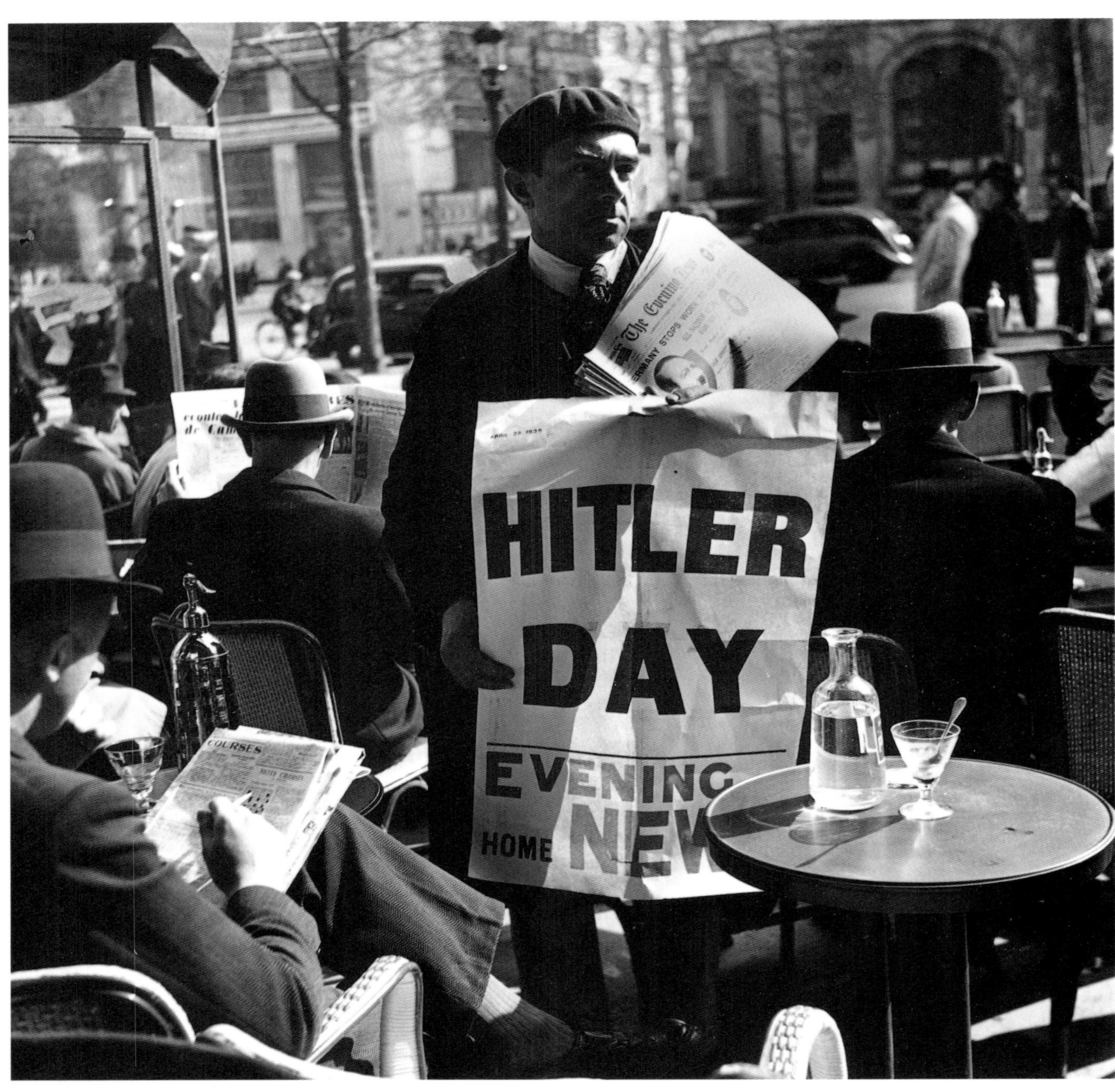

Hitler Day, 1939

The date: April 28, 1939, and a news vendor for an English-language daily is out with the news of Hitler's invasion of Czechoslovakia.

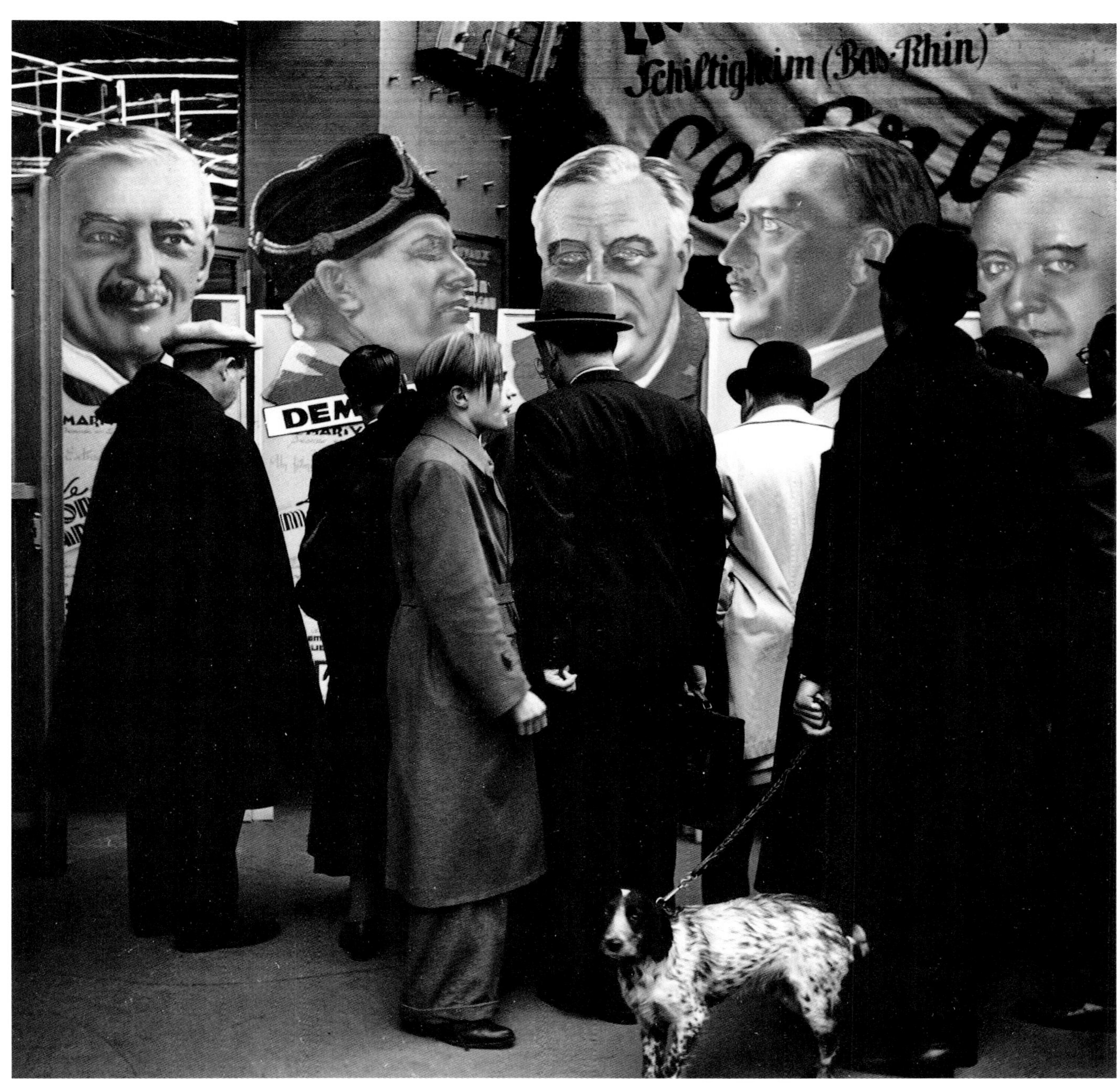

Critical Times, 1939

The five world leaders are
displayed on the wall of the
Paris Soir *newspaper building*
as onlookers crowd around
to read the latest news.

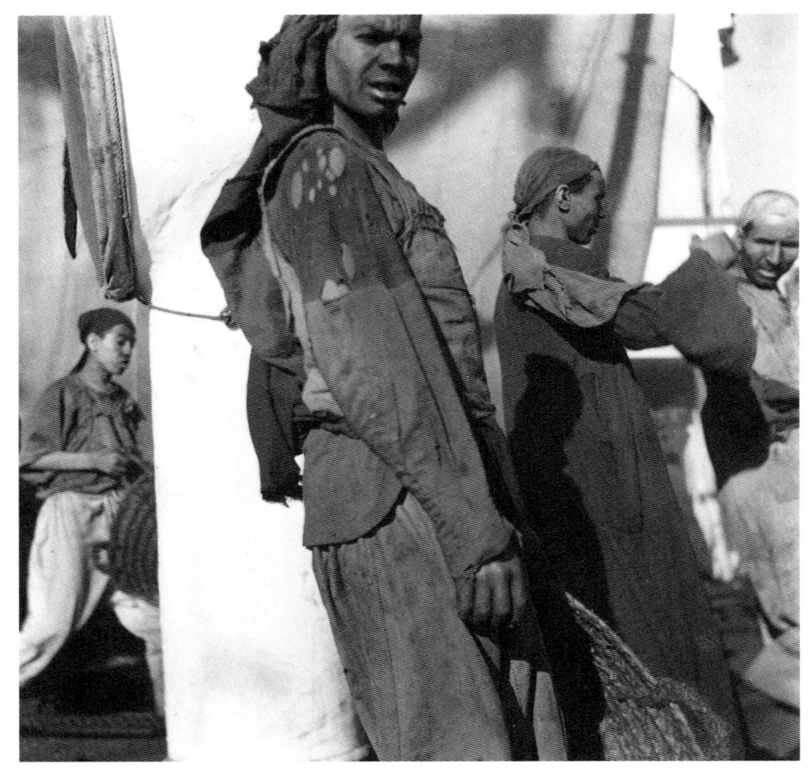

Loading Coal, Port Said, 1939

*On the way east, we had a
stopover in Port Said, where
these laborers restocked the
ship with coal for the long
voyage.*

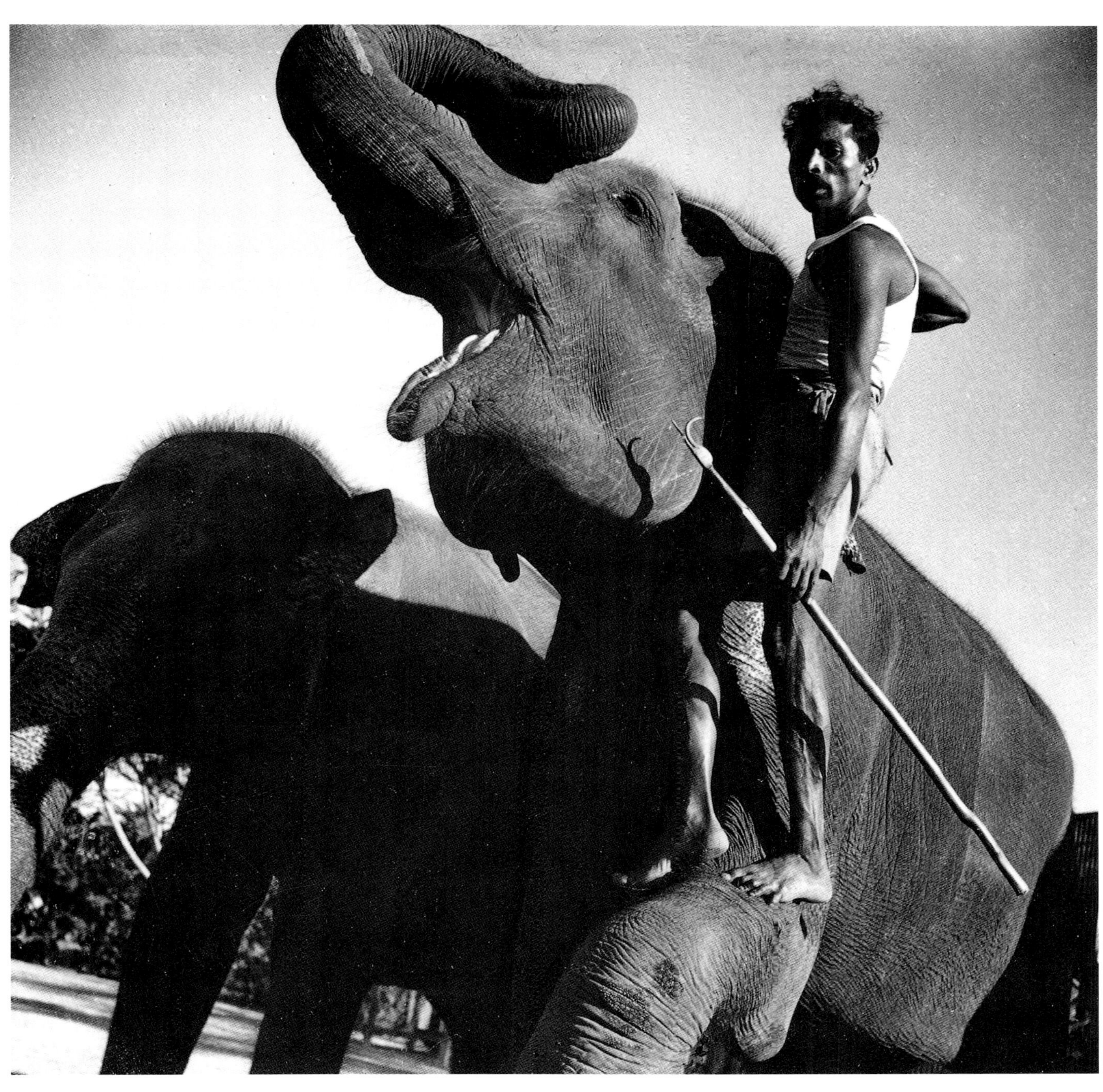

Elephant Keeper, Colombo, 1939
En route to Japan, every port of
call offered exotic locales for
the traveling photographer.

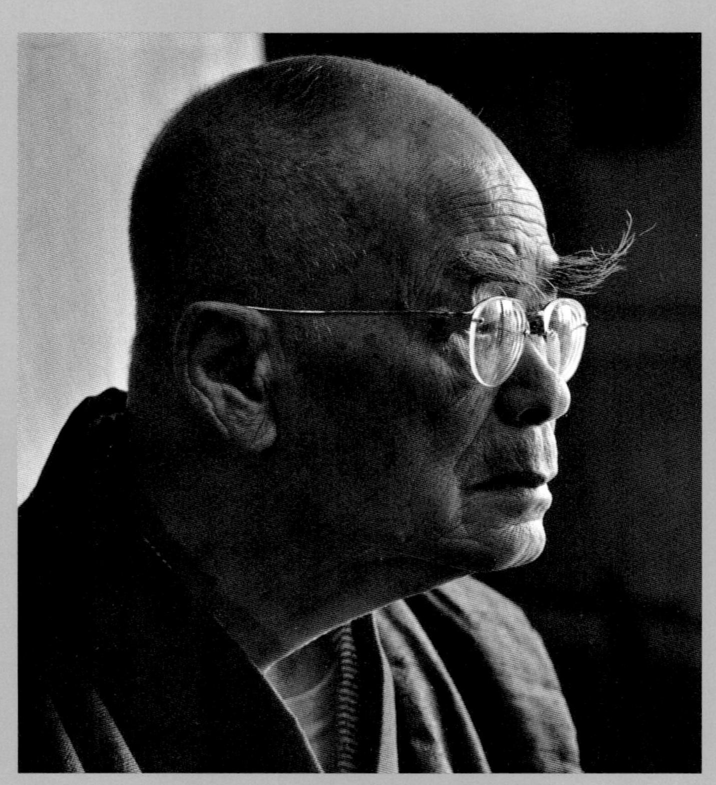

japan

D. T. Suzuki, Aged Ninety-Three, 1963

*I had the honor of visiting
the renowned philosopher and
prolific writer on Zen Buddhism
at his home in Kita-Kamakura.
He was completely unself-
conscious in front of the
camera, embodying the
'ego-less' personality
of the Zen master.*

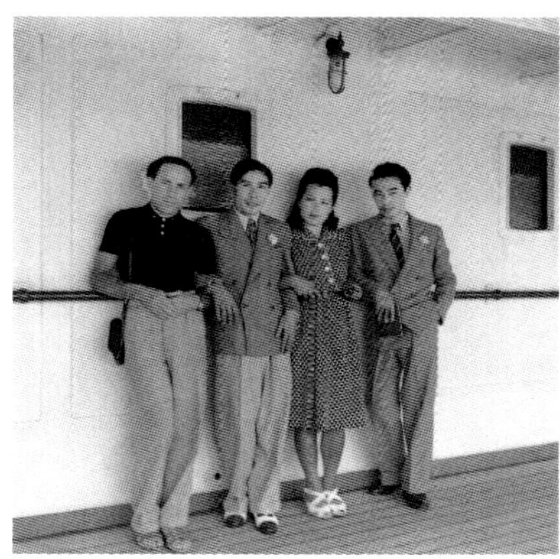

*Francis (left) on board the Suwa
Maru with his friends Chieko
and Hiroshi Kawazoe (right),
and an unidentified friend,
December 1939*

Hiroshi Kawazoe arranged my visa to Japan, and I left with him and his wife on December 1, 1939, aboard the Japanese ship *Suwa Maru*. Because Irene and I couldn't liquidate our studio quickly, and because Irene's papers were still valid, she agreed to stay behind for about six months and finish some portraits we had begun. She hired a young Hungarian woman who was also a good photographer to assist her until I could establish myself in Japan, when she could join me.

After a six-week voyage by way of the Suez Canal, Bombay, Ceylon, Singapore, and Shanghai, the ship arrived in Kobe, Japan, during the first week of 1940. From Kobe, we traveled by train to Tokyo. I stayed in a hotel while waiting for Irene to arrive, and once again I faced a language problem. I could communicate only with those few Japanese who spoke French. A little later, I was introduced to a well-known painter, Ikuma Arishima, who had lived in Paris for several years, was fluent in French, and was kind enough to rent me one of his houses located in the center of Tokyo. I was also fortunate to find a studio and darkroom facility through Junzo Sakakura, an architect friend of Kawazoe whom we had met in Paris at the opening of the 1937 World's Fair. Sakakura had worked in architect Le Corbusier's office and was the designer of the Japanese pavilion. By the time Irene arrived, I was comfortably established in Japan.

Because Francis' carte d'identité expired first, he left with our Japanese friends on the Suwa Maru in December. I remained to close our studio and pack all our belongings, since my permit was still good for a few more months. Surrounding me were war and destruction. Sirens were screaming constantly, gas masks were distributed, the outskirts of Paris were bombed, and we had to take refuge in shelters. But the city of Paris was spared, and the French seemed very confident, believing in the miracle of the Maginot Line.

After a long, anxious wait, a ticket arrived from Francis, and in April 1940 I, too, was on my way to the Far East. I had mixed feelings of anxiety and sorrow leaving France behind. I still have vivid memories of a Hungarian poet friend, his face flushed, who was running after the train I was leaving on from Paris to Marseille, shouting,

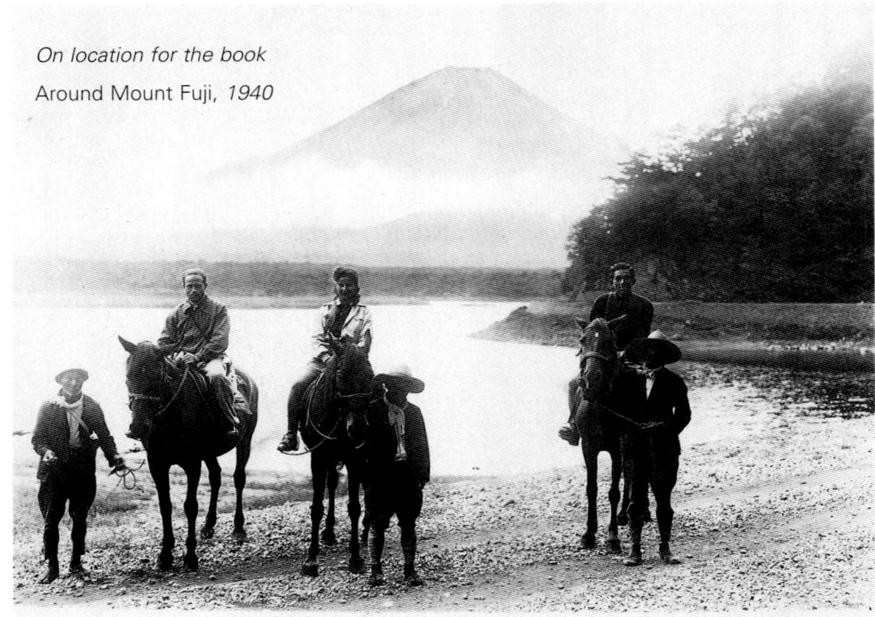

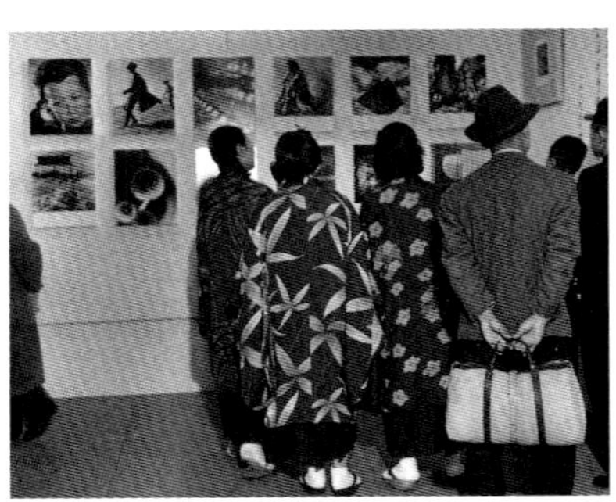

Exhibits at the Shirokiya department store in June 1940 and April 1941 attracted much interest.

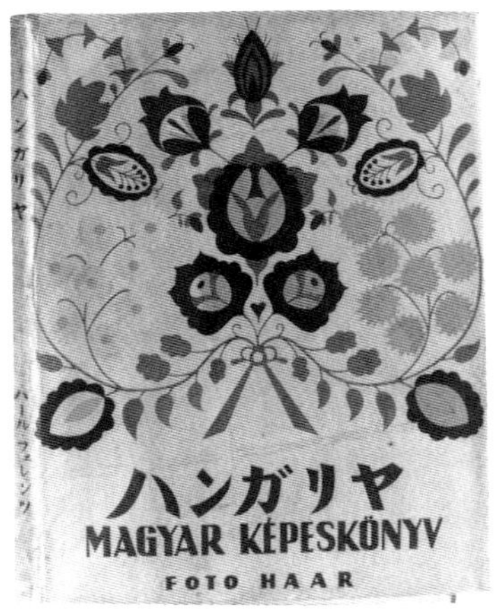

Cover for Francis' second book published in Japan, in 1941, Hungaria: Magyar Képeskönyv (Hungarian Picture Book), with cover design by Irene Haar

For a while, we were very content. Japanese people are polite and considerate, we were far away from the troubles of war in Europe, and we were confident we could begin a new life in Japan.

Kawazoe actively promoted us. Soon after my arrival, he arranged a large photo exhibit for me in the gallery of Shirokiya, one of the largest department stores in Tokyo. The exhibit was well received and led to my first book in Japan, *Way to the Orient*, which was published in 1940. In this book I presented my work from Hungary and Paris, together with photographs taken on the trip to Japan and others taken since my arrival. It was well received and quickly sold out.

I was then introduced to an art-book publisher who was interested in bringing out large-format photo essay books. The first idea I proposed to him was a book about Hungary called *The Hungarian Picture Book*, a selection from the work I had done in the Hungarian countryside before Paris. The text was written in both Japanese and Hungarian, and Irene designed the cover for the book, which has now become a collector's item in Hungary.

My next book, for the same publisher, was *Around Mount Fuji*. In the summer of 1940, Irene and I, accompanied by a student assistant, had hiked around this extinct volcano, which is regarded as sacred by the Japanese, photographing it from many vantage points.

We established a portrait studio in the Ginza, the fashionable business district in the center of the city, where I made portraits of many prominent Japanese of the day.

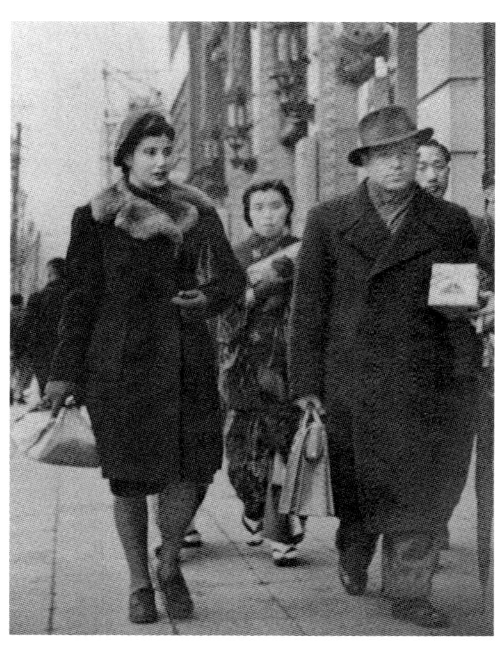

Irene and Francis shopping in Tokyo soon after their arrival in Japan, 1940

The longer we lived in Japan, the more I realized that people there held a great interest in and general sympathy for Hungary and the Hungarian people. In fact, I later discovered that Kawazoe had invited us to his country not only because he liked my work but simply because we were Hungarians. I recall one occasion in particular when we were in the Ginza; we noticed a crowd in front of a music store listening to music being played on a record player. To my great surprise, I realized they were listening intently to Liszt's *Hungarian Rhapsody*.

On another occasion, in the hot and humid Tokyo summer, Irene and I decided to go to a public swimming pool to cool off. People were waiting in a long line in front of the entrance to the pool. As we were waiting we chatted in Hungarian, and a young man in a black university student uniform turned around and asked us in broken English what language we were speaking. When he realized we were Hungarians, he was so interested in us that he bought tickets for us and resisted all our attempts to pay him back.

I became more and more interested in why the Japanese had these friendly feelings toward Hungarians. I eventually met Juichiro Imaoka, a linguist working for the Japanese Foreign Ministry, who was interested in the relationship between the two languages. He had worked in Hungary as a diplomat for eight years and not only had learned to speak the language but also had done some literary translations from Hungarian into Japanese. He followed other linguists in concluding that the languages were related, with both having common origins in the Ural-Altaic language family in Central Asia. This helped explain the identical sentence construction and other grammatical similarities. On the main floor of the large family house we had rented, Imaoka and I together established a Japanese-Hungarian Cultural Society, which enabled him to continue his publications about Hungary. We even succeeded in getting Baron Takaharu Mitsui to become the president.

Japan was everything I had hoped it would be: endlessly picturesque, with beautiful landscapes beyond imagination and delicate, fragile charm in everything. I traveled all over, starting by shooting pictures to be used for travel posters for the Japan National Tourist Organization. I liked to shoot formal compositions of the landscapes—seacoasts, mountains, the magnificent shrines. In those days, I was more interested in the pictorial possibilities of nature than in the people and human drama around me. I had to see all of this beautiful land before I could begin to see the even more powerful beauty subtly interwoven underneath.

Living in Japan was a fascinating experience for Irene and me. In Europe, I had always felt I was a modern man, interested only in looking toward the future.

I was never particularly interested in what had happened in the past. In Japan, however, I faced a living tradition.

Japanese people treasure and maintain aesthetic values from their past that inform the present—in the simplicity of their architecture, in the sparse furnishings of a traditional home, in the way the house opens onto a garden, even in the way a meal is served. The great importance placed on the family, the respect shown for the elderly—all these traditions deeply impressed me. Very quickly, I felt my outlook on life begin to change.

I also became interested in the traditional theater of Japan, including Kabuki, Noh, and the Bunraku puppet theater. People in the West knew little about them at that time, and I began to study them, taking pictures and preparing for my next publication. Then came the attack on Pearl Harbor.

A year and a half after our arrival in Japan, war suddenly caught up with us. All foreigners were ordered to leave Tokyo. Nationals belonging to the Allies had to leave Japan or be interned in a prison camp near Kobe. Those from Nazi Germany and Fascist Italy were sent to a place near Mount Fuji. Because Hungary was not considered an enemy nation Irene and I, with our two babies, were sent to the resort town of Karuizawa along with citizens of other neutral nations, including Swiss, Turks, and South Americans. Our first child, Thomas, had been born in 1941, and our second child, Veronica, was born the following year. We evacuated to Karuizawa in the spring of 1943.

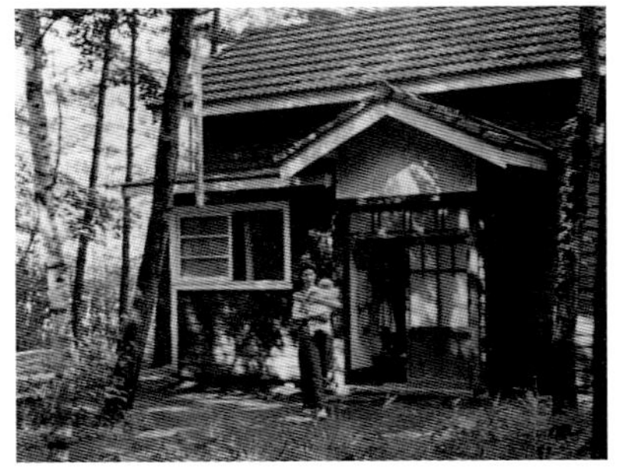

Irene holding her first-born, Thomas, in front of the house in Karuizawa where the Haars spent the war years in virtual confinement

Karuizawa is a town in the mountains northwest of Tokyo, a plush summer vacation spot popular both with wealthy Japanese and foreigners. We had been there twice before to escape the midsummer heat in Tokyo. We managed to rent the same house we had used before, but this time we had to prepare for the long, cold winter. Although it was a two-story house, basically we lived in one small room on the first floor, which was heated by a small wood-burning stove that we fed with dry branches collected from the nearby woods.

We were fortunate to have a Japanese maid, who helped take care of the children while Irene and I gathered firewood and did the domestic chores necessary to survive. Shizuko had been with us in Tokyo, but when war broke out and we had to leave the capital, we regretfully told her we would have to let her go because we would no longer have an income to pay her wages. She dismissed the idea and insisted she would stay with us. Because she had worked for us so long, she felt she was part of the family. Shizuko stayed with us in Karuizawa through three and a half years of hardship, until the end of the war.

Once the youth of Japan had been mobilized, food was rationed and soon became scarce. We received about a pound of bread a week for the whole family. Our main problem was finding a way to get milk for the children and food for us. I made a small vegetable garden beside the house, but this did not yield enough to get us through the long winter months. Fortunately, a small stream ran near our house with a lot of watercress growing in it, and this is what saved us, as it grew even in the wintertime. Irene used it in many ingenious ways—in soup, sautéed, or raw as a salad. We lived almost on watercress alone.

We managed to buy from a Japanese farmer a milking goat, which we fed with cut branches and leftovers from the kitchen. Irene milked it daily for the two young children, and for a while things seemed to improve.

We had our goat mated, and it gave birth to one kid. In the summer, when the kid was big enough to eat leaves, I would cut branches for both of them. One day, I tethered the kid with a rope around its neck at the side of the stream, where it could eat the grass growing there. A couple of hours later, when I went back to check on it, I was shocked to discover the kid had slipped into the stream and hung itself on the rope. When I touched it, it was motionless but still warm. I ran back to the kitchen, picked up a sharp knife, returned to the stream, and cut the throat of the small creature to let the blood out. This way we could eat meat, something we hadn't tasted for months. After the hide was dried, I made boots for both of our children. The soles were made from a piece of wooden board. We had to be inventive in those limited circumstances.

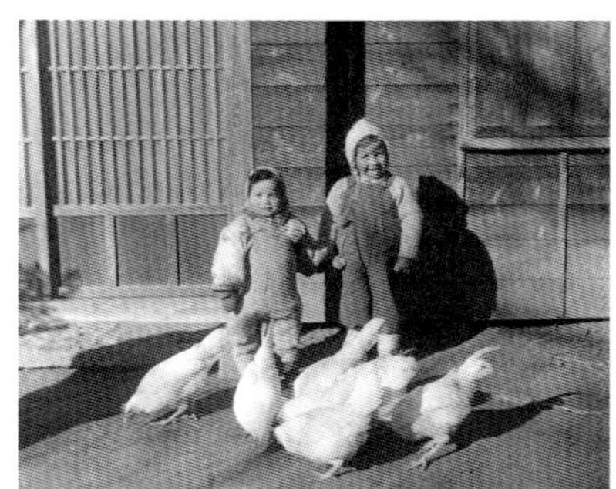

By 1943, the Haars had two children. Karuizawa was bitterly cold in the winter, and the children had to be wrapped up warmly.

Money lost its value. We could only exchange our belongings for food with farmers at neighboring villages. In this manner we got two goats, and some rabbits and chickens. The farmer showed me how to feed and take care of the livestock and how to milk the milking goat. This was something new to me, and I was nervous and clumsy at first; fortunately, the goat was patient, and after a few attempts, I succeeded. I was so proud of myself. Goat's milk was very nourishing but had a peculiar strong odor and flavor, and I had to dilute it for our children. I even made some really good cheese from it.

Winter in Karuizawa was long and cold, which made it difficult to grow vegetables throughout the year. Fortunately, there was a small stream nearby where watercress grew—a valuable food, which I used in many ways. I also became a diligent follower of horses, in order to gather their manure to enrich the vegetable garden.

We practically lived in one room in the winter, the room with the stove. We warmed up by the stove and ran upstairs to bed. For our two small children, we made boots from goatskin and coats from rabbit fur. We got our nutrition from miso (soybean paste), which was on our menu three times a day. Sometimes I traveled to faraway villages for apples, walnuts, and flour in exchange for clothing. We managed to survive.

The incident with the goat was a real tragedy for us, since it was a milking goat. Eventually, Francis became ill from malnutrition and was bedridden. I had to work and shop for food. I remember one bitter cold winter morning standing in line at the butcher shop to get soup bones at five o'clock in the morning. We were all numb from the cold. All of a sudden, the woman in front of me just turned and walked away. As I approached the counter, I found out the reason why: the butcher had run out of soup bones.

Real hardship came after two years, when our reserves of money ran out. There was only one thing left to do—barter our possessions for food from Japanese farmers. Our clothing was reduced to a minimum (by the end of the war, I owned only one pair of pants and one shirt). Next, we exchanged one of my cameras for a large sack of potatoes and some vegetables. It wasn't such a big sacrifice, because I couldn't use it anyway. As a foreign photographer, I was considered a potential spy, and we were constantly watched by the Kempeitai, the military police.

But the shortage of food had its effect. After about three years in Karuizawa, an inflammation developed all over my body, a sure sign of malnutrition. The doctor in our community was unable to help me, and I became weaker and weaker until I had no choice but to stay in bed, where I remained for several months. Tokyo was being bombed, and while I was bedridden I often thought about the stacks of photo negatives in my studio there. I was too weak to retrieve them, however, and lost many of my irreplaceable old negatives and glass plates when the studio was destroyed by the bombing.

Soon after the Tokyo bombing, we received an order from the police saying we would no longer be allowed to communicate with Japanese people. We weren't even allowed to greet each other on the street. Our neighbor used to collect the garbage from her kitchen and bring it over to us to feed our goats. The day after the new restriction was introduced, she left her container on the street in front of our house instead of bringing it to our door. An hour later, the military police were at her house, warning her to stop this kind of contact with foreigners or face imprisonment. We were watched all the time.

Although we didn't really understand the reason for this restriction, we guessed it had been caused by events on the war front. The military police wanted to prevent the Japanese from hearing any rumors about the course of the war.

We could hear the bombs exploding nearby, night and day. The earth was shaking and everybody was scared. The windows were covered with black paper to prevent any light shining out at night. No one seemed to know what was happening. There was a rumor that the Americans would invade Japan and everyone should fight with whatever they could lay their hands on or escape to the mountains. We filled our backpacks with a few cans of food, rolled up blankets, and put on as many layers of clothing as we could and waited—but for what, we did not know.

A complete stillness awoke us on the morning of August 15 [1945], a beautifully bright sunny day. It was so still that it was frightening. About ten o'clock that morning a good friend from the Swiss Embassy came running into our garden. Her face was flushed and tears were rolling down her cheeks. She hugged me and whispered into my ear, "The war is over, the war is over, MacArthur is in the Philippines!" Before I could say anything, off she went, carrying the good news to other friends.

Then the police went around with loudspeakers telling everyone to listen to the radio at 12:00 noon to hear the Emperor speak to the nation. When the time came, our maid went to the neighbors' to listen to the radio. When she returned, she was crying. "Hiroshima and Nagasaki were bombed and are in ruins. Japan has surrendered!"

The surrender was a great shock for the Japanese people. It was the first military defeat they had experienced in the country's long history. Several military officers committed suicide, unable to accept the humiliation. For us, however, it meant the end of our misery, and we were overwhelmed with joy. From this time on, all the restrictions we had been forced to face disappeared. We heard from a foreign diplomat that the Americans would soon be arriving in Japan. In a few weeks, Foreign Minister Shigemitsu signed the surrender document and peace treaty with General MacArthur aboard the battleship *Missouri*.

Some foreigners, including one of our friends, managed to obtain special permission to visit Tokyo. We waited anxiously for his return to hear news of what happened to Tokyo. He returned very late at night, utterly exhausted from the trip. "The train was so crowded that I could hardly stand," he began in an excited voice. "The city was in ruins except for some large buildings." As he was speaking, he began to shake out the contents of his backpack. "The large buildings are being occupied by the American Occupation Forces as headquarters." Out poured chewing gum, cube sugar, K-rations, a can of ham, and even a couple of bars of chocolate. We couldn't believe the things we were seeing.

In a few days, American jeeps were running on the roads. Two American soldiers were guided to our home by the English-speaking young son of a family friend of ours. They were correspondents for the military magazine Yank, *and they were looking for a photographer to work with them. They brought with them some K-rations, and we had a festive dinner together. The baked beans and chopped ham tasted heavenly. Francis got the job, and the two Americans asked him to join them in Tokyo. They become instant friends.*

Within a week or so, I felt strong enough to go down to Tokyo with the American reporters. There I was examined by an American doctor, who attributed the inflammation on my body to undernourishment and lack of vitamins. He gave me some injections and pills and saw to it that I received good, nutritious food. Three weeks later, I was ready to begin work.

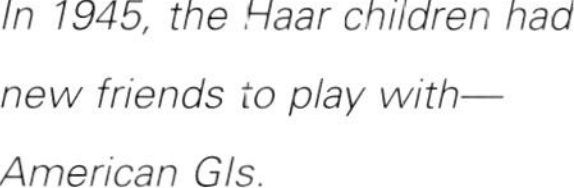

In 1945, the Haar children had new friends to play with— American GIs.

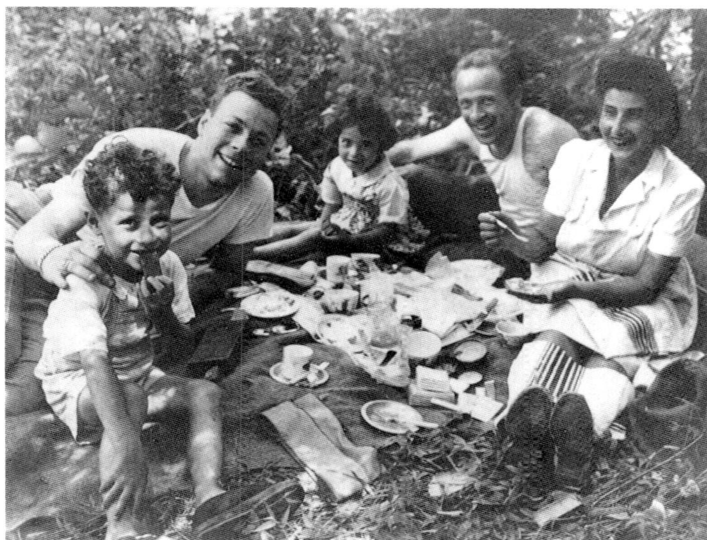

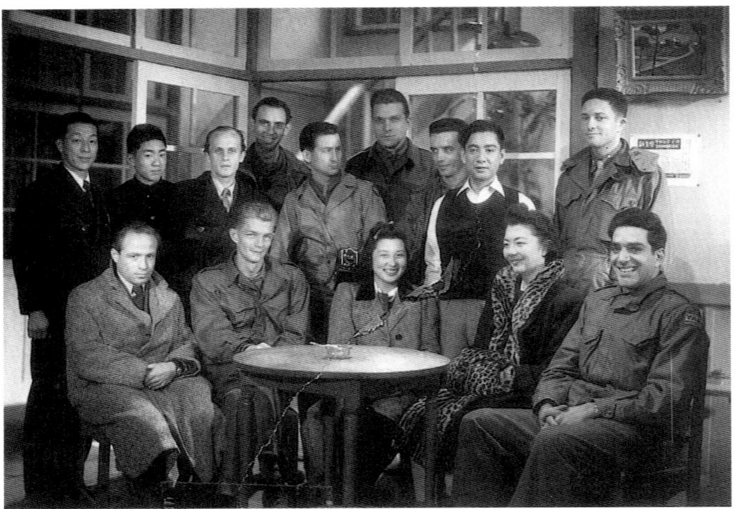

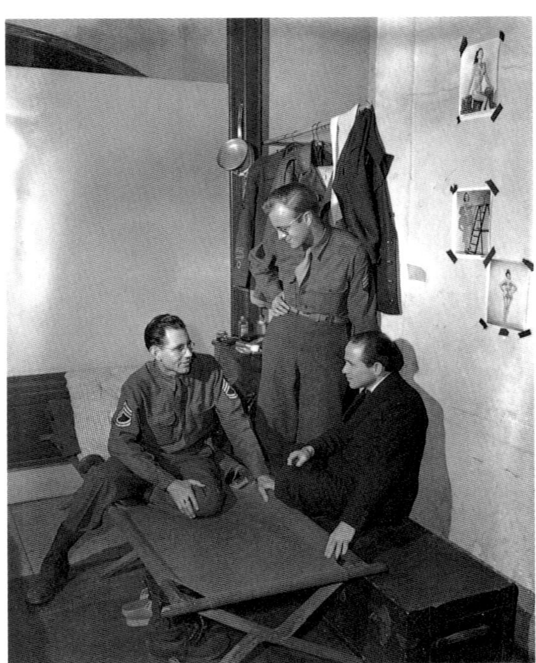

Francis Haar (seated, left) with
the U.S. Signal Corps in Tokyo,
1946

My job was straightforward. We were simply expected to go around reporting on what was happening in newly occupied Japan, and I was to take photographs to illustrate the Americans' stories. I worked for them for six months on this assignment and then had the resources to move my family from Karuizawa, first to Tokyo and then to Kamakura, an hour's train ride from Tokyo. Our third child, Andrew, was born in the spring of 1946, just before our move to Kamakura.

My next job was with the Public Health and Welfare section of General MacArthur's Headquarters, shooting 16 mm motion pictures. One job I remember well was filming Japanese soldiers, recently repatriated from China, who were suffering from all kinds of infectious diseases, including typhus and cholera. The doctors dressed me up in rubber boots and rubber gloves, and I wore a mask over my face. This was the only way I could go on board the quarantined ship.

This work lasted three months, after which I became an advisor in audio/visual education with the Civil Information and Education Division at U.S. General Headquarters, or GHQ, working in a program to educate the Japanese about democracy. Compared with my early work for the occupation authorities, this was an excellent job, a real promotion for me. On occasion, I was even asked to act as interpreter for the American education officers, even though my English was limited. We traveled around Japan in our own train, complete with restaurant car. We would pull into a station and stay there until the education program was finished, showing films and giving talks.

Only one problem remained: as a foreign national, I received a very low salary, which was not enough to feed my family. When we returned to Tokyo, I had to look around for additional income.

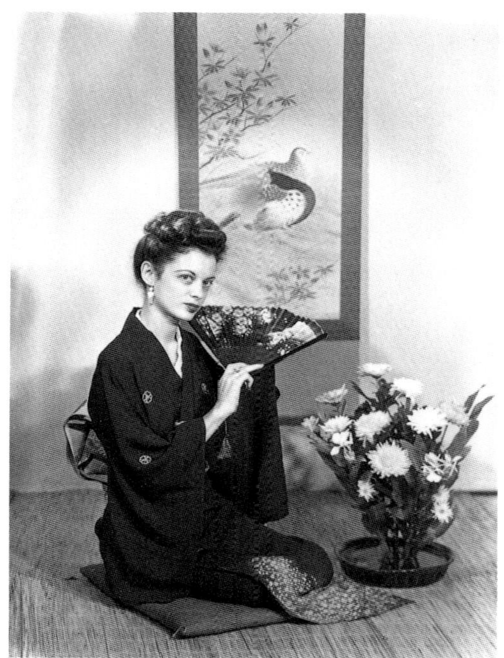

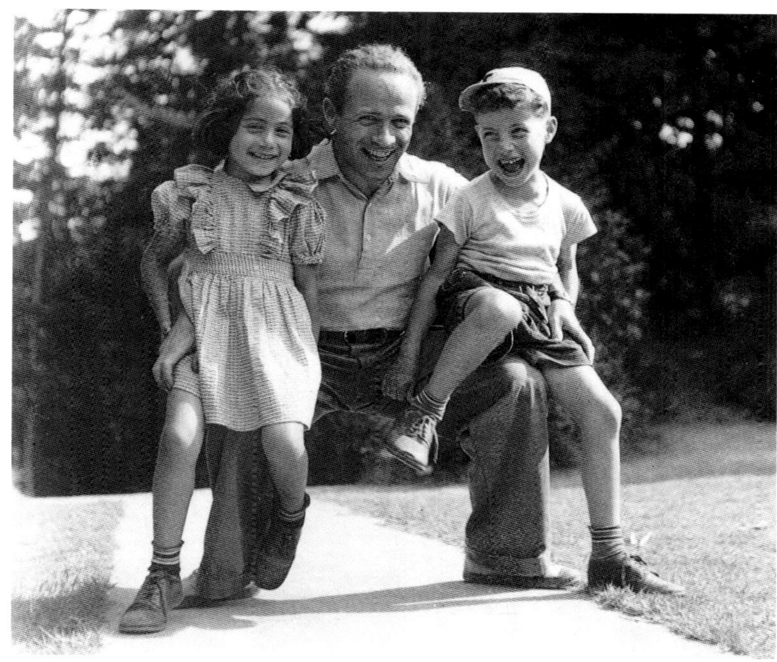

Some of the large buildings in the city had been taken over by the American occupation forces. One of these was the Mitsubishi Shoji Building, which was being used as a billet for the women's corps. As an employee of the occupation forces, I managed to get permission to set up a photo studio in this building. Because Irene was already an experienced photographer, I let her run the studio while I was away on assignment with the Americans, and I went to help her every day after work. We were especially busy around Christmas, when the American women liked to have their photographs taken dressed up in kimono, kneeling on a Japanese cushion, to send home as a Christmas card.

With the help of an American naval officer, we were lucky enough to rent an attractive little house near the seashore in Kamakura. Many American friends visited us there on the weekends, and Irene, who is an excellent cook, treated them to Hungarian dishes. These went down so well that she received repeated suggestions to open a Hungarian restaurant. Initially, she took this as a simple compliment, but later we started to think seriously about the idea, as my income was still limited, not sufficient to support the family.

Irene eventually found a wealthy Japanese partner to provide the necessary financial backing, and in 1950 she opened a restaurant called "Irene's Hungaria," in the Ginza. She painted the walls with scenes of Hungarian peasant life and decorated the furniture with colorful Hungarian flowers. The Japanese waiters were dressed in Hungarian shirts, and the cooks were taught how to prepare such Hungarian delicacies as goulash and chicken paprika, together with other European dishes. She had created an authentic Hungarian atmosphere, and the restaurant quickly became popular. There were only a few foreign restaurants in

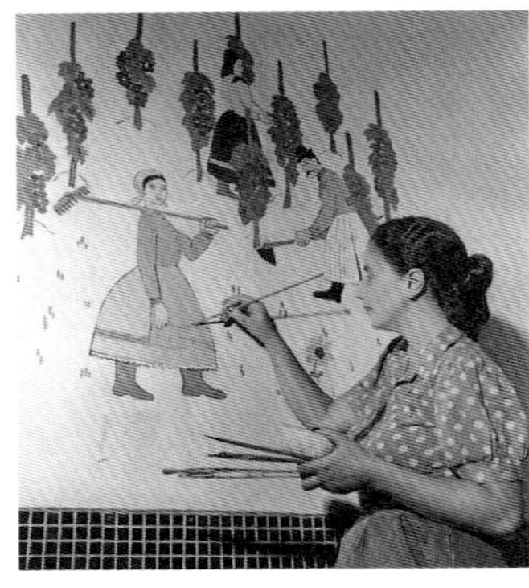

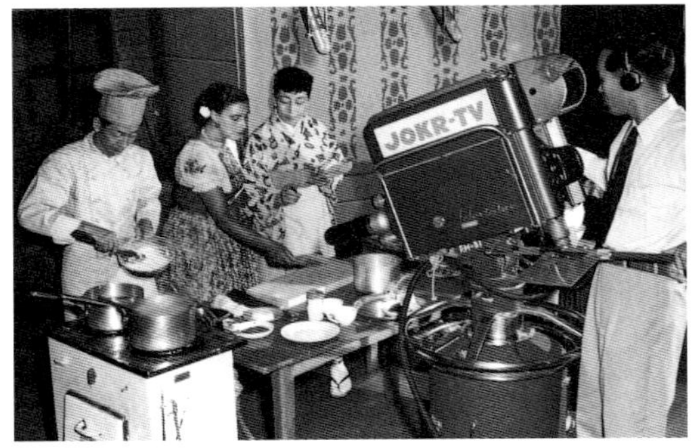

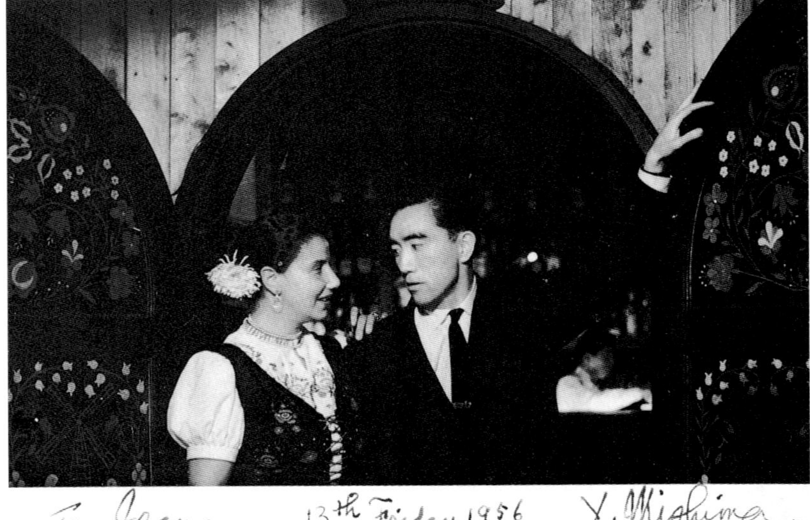

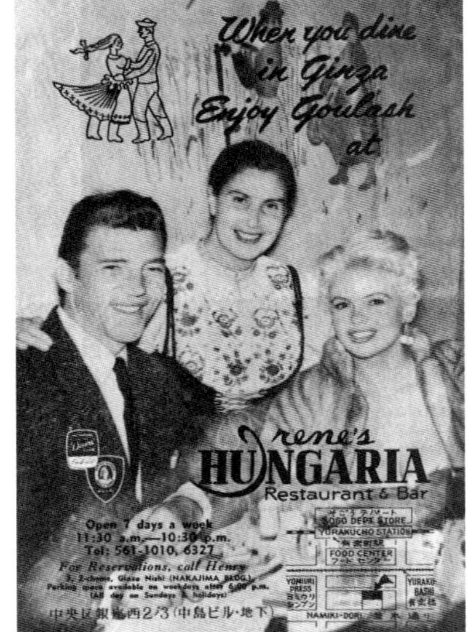

Irene personally painted the walls of her restaurant in Hungarian folk style, 1951.

A cooking demonstration on television with Chef Saito

Famed novelist Yukio Mishima visited "Irene's Hungaria" restaurant in Tokyo, 1956.

The restaurant became a favorite with celebrities visiting Japan, such as Jayne Mansfield and her husband, Mickey Hargitay, who posed for this publicity photo.

Tokyo in the 1950s, and "Irene's Hungaria" soon became a meeting place for artists, writers, and actors, both Japanese and foreign. Celebrities visiting Japan dropped by regularly: I remember William Holden, Danilova, and James Michener. On one memorable night, Prince and Princess Chichibu of Japan came to be served in a special party room, where they could enjoy their meal in privacy.

It was a difficult task to build up a restaurant, especially in a foreign country. Although I was confident of my skills and spoke fluent Japanese by then, teaching the Japanese cooks the art of Hungarian cooking was a real challenge. They had never before seen paprika, let alone used it for cooking. Their approach and style of cooking was so Japanese. One morning when I went into the kitchen to survey how the cooks were getting along, I found the chief chef placing boiled onions in a separate, neat group next to the cooked meat, saying, "Goulash looks much nicer this way, doesn't it?" I had to gently convince him that it did not taste like a Hungarian dish should, though it might look attractive to the eyes. But as the cooks learned to enjoy the flavor and appreciate the art

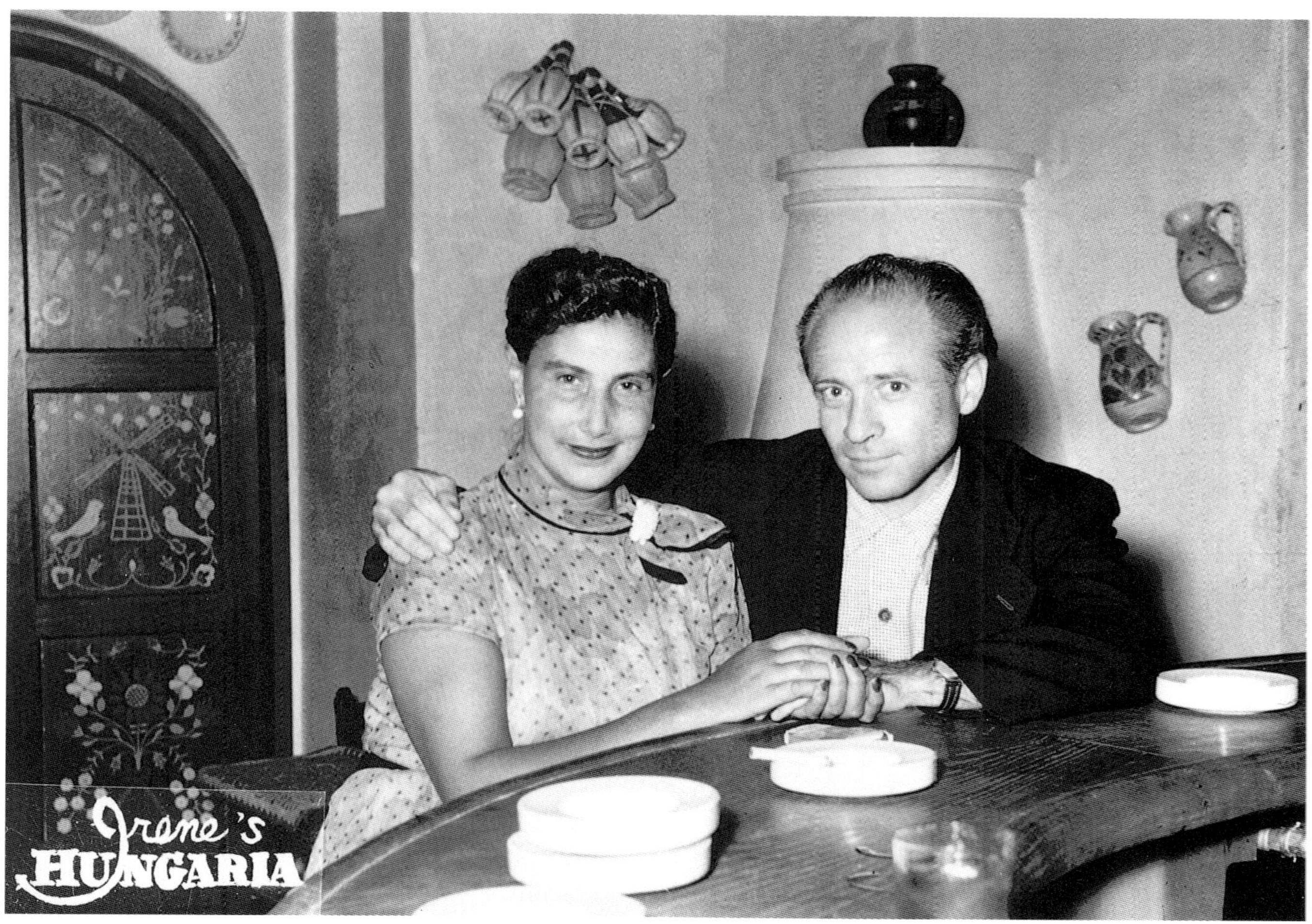

of Hungarian cooking themselves, they began to love it, especially the aroma, taste, and pretty red color of the key ingredient, paprika.

My whole staff was wonderful. They worked with me like a team—no, more than a team, like a family, with loyalty and understanding. I designed handsome white shirts with Hungarian embroidery, red ribbon neckties, and black slacks for the waiters. The waiters even learned a few Hungarian words and phrases. When Hungarians came to dine at the restaurant and heard Japanese waiters greeting them in Hungarian, they were thrilled. The restaurant developed a character of its own.

By 1948, I was ready to resume my career as a creative photographer. One of the first nonmilitary projects I was involved in was a tourism promotion film called *Picturesque Japan*, made for the newly revived Japan Travel Bureau in 1950. I made a documentary in 1951 called *Students Today—Japan's Tomorrow*, which was financed by the Australian Mission. This project was a look at the pressures on university students in Tokyo and was the closest I ever came to using actors, as I had real students recreate incidents from their lives.

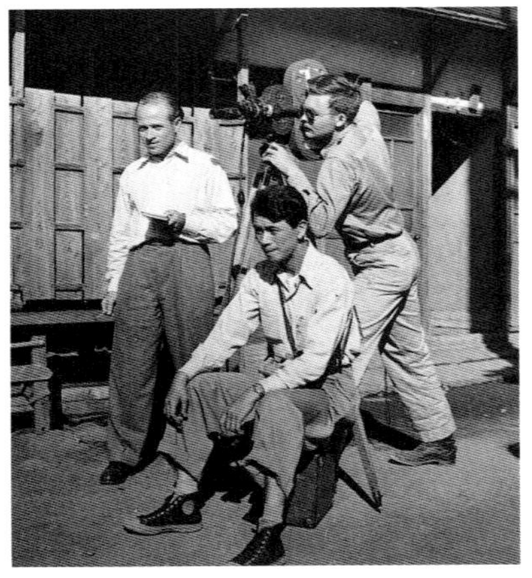

I discovered changes in my ideas and attitudes toward my work. I was growing more interested in people. Pictures of people have much to say, and say it strongly. I realized I was not saying things as strongly as I felt them.

As the occupation neared its end, in 1952, I became especially interested in photographing traditional Japanese activities, such as pearl diving and artists at work in ceramics and calligraphy. My interest in the centuries-old theatrical traditions that I had developed before the war was also reawakened. I resumed my studies of the puppet theater Bunraku, and Kabuki and Noh, and began to take pictures with publication in mind. I proposed several ideas for books to Charles Tuttle, who at the time was working for the U.S. Department of Information

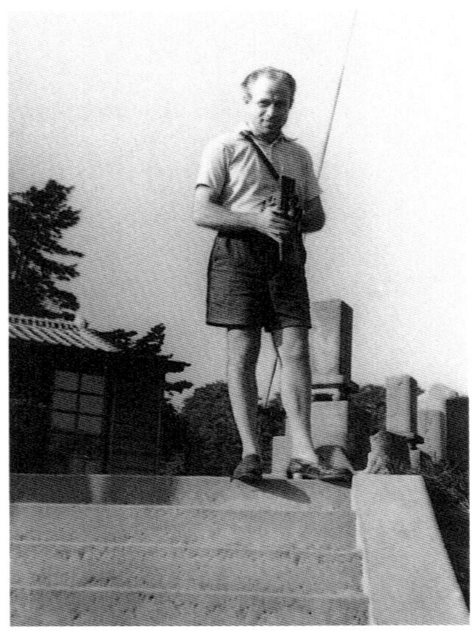

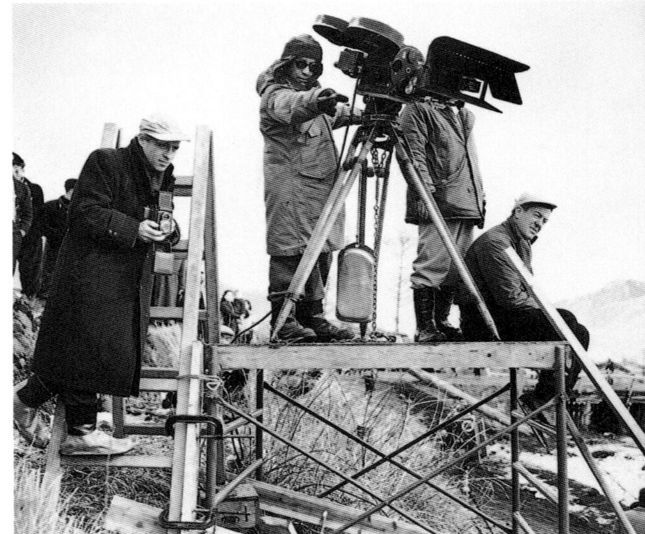

Francis developed a keen interest in film production. Here, he is directing Students Today— Japan's Tomorrow, *1951.*

Touring the Japanese countryside with his trusty Rolleiflex, 1952

Francis (left) doing location stills for House of Bamboo, *which starred Robert Ryan, 1955*

and Education in Japan. He had decided to stay in Japan after the occupation came to an end, with the idea of starting a book publishing company. Today, the company he founded is still the leading English-language publisher in Japan. He later published three of my books. The first was *The Best of Old Japan*, taken from my collection of photos of the people and customs of Japan. The next book was *Japanese Theatre in Highlights*. Once again, Kawazoe helped me, by introducing me to the theater groups, after which I could shoot freely. The third was *The Tokyo You Should See*, a little booklet guide for the visitor to Tokyo.

Traveling around Japan, I realized my two main interests were then people and the landscape. Both are fascinating. Fortunately, Japanese people are friendly and accepting of photographers. In some lands, people are hostile to the idea of having their picture taken, but not in Japan. Everyone has a camera of some kind in Japan. I think it is an excellent illustration of the intense absorption with art in everyday life that is so much a part of the Japanese way of living. They have a general sensitivity to beauty unmatched anywhere else in the world.

My approach was a kind of realistic documentary style, to capture real life as deeply as I could. Never posed: I aimed to present life as it is. I believe the aim of the photographer should be to record his visual experience.

For example, I heard of a peninsula in Japan where diving girls were working. I went there with a Japanese friend who introduced me. This was important, as the girls used to work topless. Because of the introduction they let me photograph them—their whole lifestyle, which included their husbands working as fishermen, and the grandmothers who stayed home to look after the children. Photographs from this project were published in book form as *Mermaids of Japan*, in 1954.

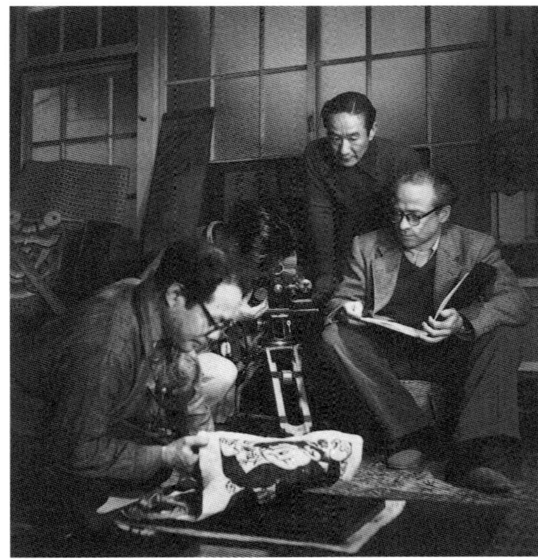

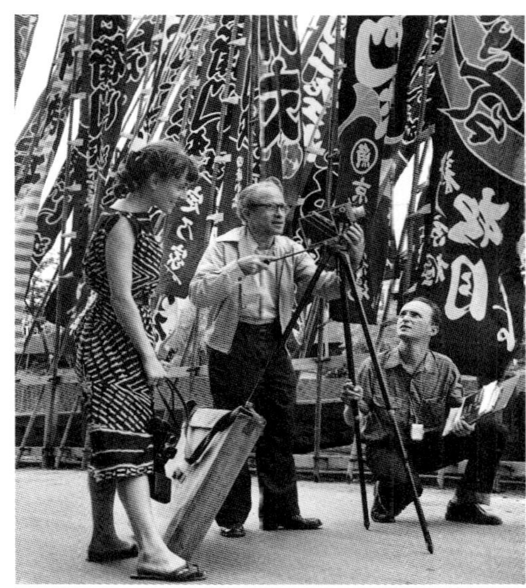

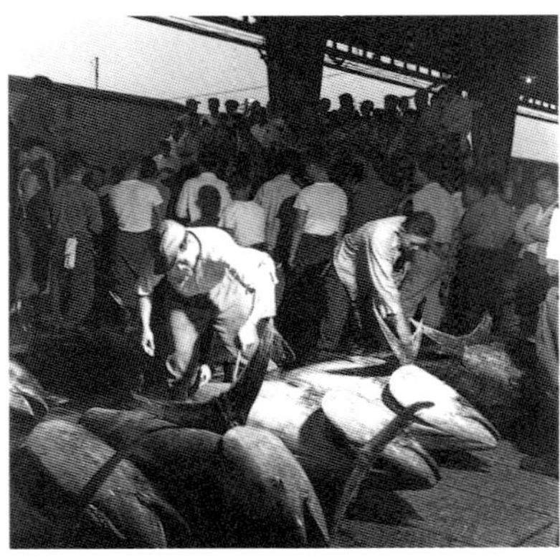

The next book was the *Geisha of Pontocho* (pp. 99, 100). I went down to Kyoto and found an American man who had married a geisha. I had the idea of doing a book about her life. The man was interested and offered to help write the text. Through his wife, we had access to the innermost circle of geisha life, even shooting a large geisha union meeting.

When I heard that the Motion Picture Department of the U.S. General Headquarters was looking for proposals for documentaries designed to improve American-Japanese relations, I already had a project in mind. I envisioned a film about Japanese traditional arts, which I proposed to George Gercke, head of the department. He was openly skeptical about the subject: "What good can a film about Japanese arts do to promote friendship and understanding between Americans and Japanese?" I argued that Japanese people are exceedingly proud of their traditional arts, and if they could see that Americans also appreciate their own culture, it would encourage feelings of mutual respect. I somehow managed to persuade him to finance the production.

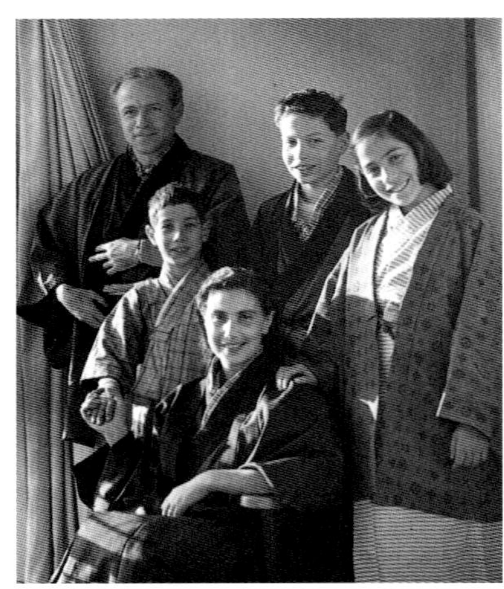

The Haars at Atami, a hot spring resort, in 1955. Clockwise from the bottom: Irene, Andrew, Francis, Thomas, and Veronica.

We built the scenario around a young American, a former GI named J. B. Blunk, who had decided to remain in Japan after the Korean War ended to study ceramics. The film followed him as he visited several renowned Japanese artists at work. We shot all over: architecture in Kyoto, pottery in Mashiko, theatrical arts like Noh and Bunraku, and even the tea ceremony performed by the Grand Master. When this film, *The Arts of Japan*, was completed in 1953, George Gercke called in some Japanese film critics and journalists for a special screening. I was anxious to hear their reactions. When the film ended, they told us, "No Japanese filmmaker could have done it better." For me, it was the highest praise I could have hoped to receive.

This was a period when I made two other short films. One was for Sophia University, called *Awakening*, shot in 1954. The next project came about when an artist from Europe received a grant from the Belgian Education Ministry to produce a film on Japanese calligraphy. His name was Pierre Alechinsky, and he was looking for a filmmaker in Tokyo. I was recommended to him, and together we started looking for the best calligraphers in Japan. We photographed them in action, at work. Calligraphy is fast, spontaneous, completed in seconds. Many calligraphers liked to work on the floor, horizontally. Others worked vertically, on the wall. It was a challenge to capture the immediacy and Zen-inspired ferocity of the medium. The film, completed in 1955, received a Special Citation at the International Festival of Art Films in Bergamo, Italy, and at the Cultural Film Festival in Tokyo.

Still photography and cinematic photography are distinctly different. The still photograph is like a little poem. The movie is more like a novel. In the still photograph, we expose at the climax of an action; it is a single, precise instant. In the movie, the action follows a curve. We pick up the start, follow the development to the climax, and then on through to the end; it is a building process—a peak is reached and left behind, and a sense of completion results. My greatest joy is if I manage to communicate a valuable message.

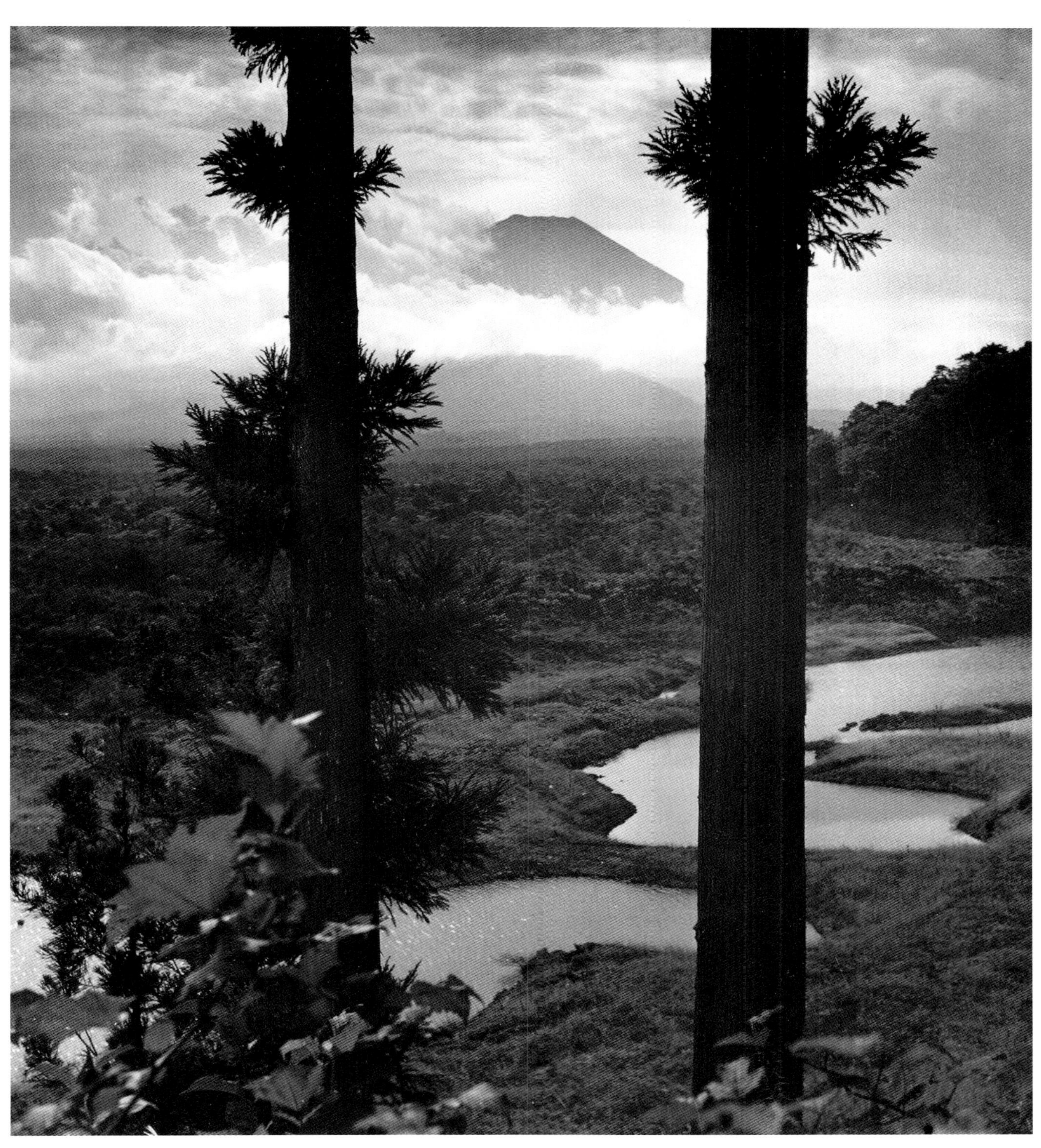

Mount Fuji from Lake Shoji, 1940

The summer after arriving in Japan, Irene and I hiked around Mount Fuji, enjoying the scenery and taking many photographs of this sacred mountain.

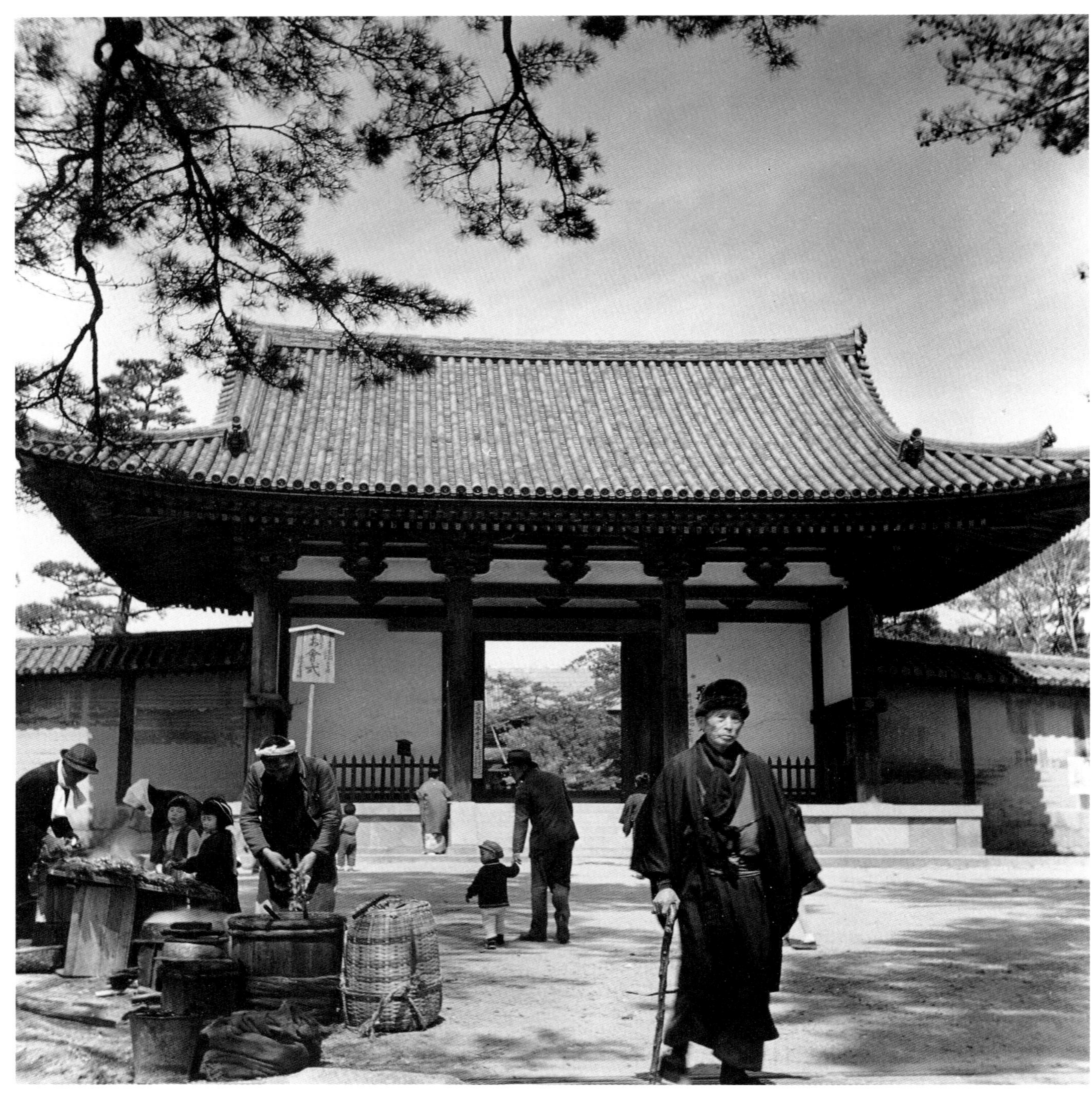

Horyuji Temple, Nara, 1940
Many scenes captivated
my interest as I traveled the
Japanese countryside, including
this entrance gate to Horyuji
Temple, the oldest wooden
structure in the world.

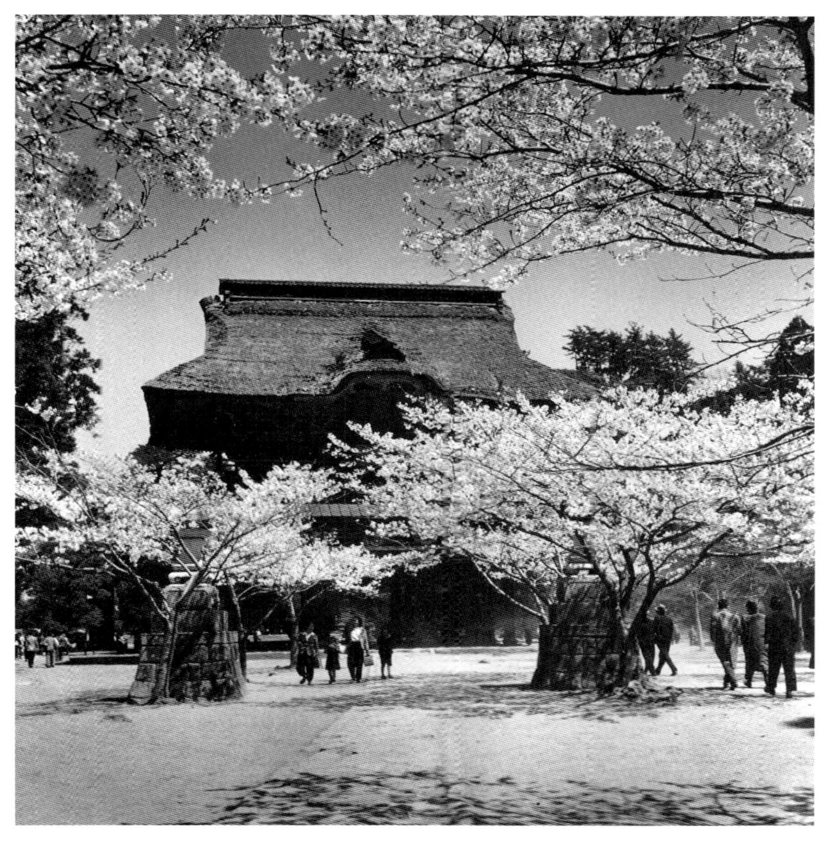

Kenchoji Temple,
Kamakura, 1940
At cherry blossom time,
temples and shrines
throughout Japan are
thronged with visitors.

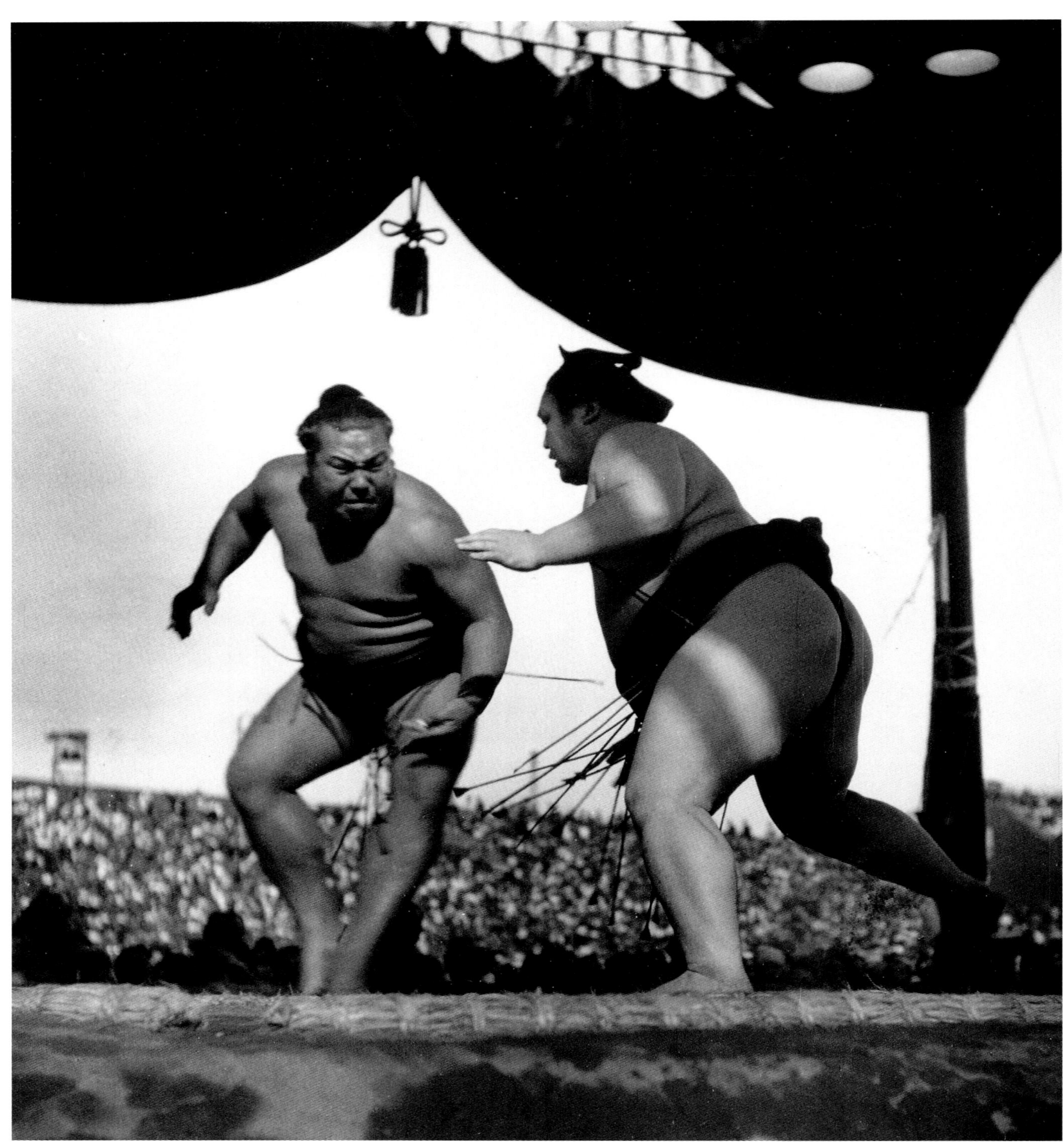

Sumo Wrestlers, 1940
After the major tournaments,
sumo wrestlers tour the
countryside putting on
exhibition bouts for
the public.

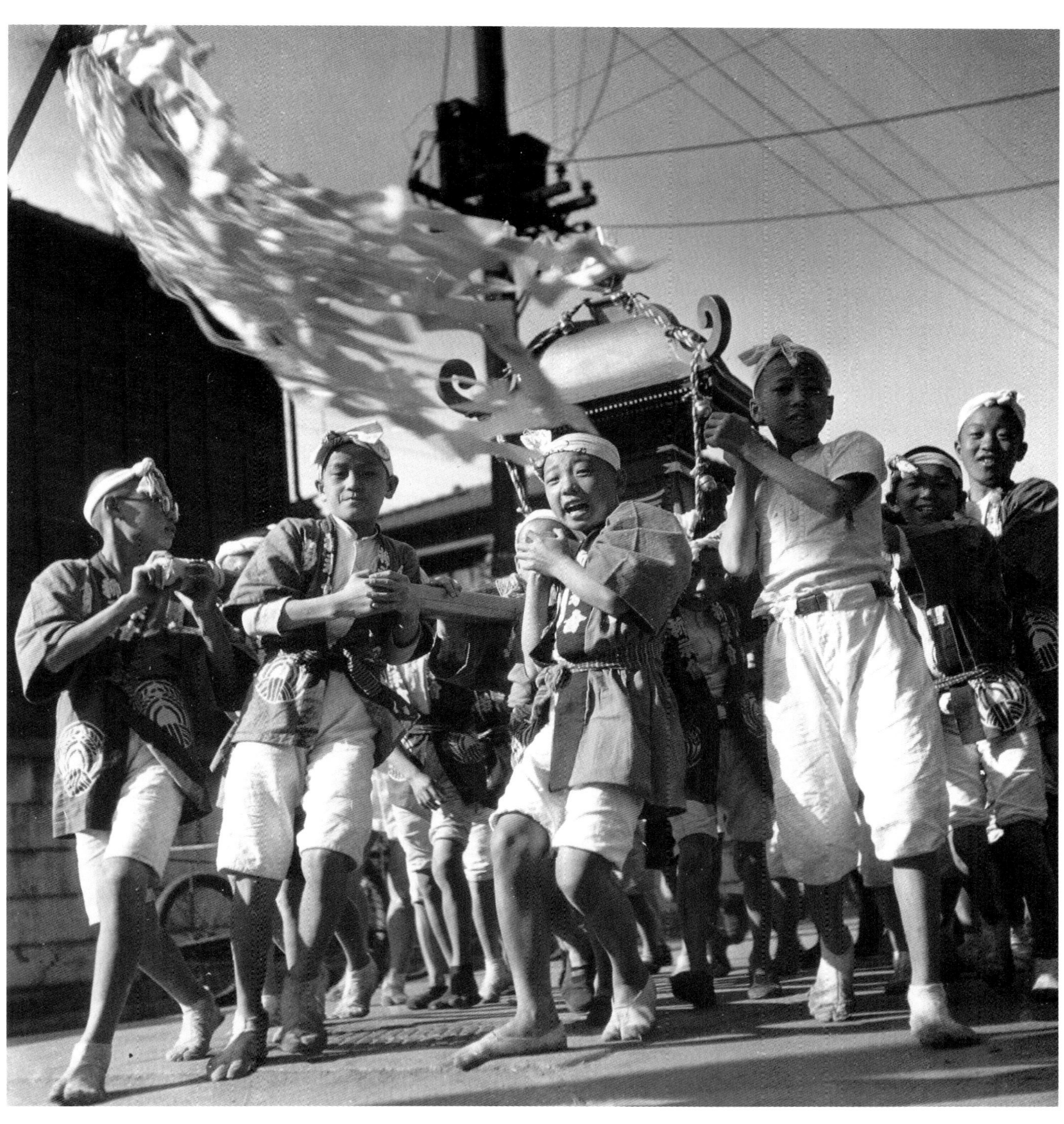

Festival Day, 1950

Boys carry a mikoshi (palanquin)
during a summer festival in
Kamakura.

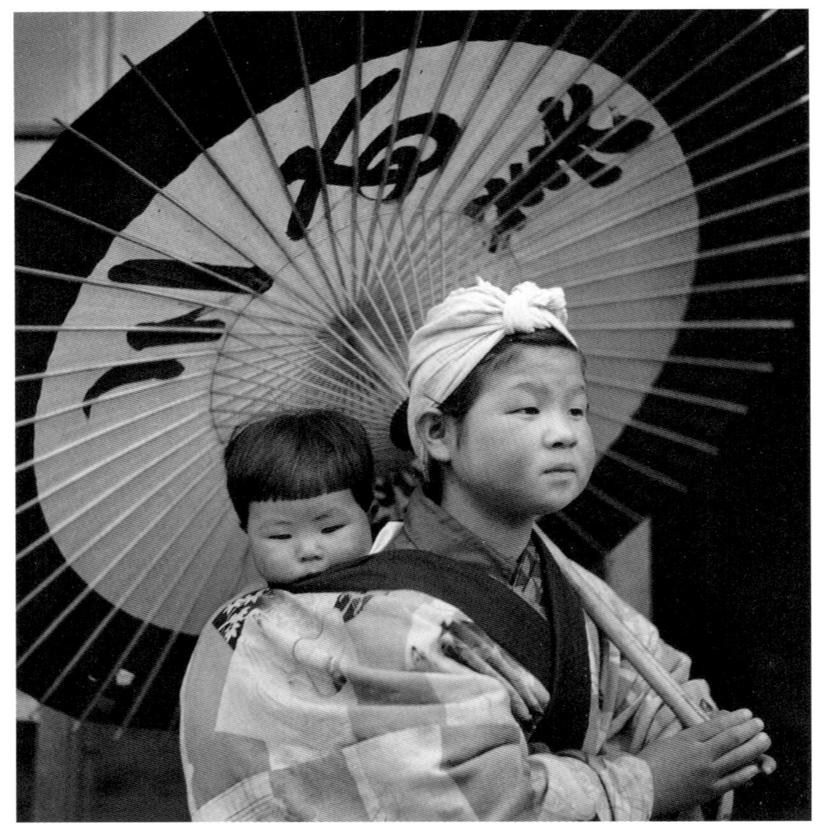

Sisters, 1940

Small children were—and still are—often carried on the back in this manner.

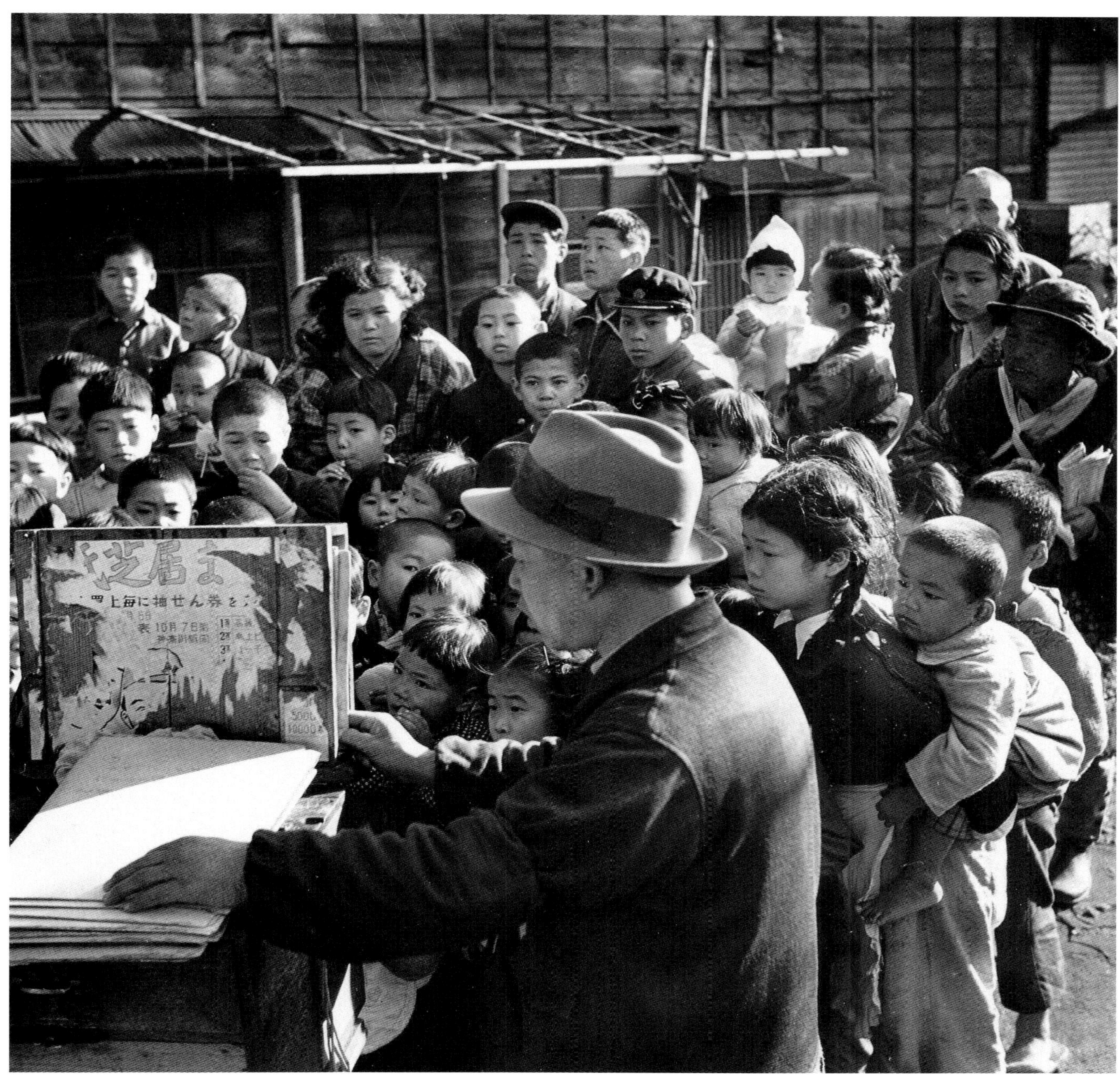

Picture Story Show, 1948

The kami shibai *(literally, paper theater)* was still a popular entertainment for children after the war, before television took over. A storyteller would visit the neighborhood every week to sell candy and tell the latest episode of a dramatic story using illustrated cards

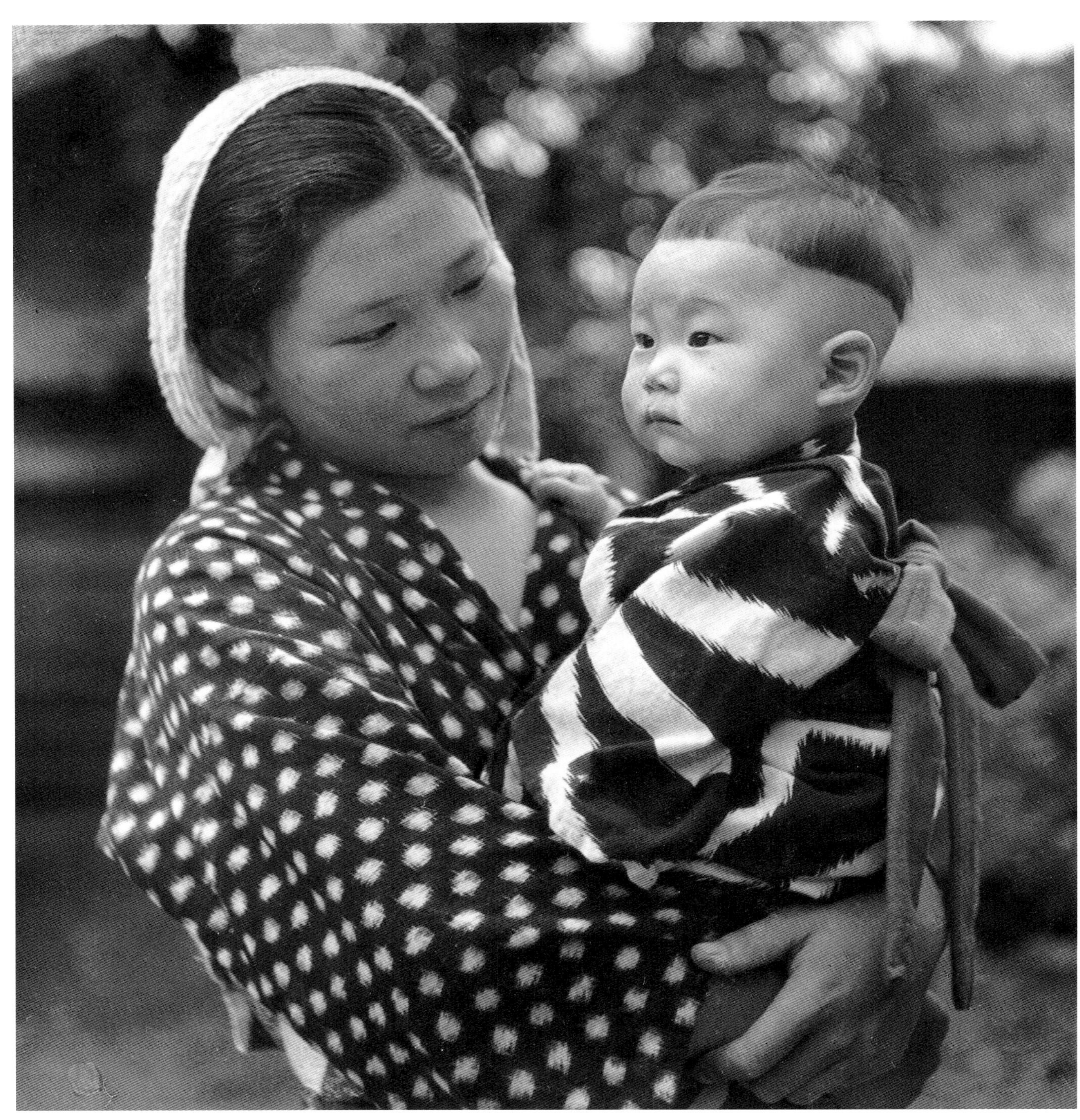

Mother and Child, 1940

*During our trip around Mount
Fuji, this village mother and
her son, wearing handwoven
clothing, caught my eye.*

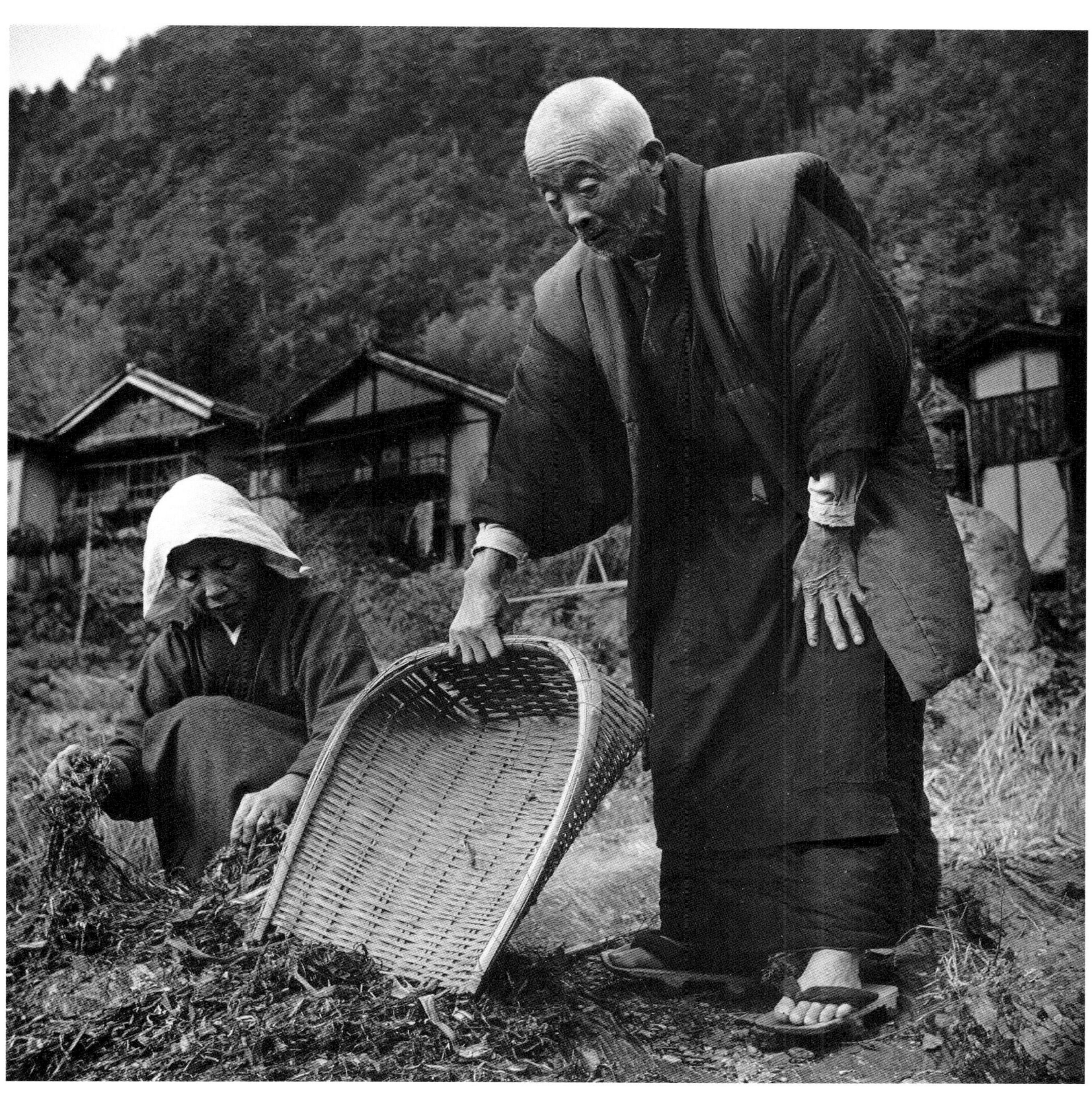

*Kuzumura, a Papermaking
Village, 1948*

*An old couple dry mulberry bark
for making paper.*

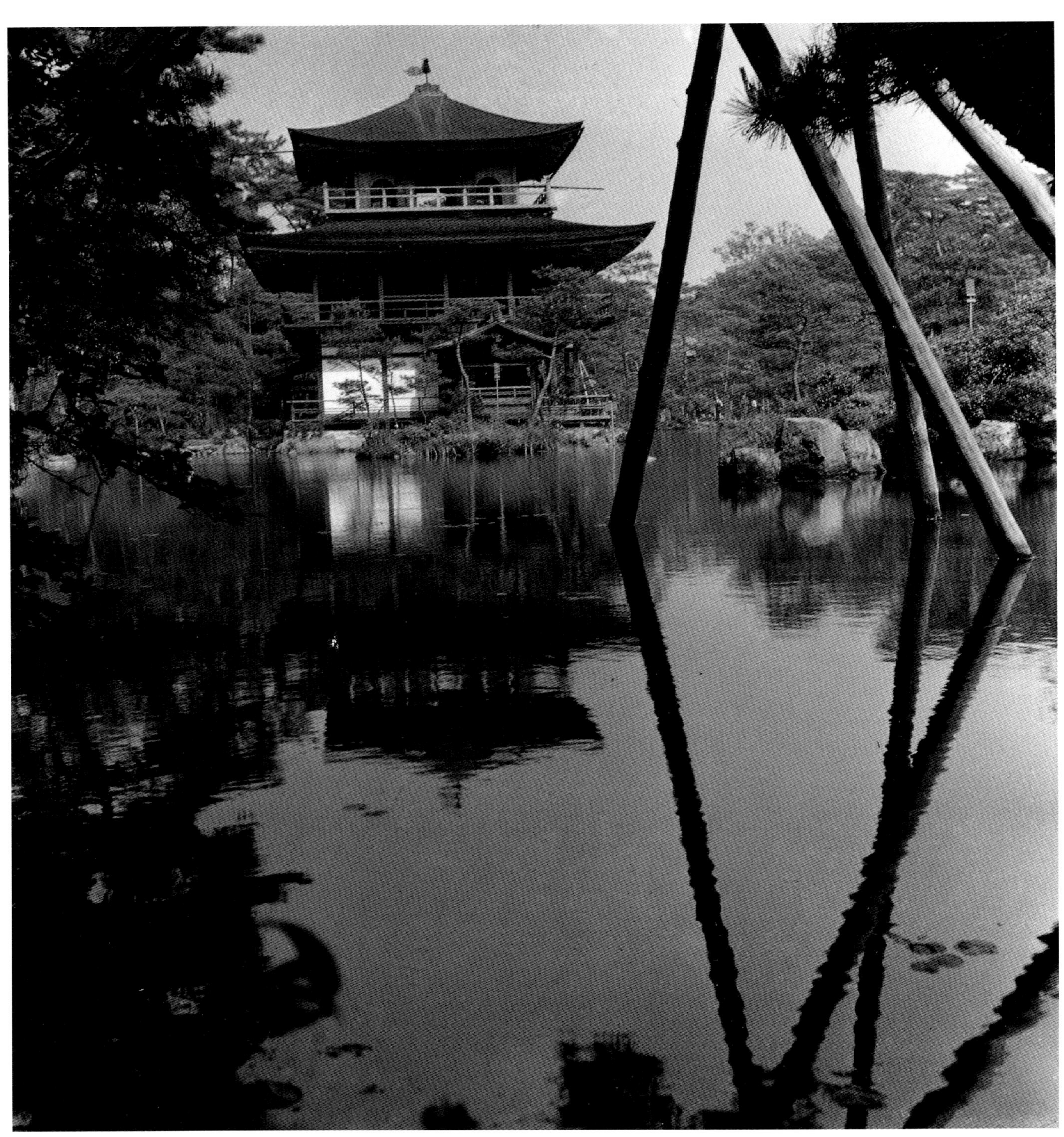

Kinkakuji, 1948

Kinkakuji, the Golden Pavilion,

was burned to the ground in

1952 and later was rebuilt.

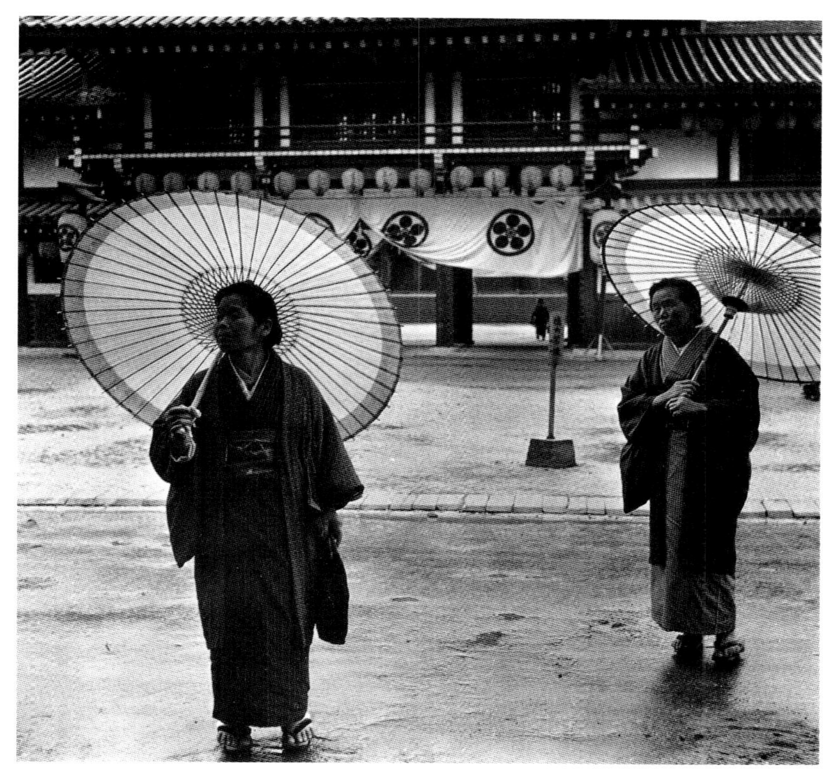

Tenrikyo Temple, Nara, 1950
Women in kimono and geta
(wooden shoes) visit the head
temple of one of the many new
religious sects that developed
in Japan.

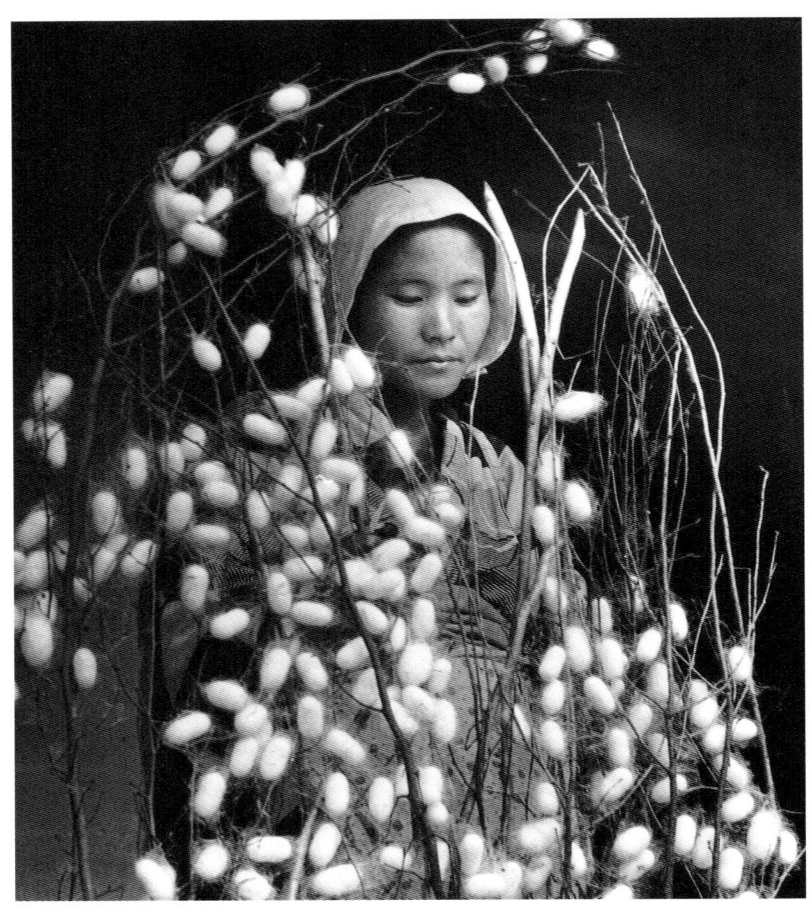

Harvesting the Silk, 1949

A farmer harvests silk cocoons

that will be used for weaving

kimono fabric.

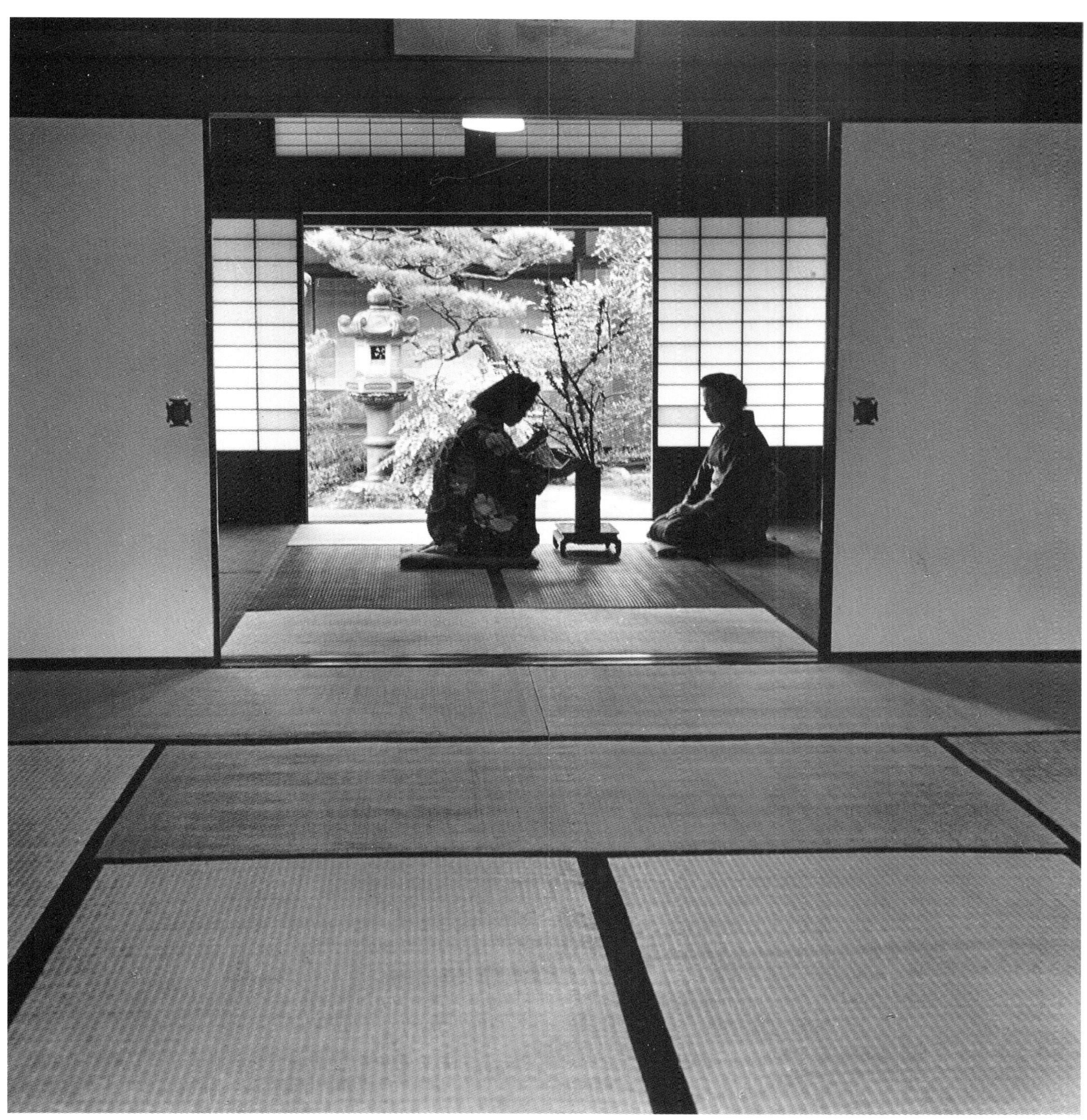

Flower Arrangement Lesson, 1953

The photo shows the beautiful simplicity of a large, traditional Japanese interior space—in this instance, of a temple.

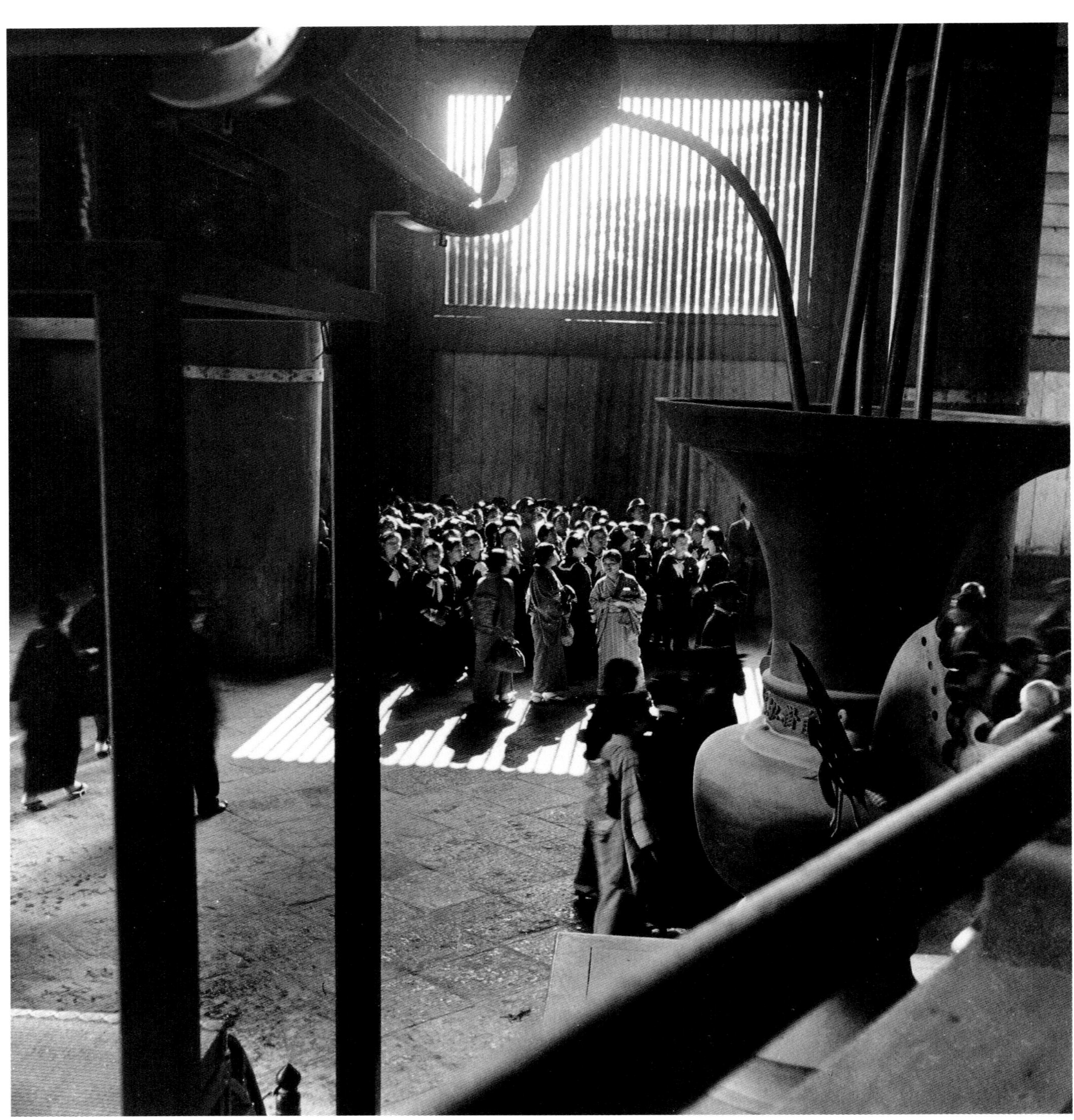

▶

Todaiji, Nara, 1949
Devotees come to make
offerings at one of Japan's
oldest and most famous
temples.

The Great Buddha, Kamakura, 1948
Soon after the war, we moved to
Kamakura. This bronze statue was built
when Kamakura was the feudal capital
of Japan, in the twelfth and thirteenth
centuries.

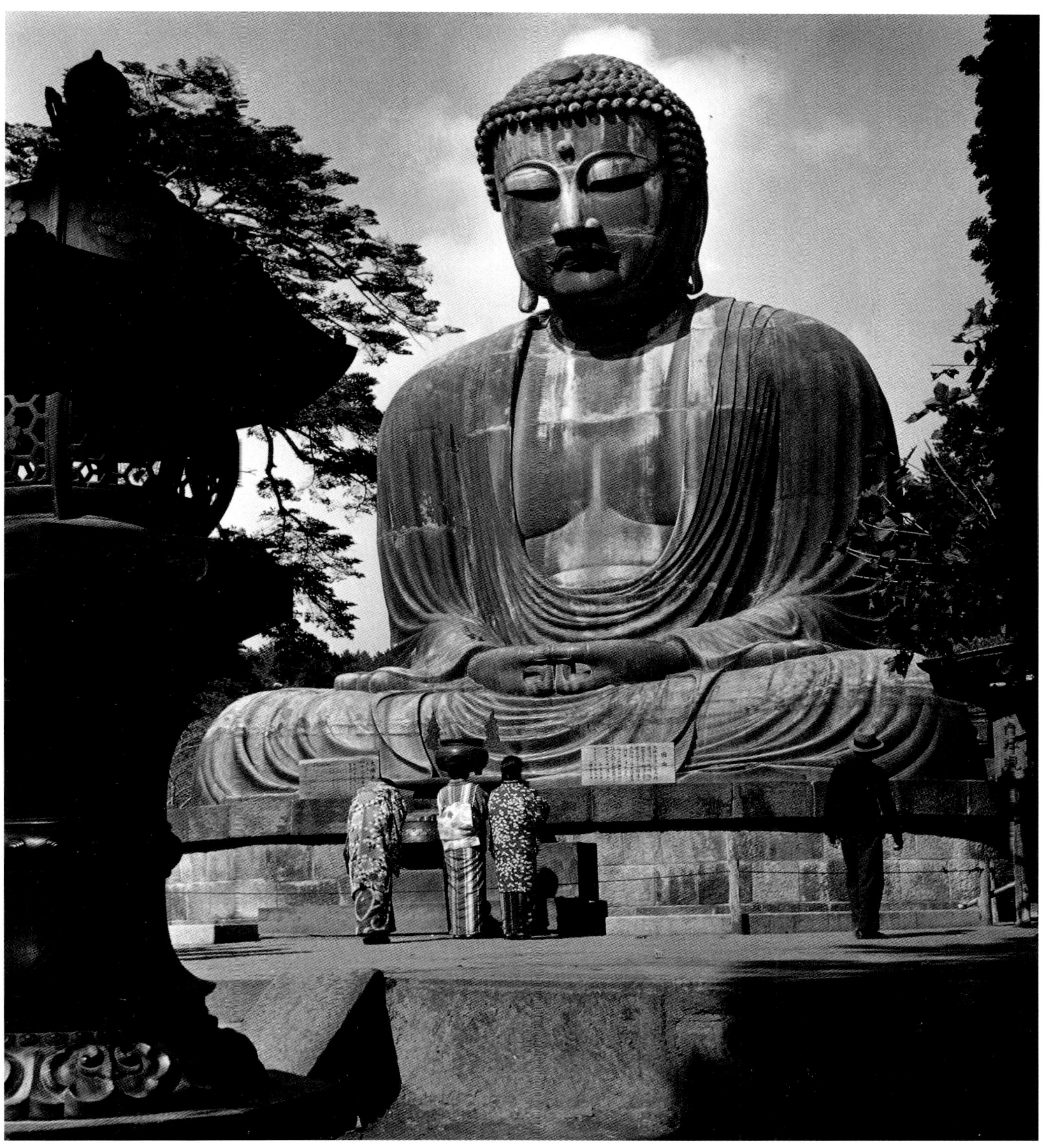

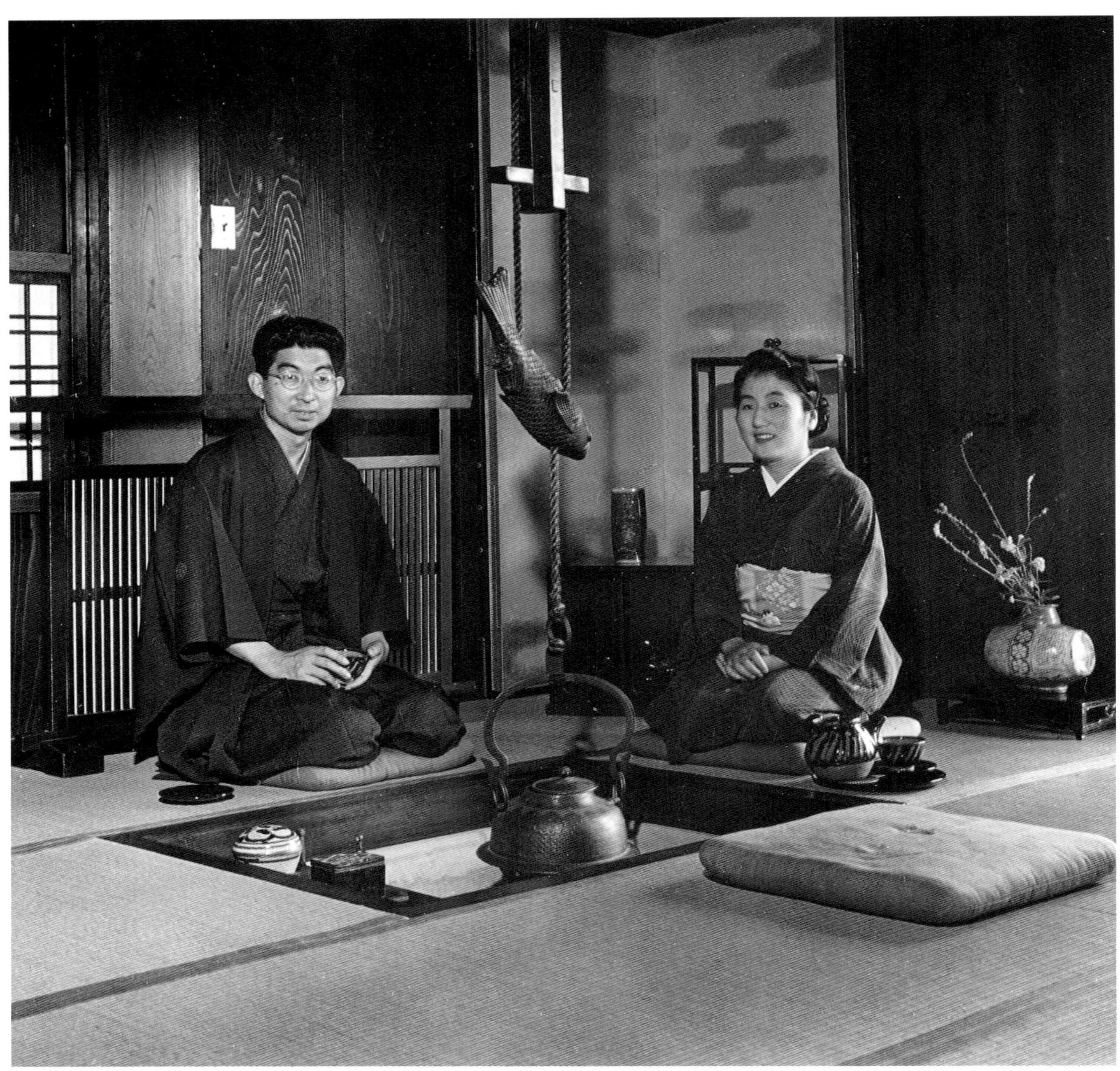

Prince and Princess Chichibu, 1950
Emperor Hirohito's younger brother and
his wife are having tea in their summer
villa at Gotemba, near Mount Fuji.

Prince Takamatsu, 1950
Prince Takamatsu, the second
younger brother of Emperor
Hirohito, preferred to be
photographed in a suit while
holding a book written in
English, emphasizing his
cosmopolitan nature.

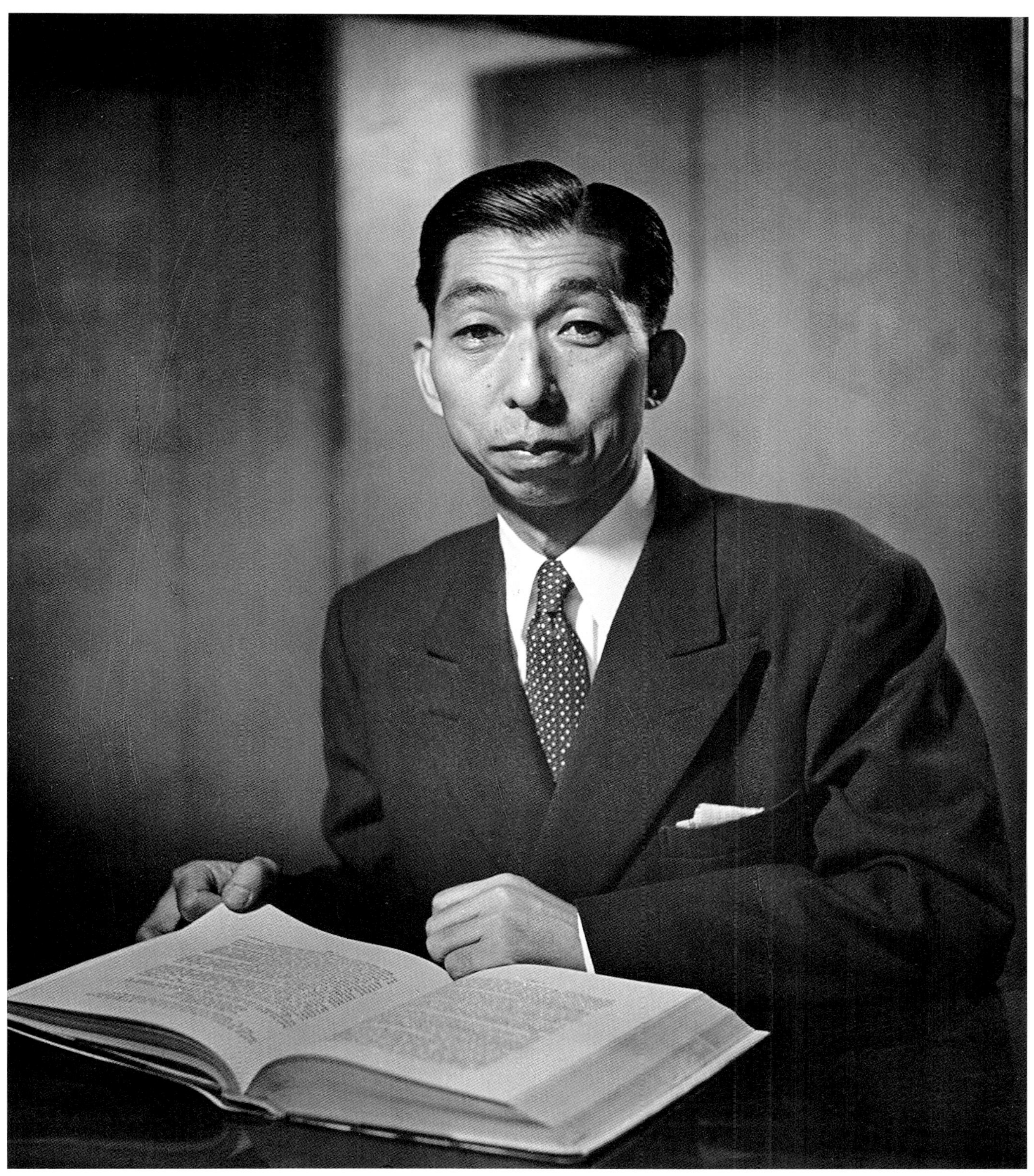

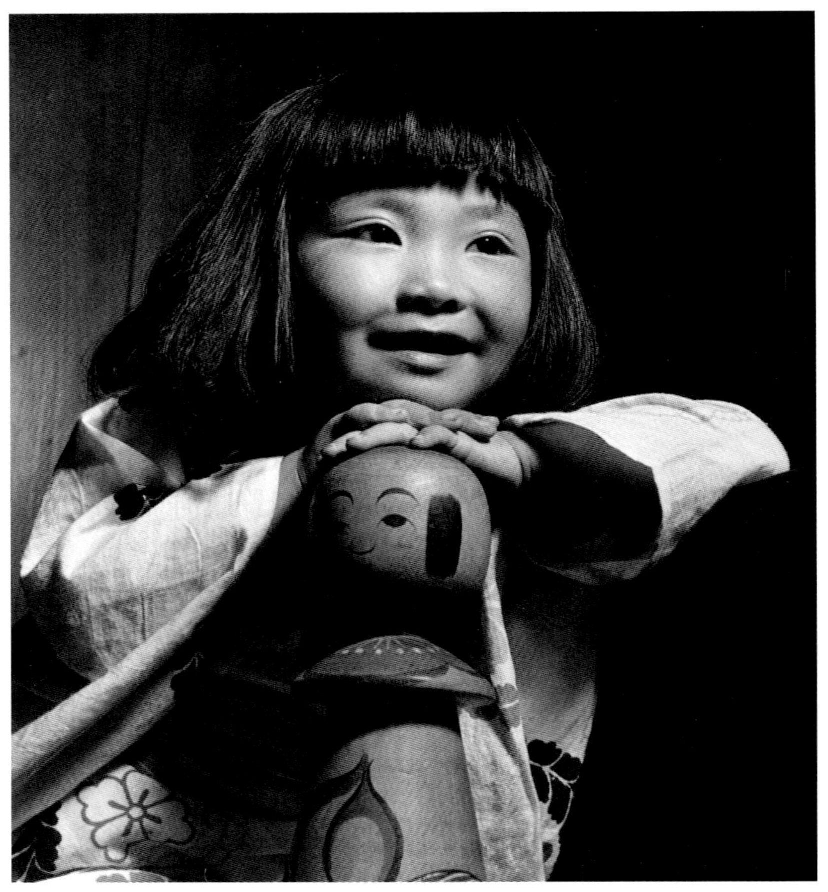

►

Living Doll, 1953
The granddaughter of the
famed Japanese ceramicist
Kanjiro Kawai poses with
a folk toy, a kokeshi.

Lotus Boy, 1953
These inventive outfits were
fashioned from lotus leaves
from the pond at Kamakura's
Hachiman Shrine.

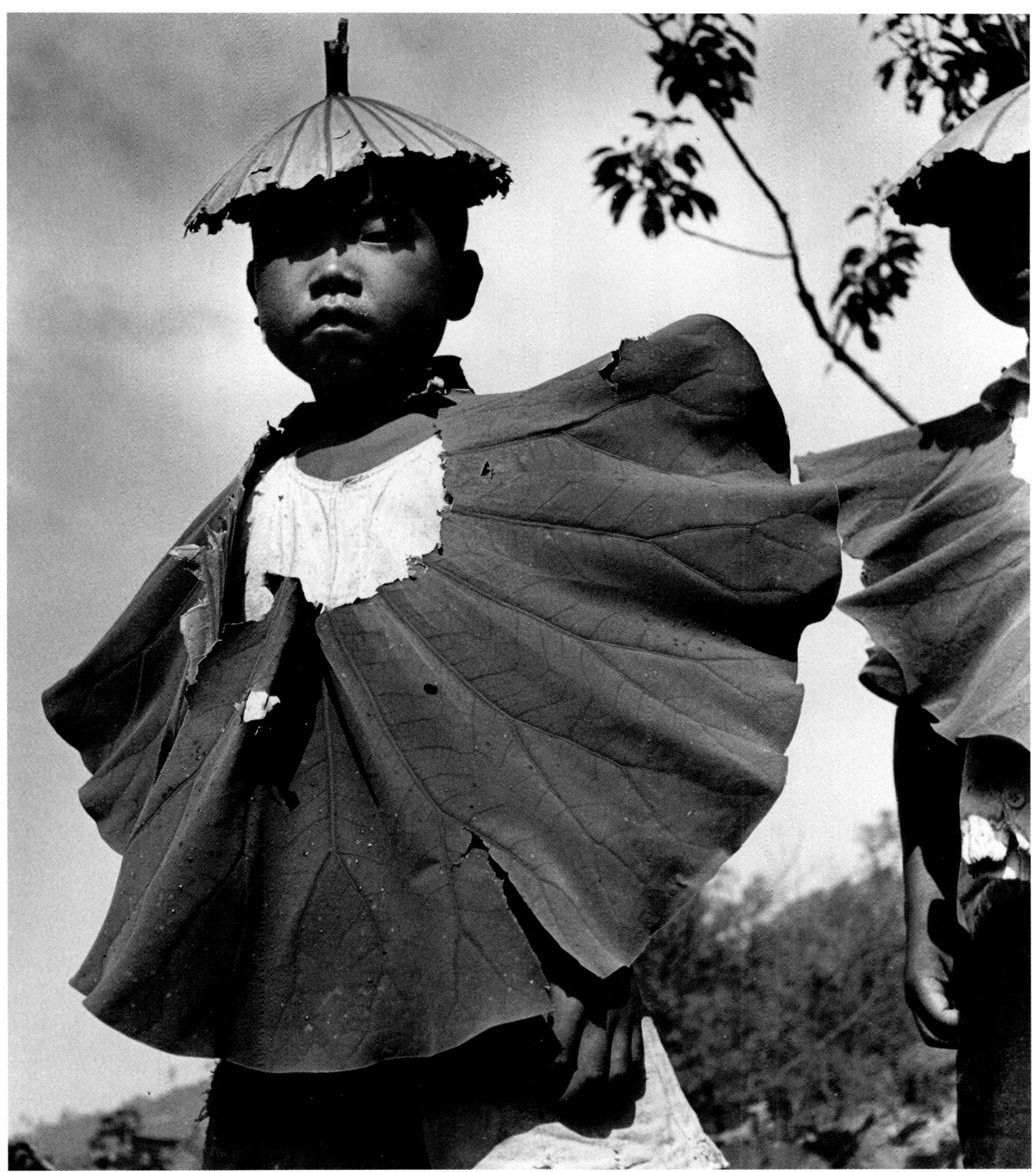

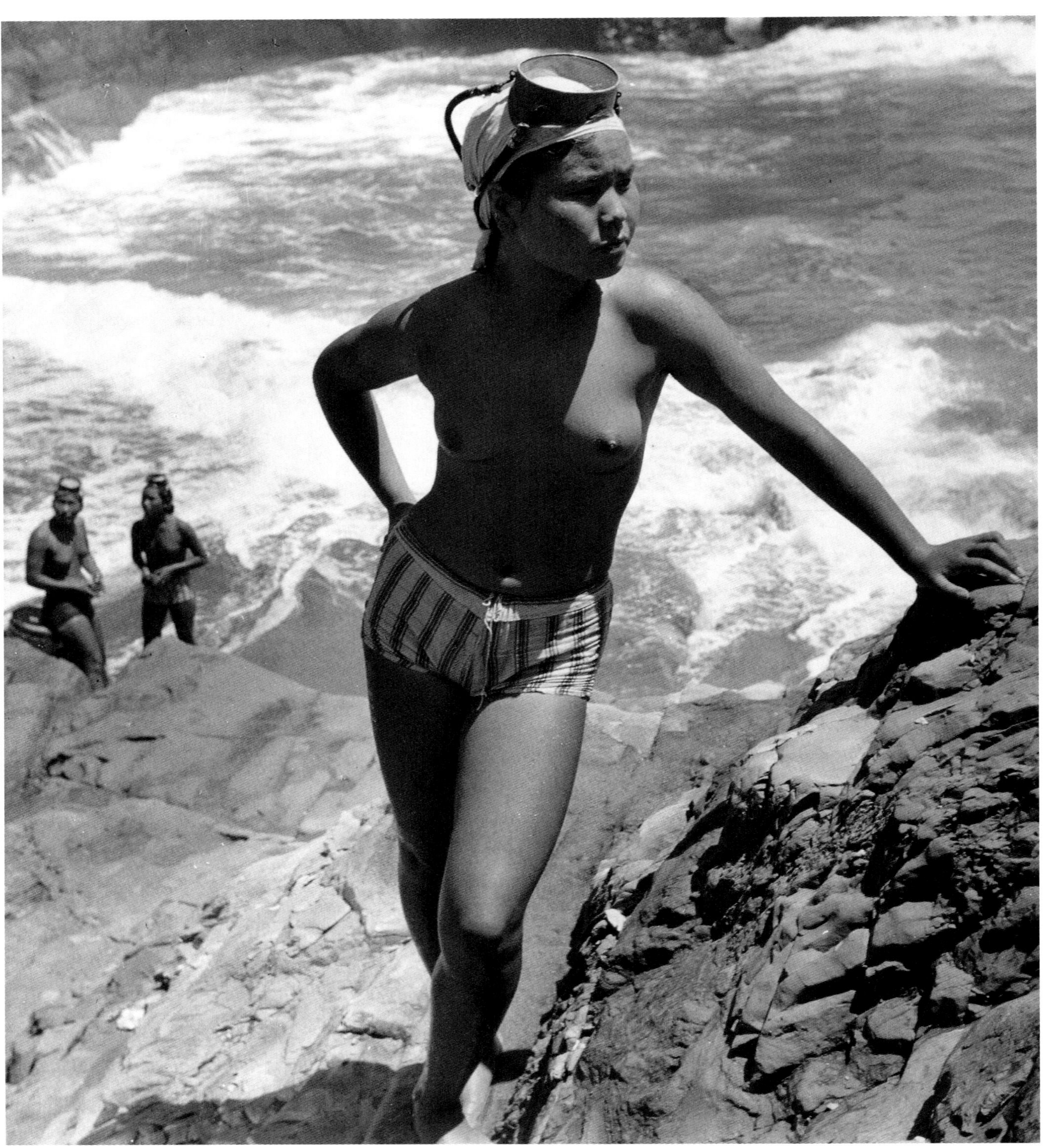

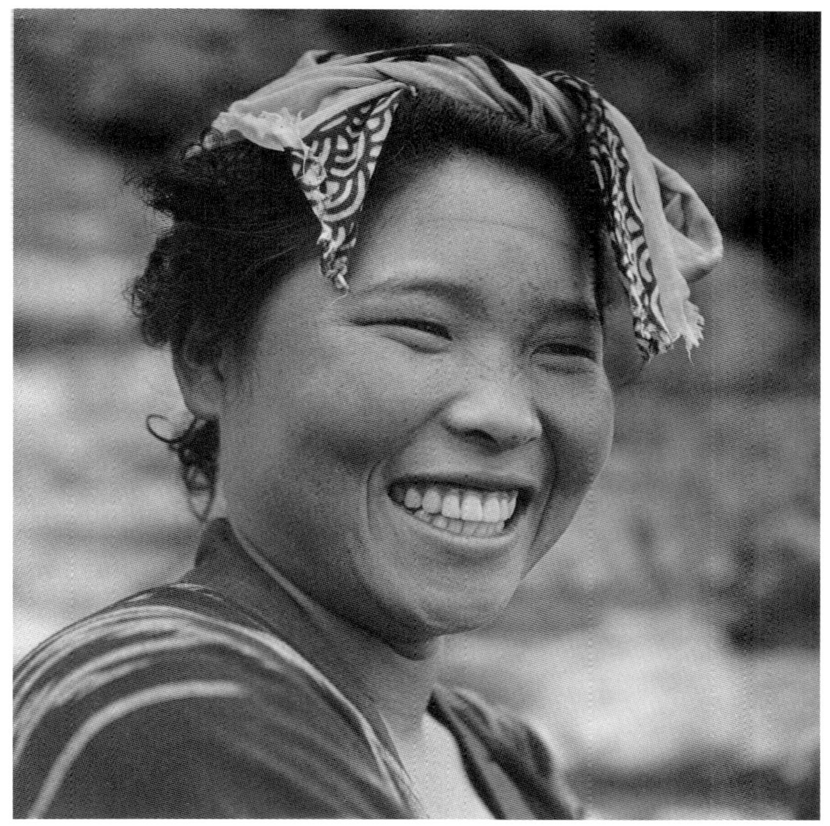

Abalone Diver, Chiba, 1952
Traditionally, nudity was
nothing to be embarrassed
about in Japan, and the insou-
ciant pose of this young diver
resulted in one of my favorite
images from the photo book
Mermaids of Japan, *which*
appeared in 1954.

Before the Dive, 1952
The life of the divers was full
of dangers, as they dived year-
round for abalone and sea-
weed, but they were always
full of good spirits.

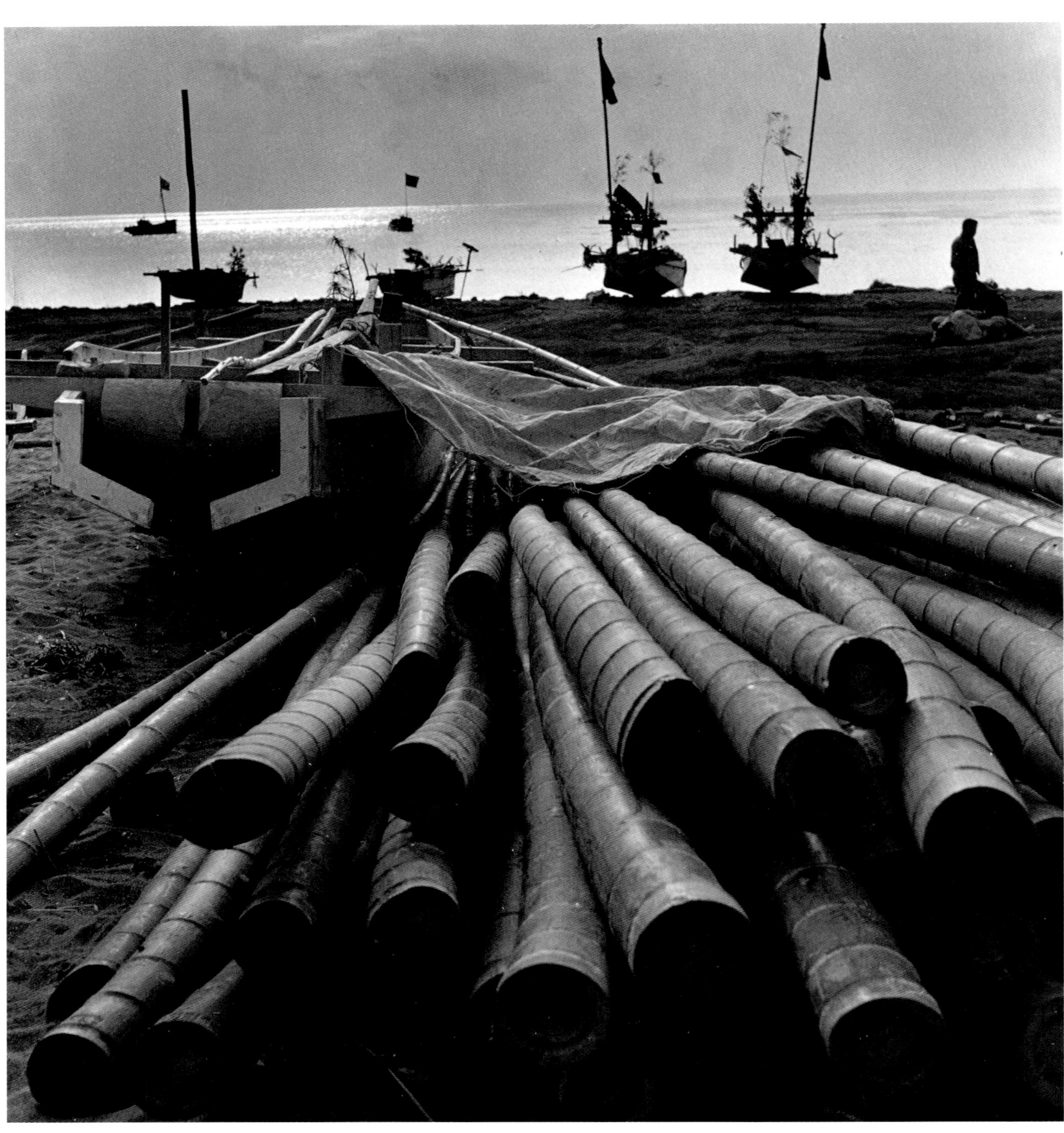

►

Fishing Boats at New Year's, 1953
During the New Year's holidays, fishing
boats were decorated with flags.

Taking Care of the Children, 1952
In the diving villages, grandmothers
cared for the children while their moth-
ers were diving and their fathers were
at sea fishing.

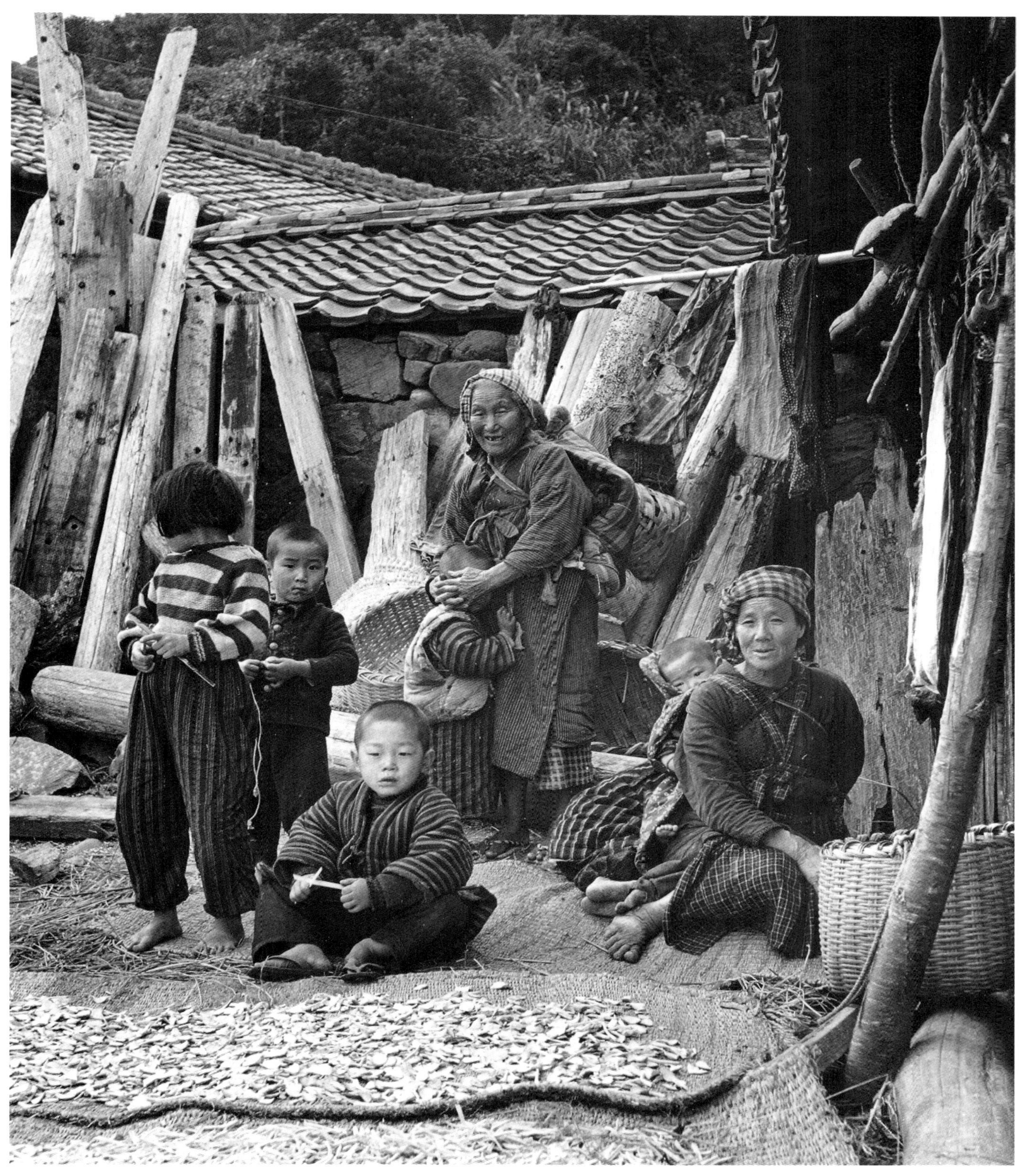

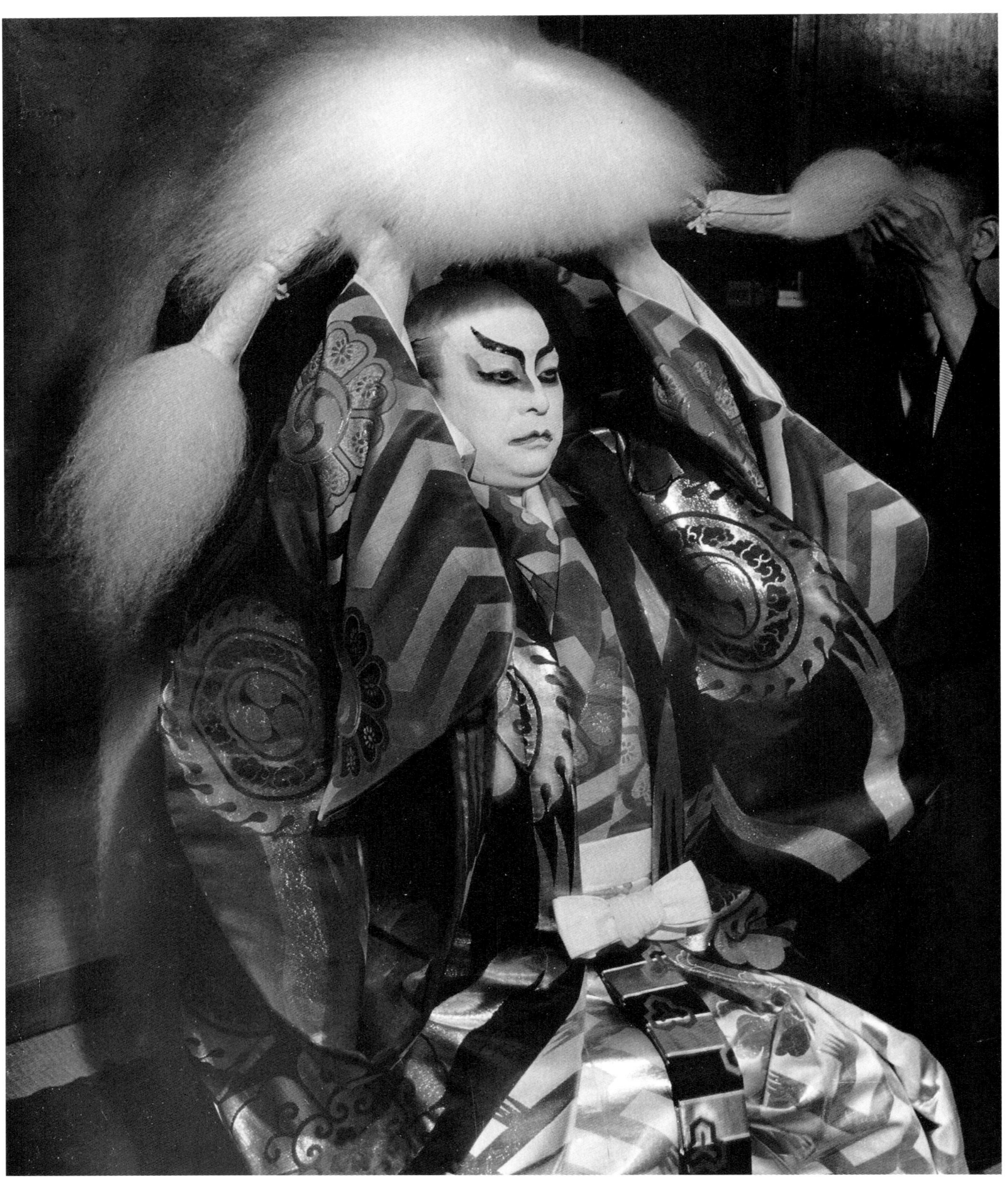

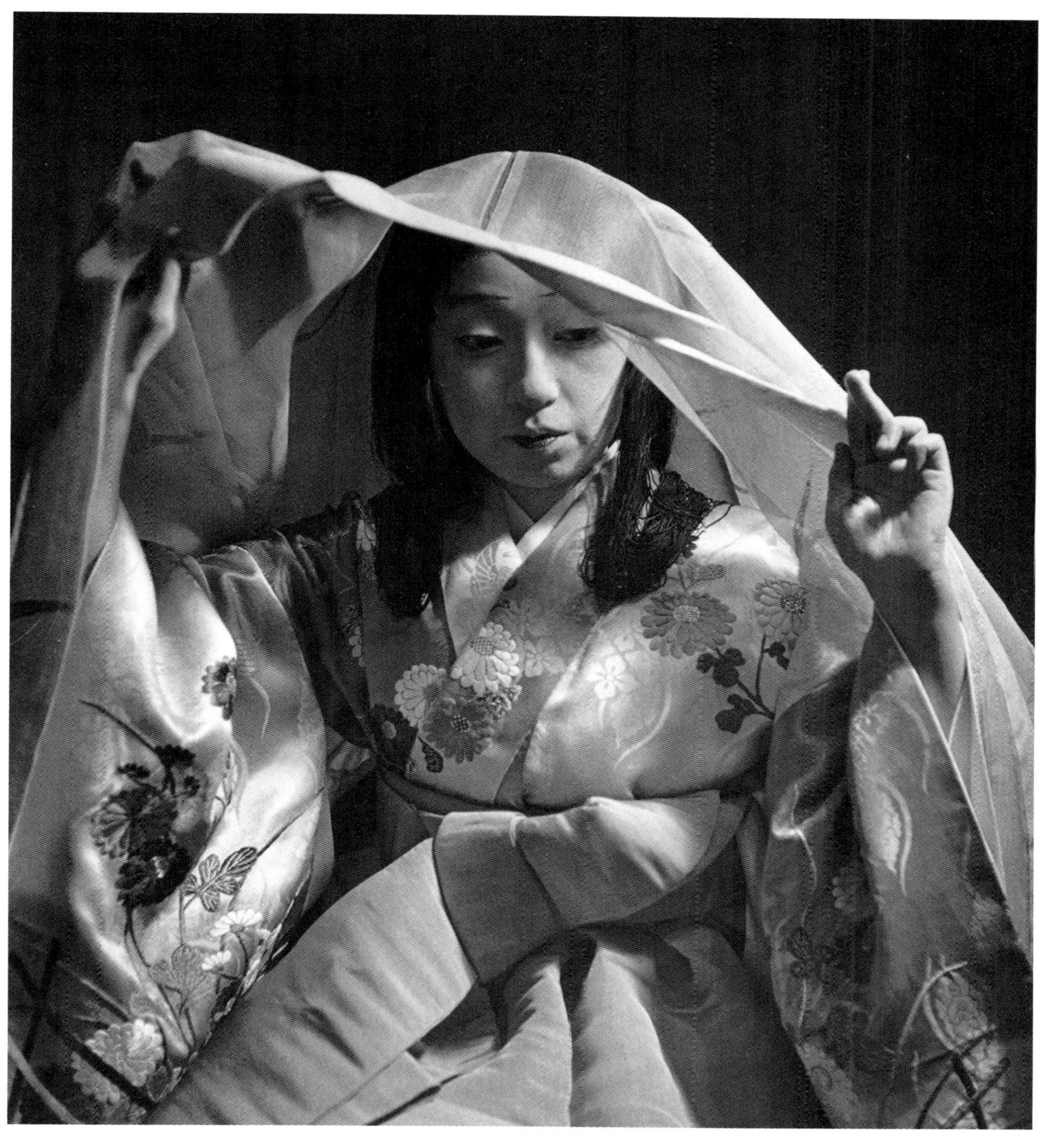

◄

Kikugoro VI, Kabuki Actor, 1951
I was deeply impressed by how the
traditional arts had been kept active
and passed on from generation to
generation. Kikugoro VI was one of
the most respected actors, famed for
the role of the Kagami Jishi lion.

*Tokuho Azuma, Traditional
Dancer, 1951*
Tokuho Azuma was one of the
most renowned performers in
classical Japanese dance.

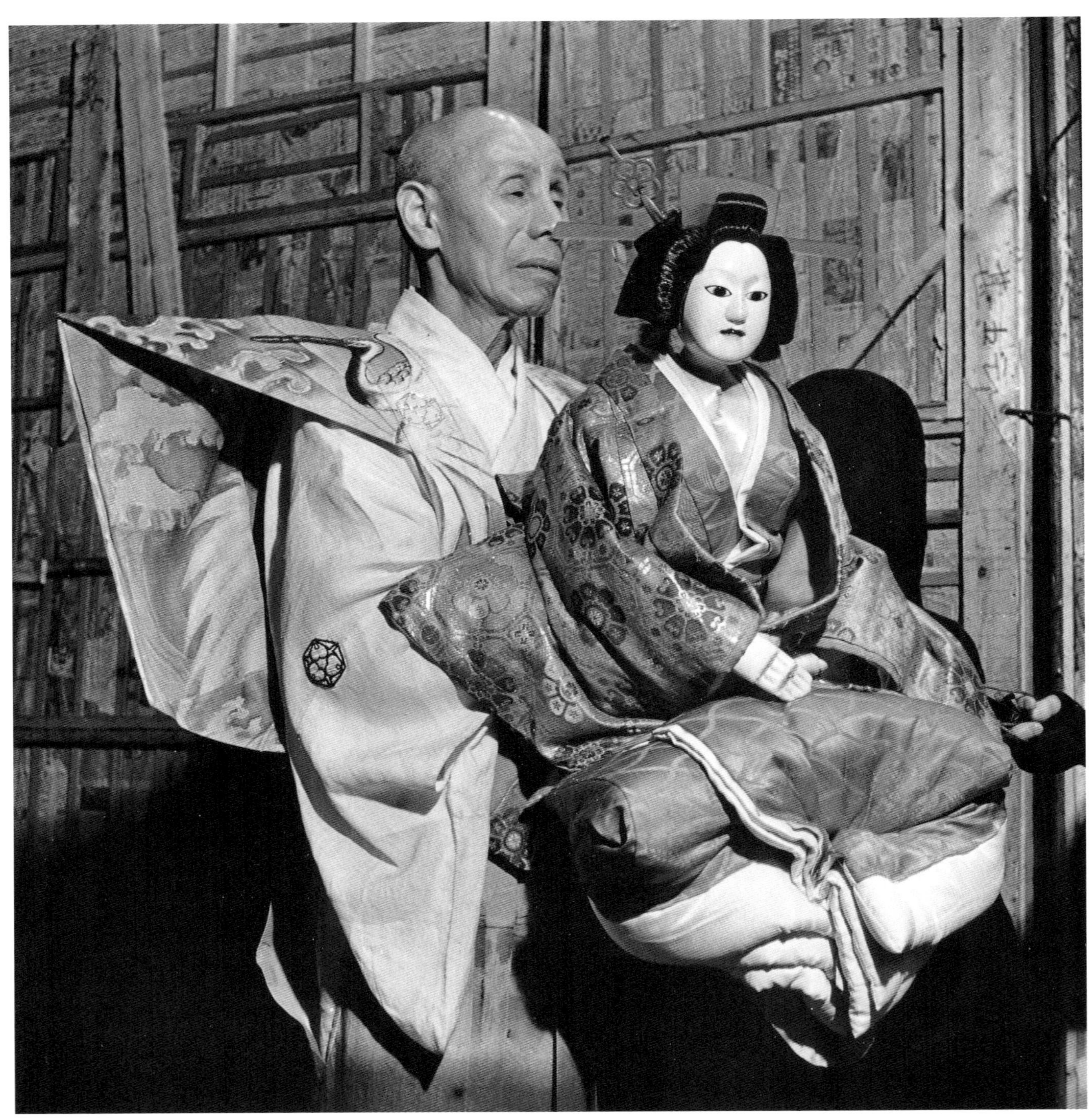

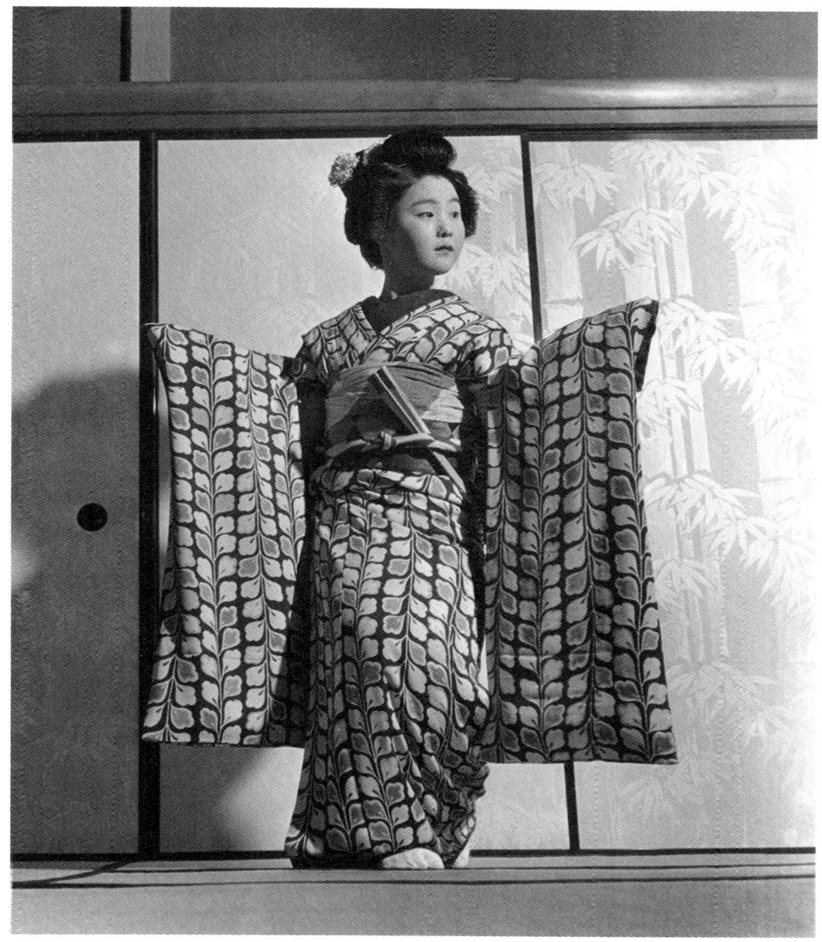

◄

Bungoro, Bunraku Puppet
Master, 1951
This Living Treasure of Japan
was already in his eighties and
almost blind when I photo-
graphed him backstage in
Osaka, waiting for his entry.
The performance was
impeccable, magical.

Dancing Maiko, 1953
A young apprentice geisha
dances for guests.

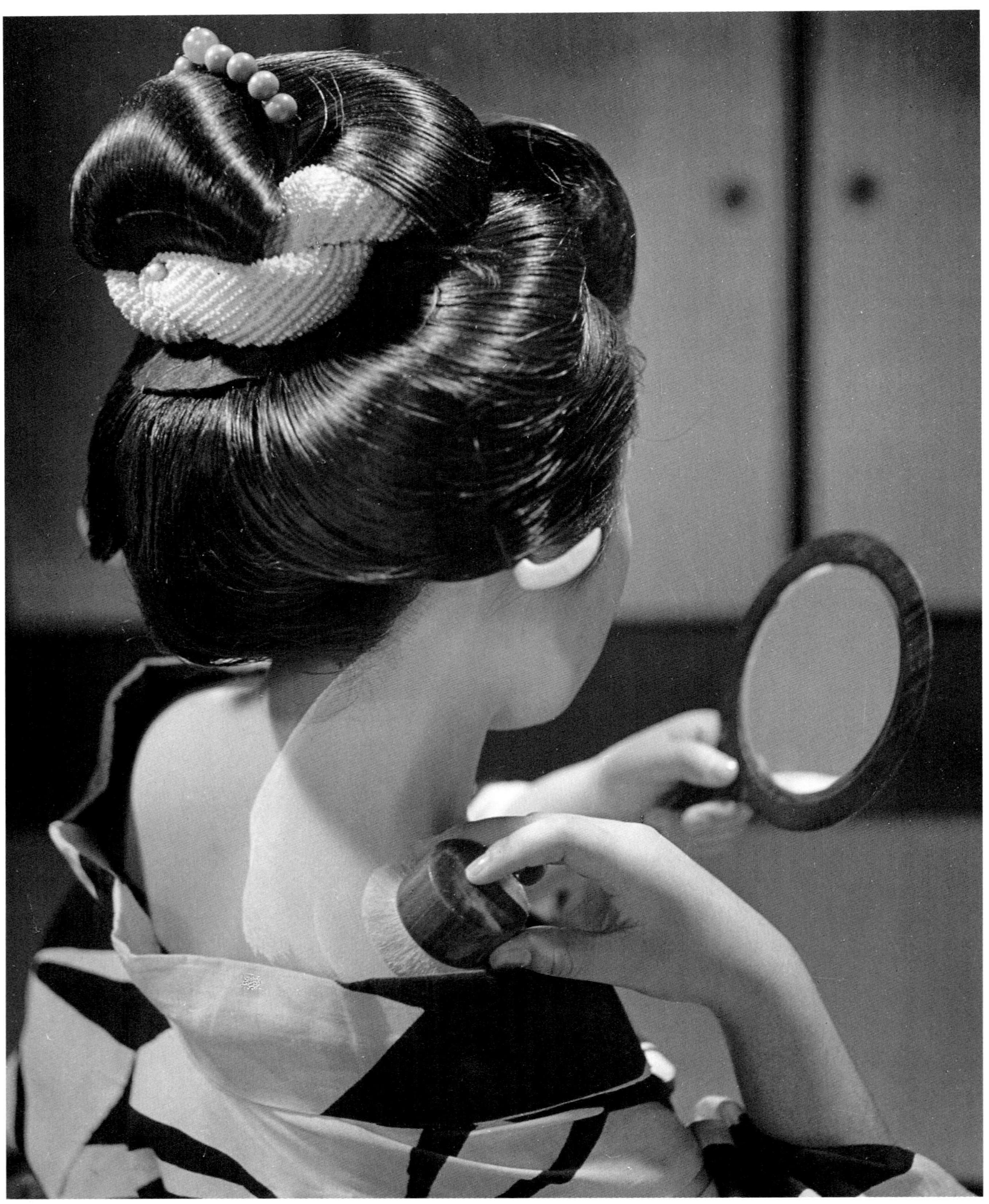

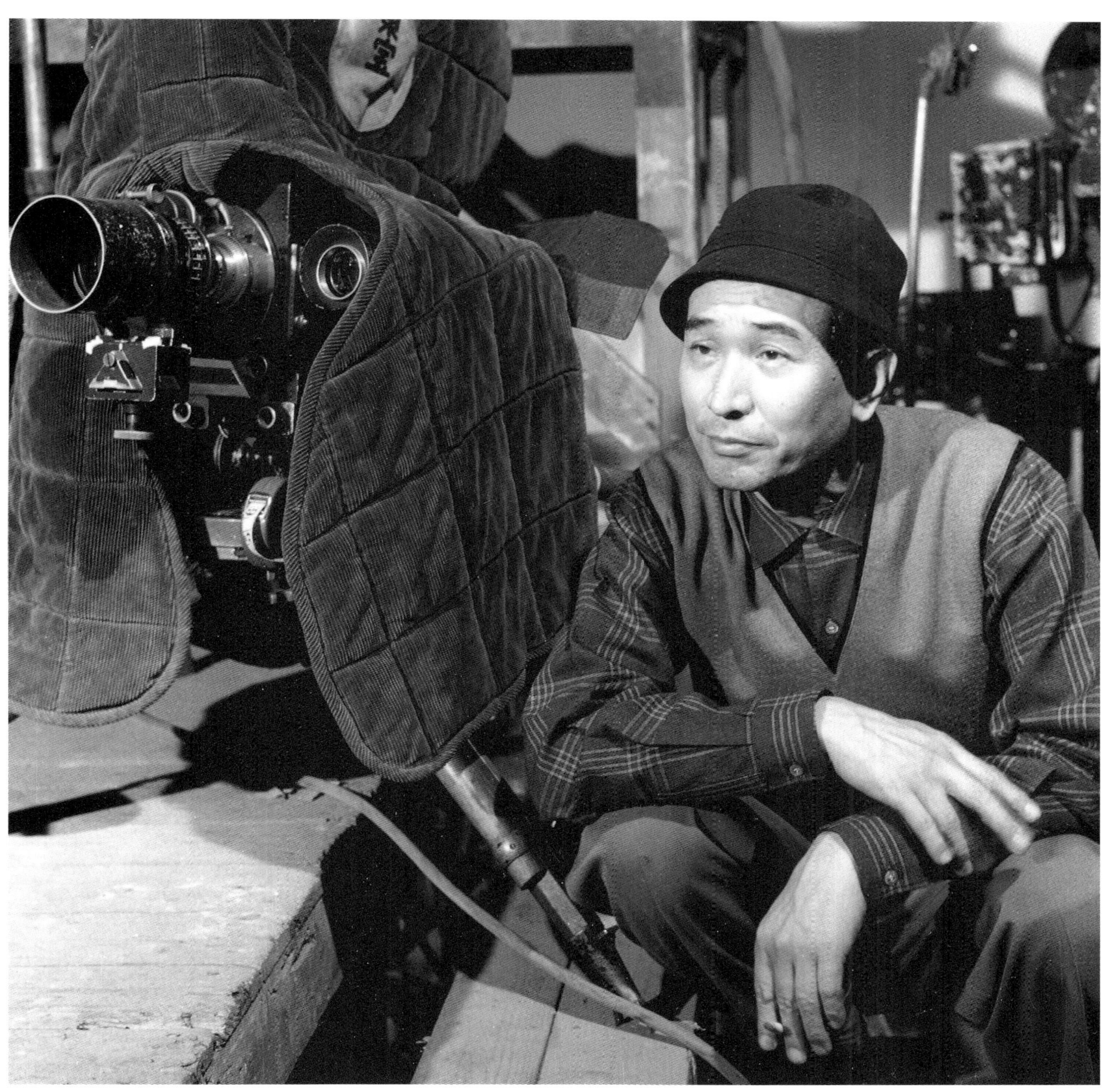

Geisha, 1953
A geisha applies white make-up
in preparation for a dinner party.

Akira Kurosawa,
Film Director, 1954
Kurosawa was at the peak of
his career when I photographed
him at the Toho studio in Kyoto
on the set of The Seven
Samurai.

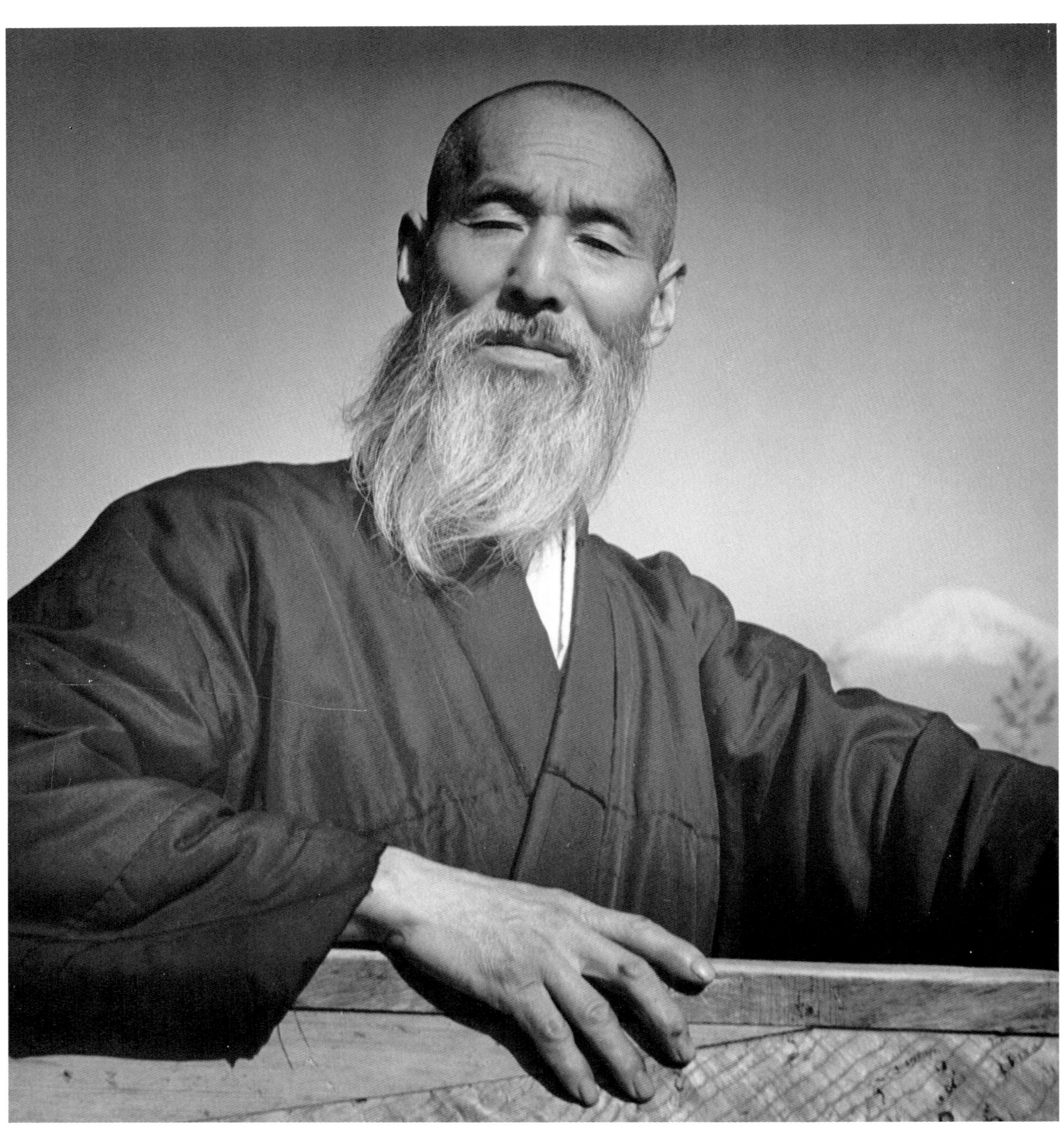

The Painter, 1950

This traditional painter lived

near Mount Fuji and painted

nothing but the sacred

mountain all his life.

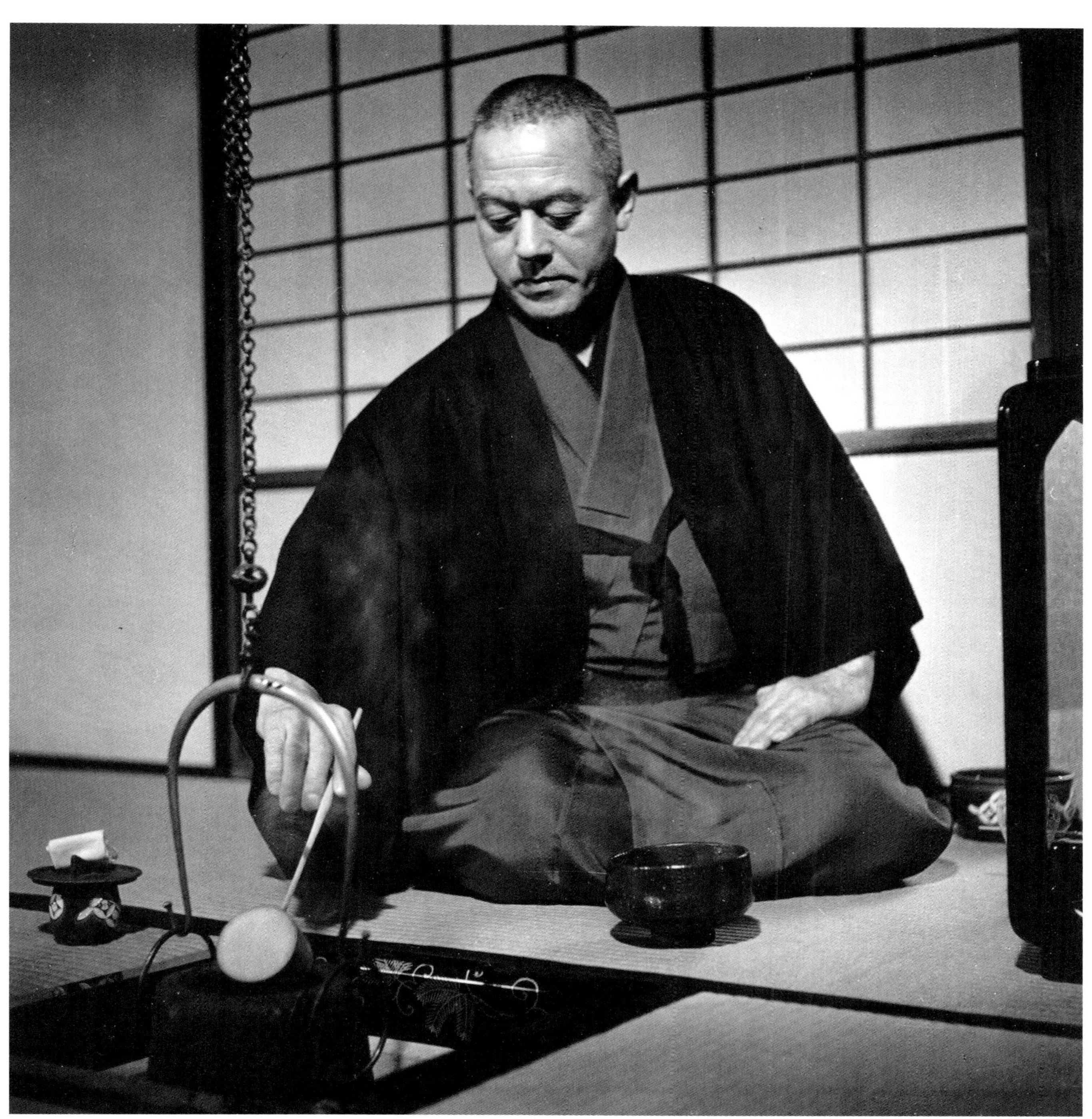

Soshitsu Sen XIV, 1952
I photographed the Grand
Tea Master of the Urasenke
School in Kyoto during the
production of the docu-
mentary Arts of Japan.

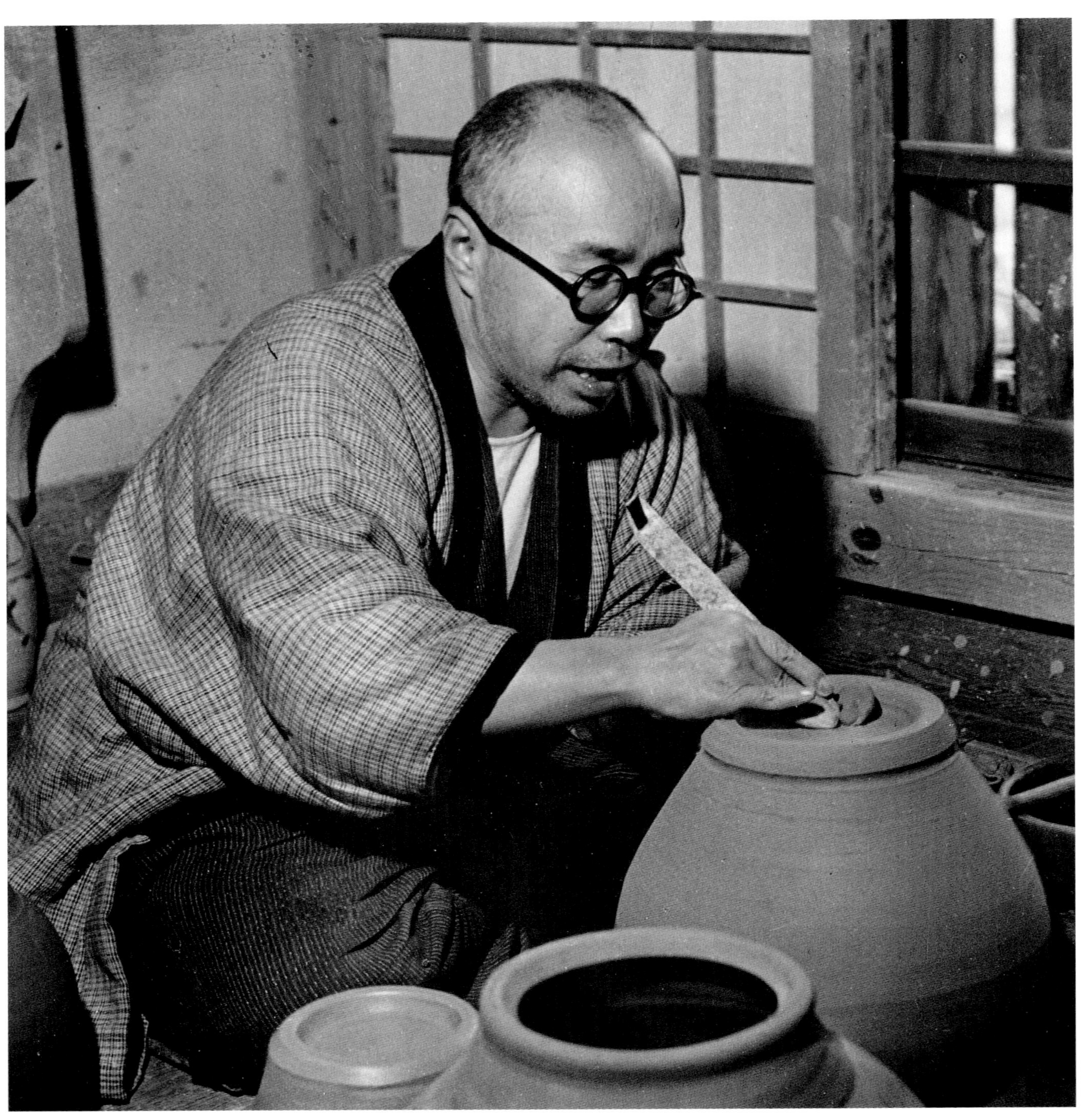

Shoji Hamada, Potter, 1953
The Arts of Japan *also*
featured this famous potter
from Mashiko.

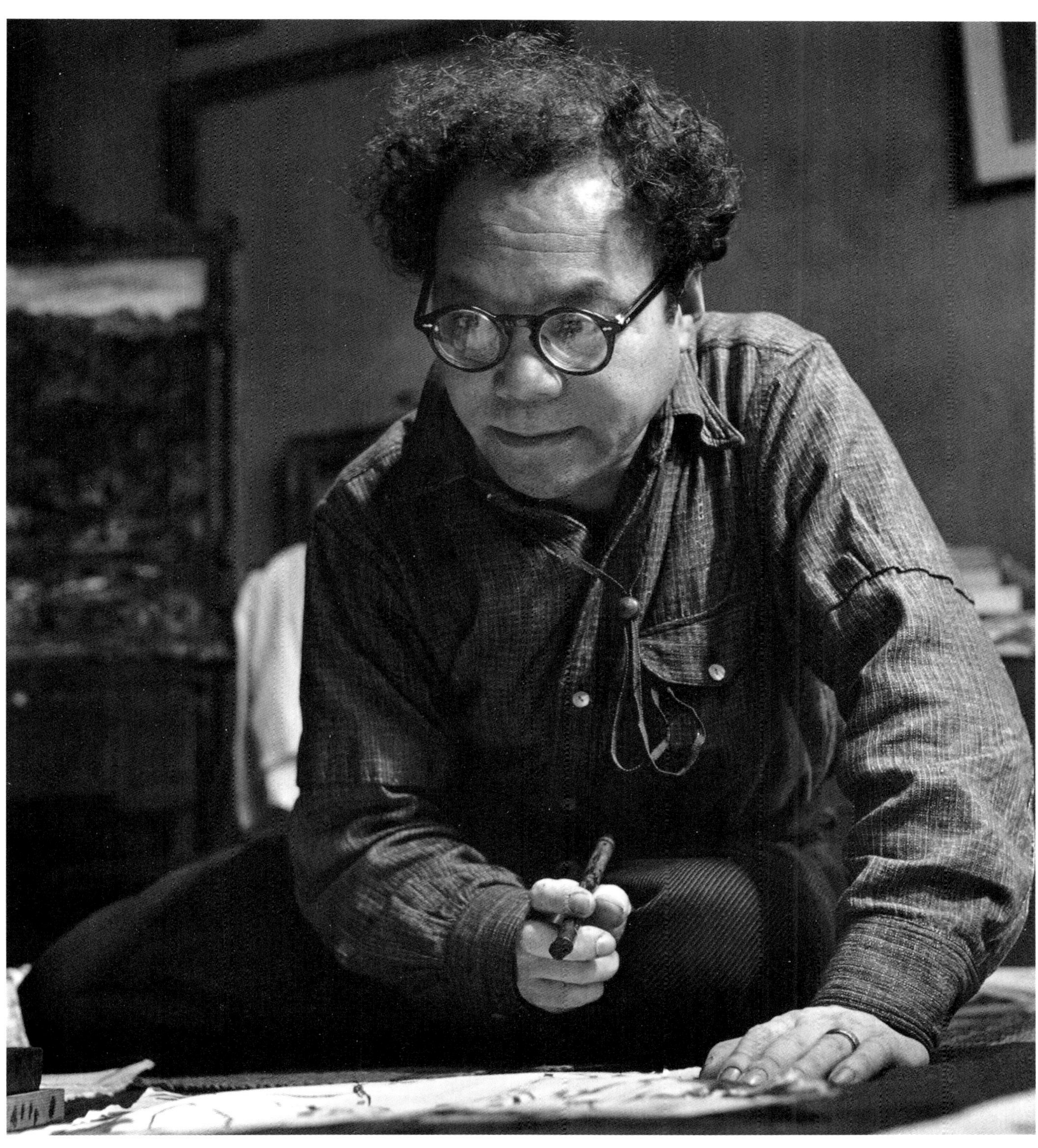

Shiko Munakata, Wood-Block
Artist, 1953
This luminary folk artist was
acknowledged as a Living
Treasure of Japan.

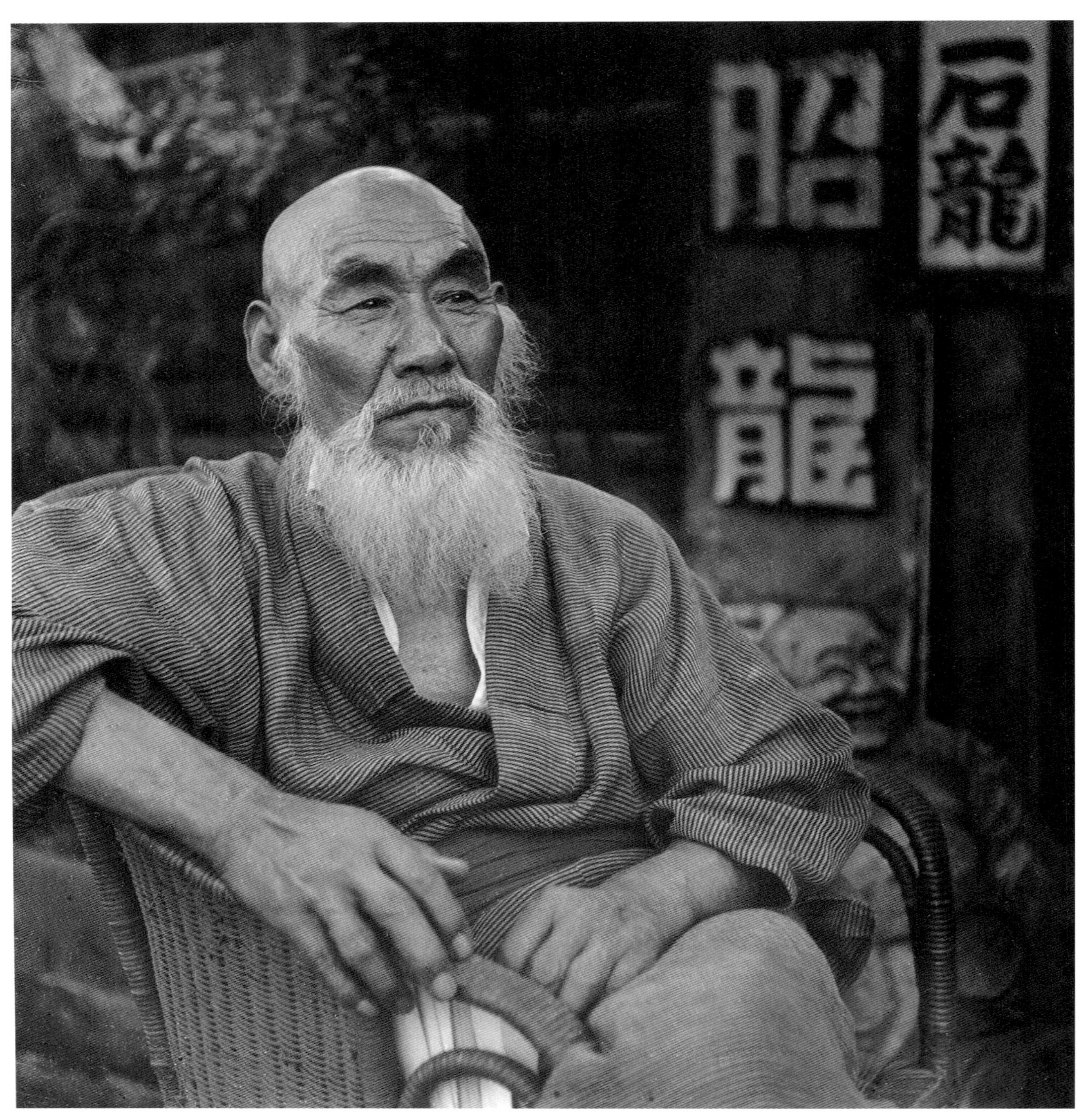

Fortune Teller, Kamakura, 1955
A fortune teller, who worked by study-
ing a person's face, looked at mine and
said I would travel overseas in the near
future, which really happened.

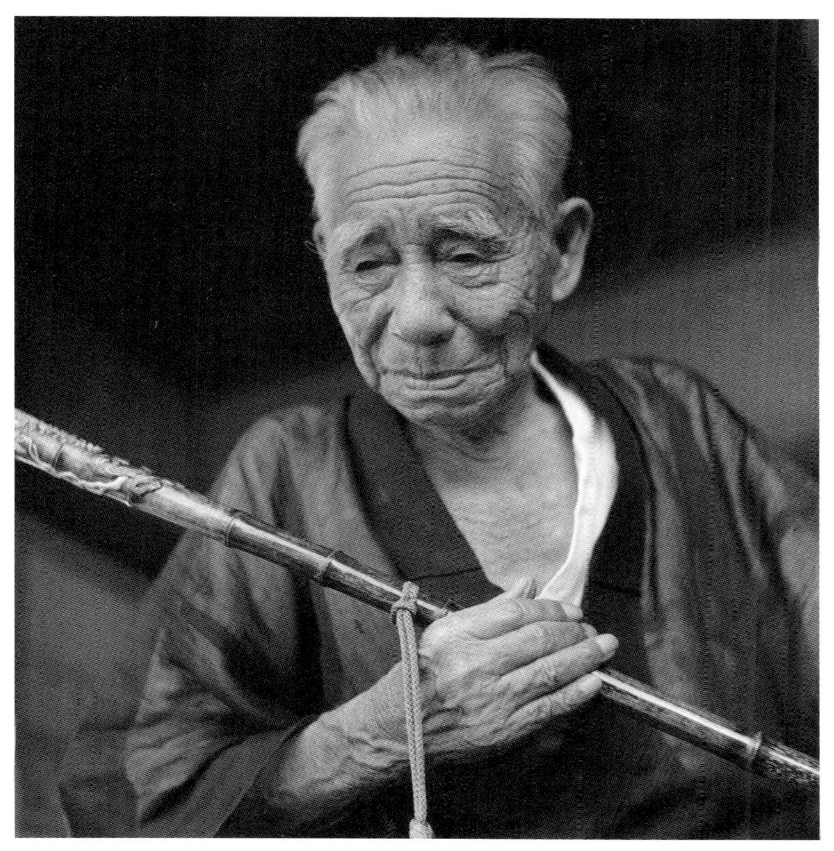

Mikimoto, the Pearl King, 1952
This stately gentleman, who
introduced cultured pearls to
the world, was already in his
nineties when I photographed
him, holding a staff he had
received from the Emperor.

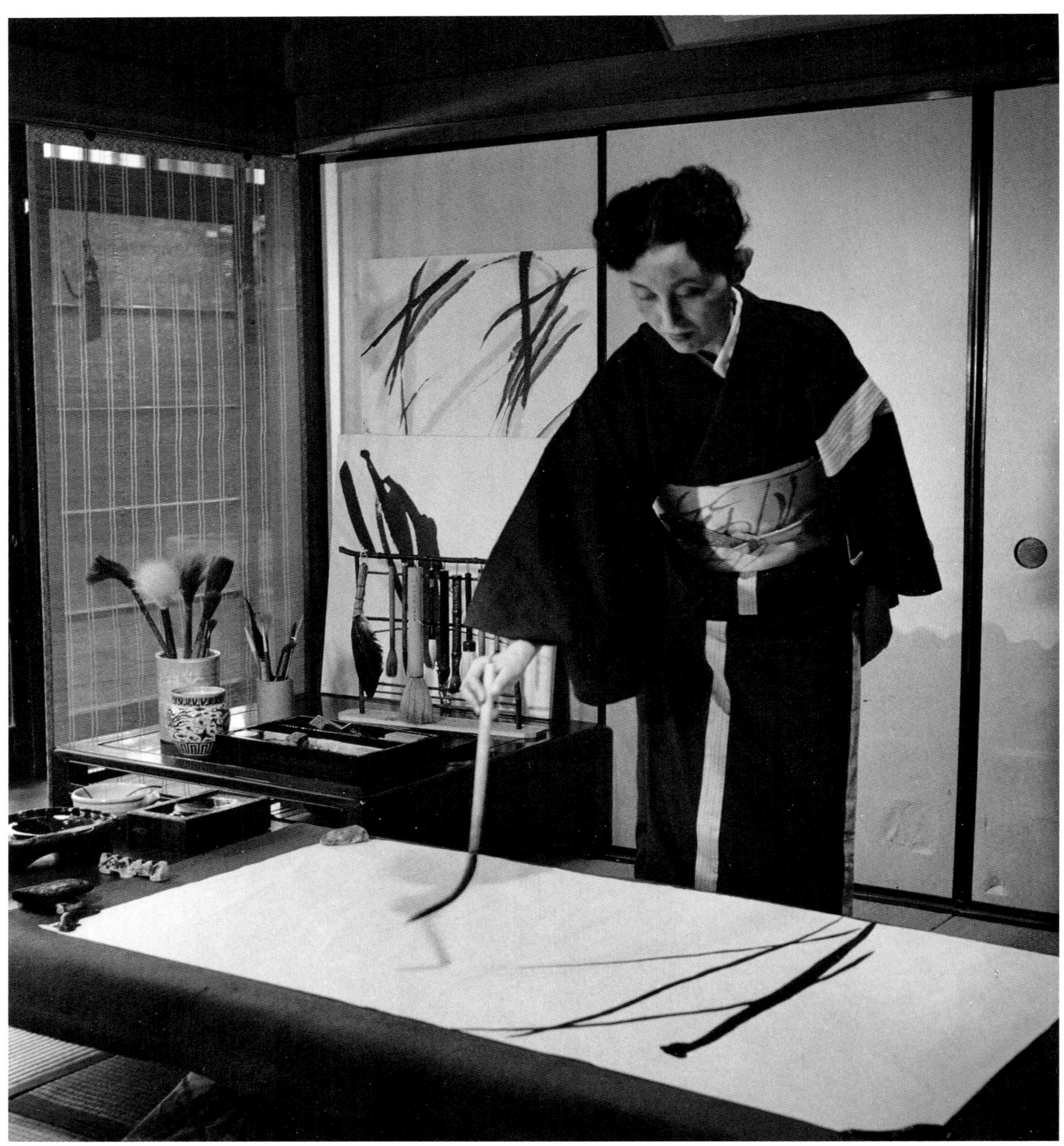

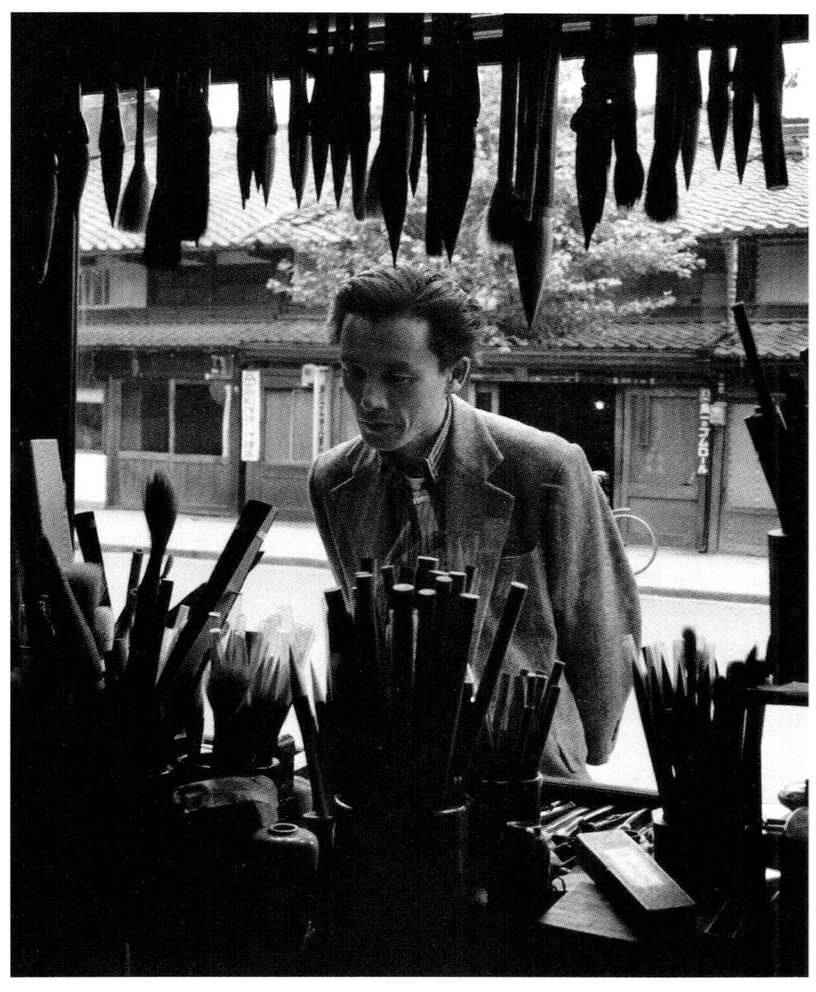

◄

Toko Shinoda, Calligrapher,
1955
Renowned calligrapher, painter,
and printmaker Toko Shinoda
was featured in the documen-
tary Japanese Calligraphy.

Choosing a Brush, Kyoto,
1955
This shot also appeared as a
scene in the film Japanese
Calligraphy.

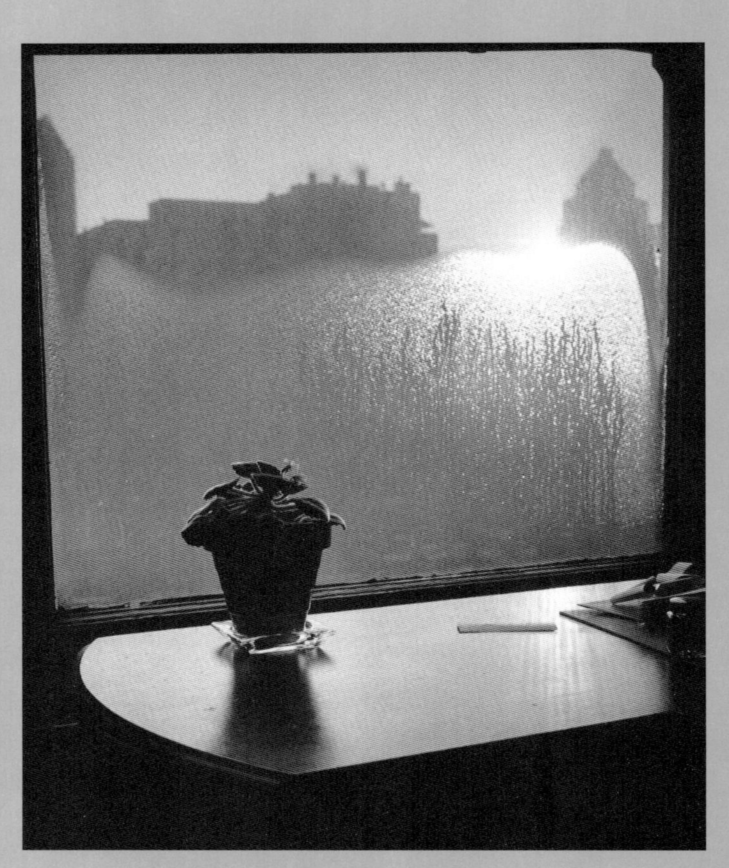

chicago

Hotel Window, 1956

Soon after arriving in Chicago, I captured this image of frost melting in the early morning light. It was later purchased by the New York Museum of Modern Art for their permanent collection.

Our three children, all born in Japan, were growing up, and Irene and I began to think they would have a better future if we were to move to America. When I applied for a U.S. immigrant visa in 1956, U.S. Embassy officials cautioned me that it might take a long time to receive one because of the strict limits on the number of foreign nationals allowed to emigrate to the United States each year. We had an additional problem. Our Hungarian passports had expired during the war, and with Hungary having become a Communist nation after World War II, we were officially "stateless."

Sometime afterward, the commercial attaché at the American Embassy called to say that a businessman from Chicago had asked him to recommend a motion picture photographer and my name had come up. I found out he was the publisher of two architectural magazines, and he needed some footage of good modern Japanese architecture for showing on American television.

I was familiar with good architecture in Tokyo and took him with me while I filmed several locations. As we were driving around Tokyo he began discussing the possibility of my going to Chicago to work for him. I told him I would be interested but I was on a waiting list for an American visa. He said he could easily help me. He must have been satisfied with my work because after the filming was over and he had returned to Chicago, I received a letter from him within three weeks offering to sponsor my visa and inviting me to go and work for him in Chicago. Because such a move would involve a lengthy separation, Irene and I talked over the idea for a long time. Her success with the restaurant meant we did not have to worry about her financial situation. We decided I should take the job offer and look around for the best place for the family to settle.

The twenty years we spent in Japan affected me profoundly. Not only did my work change, but I felt that I literally became a different man, eventually becoming a Zen Buddhist.

I arrived in the United States alone in the fall of 1956, leaving Irene in Japan with the children. I did not know how long we were going to be separated. I only knew I wanted to look around in this country carefully before making a permanent move. After a few months in Chicago, I began to realize it would not be the place where our family could easily adapt. The climate was not particularly agreeable. It was bitterly cold in winter and too hot in summer. I was busy with my work from the beginning, though, and time passed quickly. I could not decide what to do about my family. I only knew I missed them more and more.

I continued making 16 mm films in Chicago for my sponsor, which were used to promote architectural magazines on TV. I also did some still photography to illustrate them. After about a year, I found some Hungarian friends there, including Gyorgy Kepes (p. 117), who was teaching at the New Bauhaus, located at the Illinois Institute of Technology, and Albert Kner, for whom I had done the large

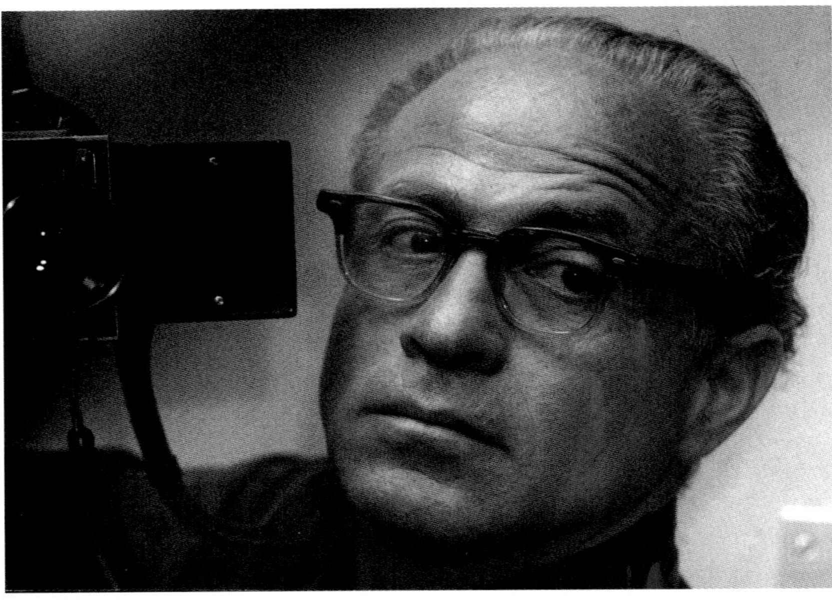

Self-Portrait, Chicago, 1958

printing exhibit in Budapest. Kner had moved to Chicago in 1938 and was art director of a large paper company, the Container Corporation of America. When my work with the architectural publisher slowed down, Kner invited me to do promotional photography for his company.

I was pleased to learn in 1956 that the Museum of Modern Art in New York had purchased one of my Chicago photographs for their permanent collection (p. 110). For me this was particularly gratifying because decades earlier, art critics would not accept photography as a legitimate form of art. Their major criticism was that the camera is a machine and is limited to merely copying the reality in front of the camera. Later that year, I entered a Chicago Modernization Photo Contest, for which I shot a large Mies van der Rohe building bathed in early morning light. For this I received first prize and one thousand dollars (p. 116). After receiving the award, as further confirmation of the acceptance of photography as an art, I managed to have a one-man exhibit at the Art Institute of Chicago.

When the curators at the Art Institute learned of my personal history and that I was also a filmmaker, they gave me an assignment to produce a documentary film on their Japanese woodblock print collection. This collection had been donated to the museum by well-known novelist James Michener, whom I had met in Japan during the occupation. After I completed the filming of the *ukiyo-e* wood-block prints, the Institute told me the narration of the film was going to be done by Michener himself, who was then in Hawai'i working on his book *Hawaii*. I was asked to go to Hawai'i to film him for the introduction and to record his voice for the narration.

After arriving in Honolulu for the *ukiyo-e* assignment, I was in need of a film technician and a studio where we could do our filming and recording. George Tahara was recommended to me, and we completed the work in two weeks. Mr. Michener was most cooperative. He also introduced me to the director of the Honolulu Academy of Arts, Robert Griffing, who, when he learned I was going to do a film about *ukiyo-e* with Michener, told me he had been wanting to produce a film on a remarkable traditional dancer of Hawai'i, 'Iolani Luahine. Shortly afterward, he held a dinner party for 'Iolani and me where we could discuss the project. 'Iolani was very inspiring, and I told Mr. Griffing I was enthusiastic about making the film with her.

I returned to Chicago to finish up the *ukiyo-e* film and delivered the work I had done with Michener to the Art Institute. Three weeks later I received a letter from Mr. Griffing: the Academy had received a grant of $30,000 from the Rockefeller Foundation to finance the dance film on 'Iolani Luahine.

During my brief stay there, Hawai'i had impressed me as an attractive place. It had a large university, which I learned could provide work for me, but most important, it had a wonderful climate. I wrote to Irene in Japan, suggesting she and the children move to Hawai'i. The family was able to secure special immigrant visas in late 1959, with the help of the International Red Cross.

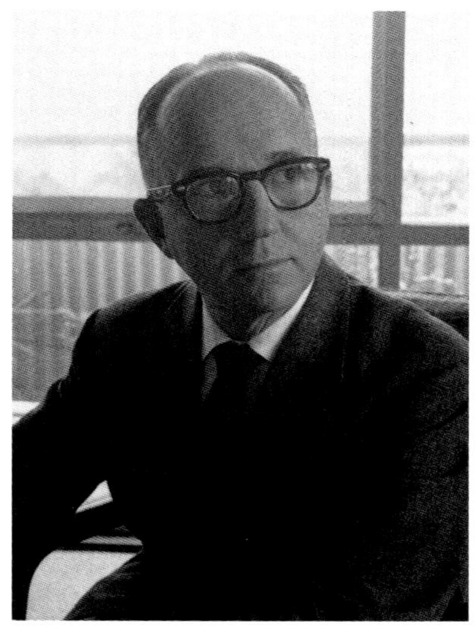

James Michener, Honolulu, 1958

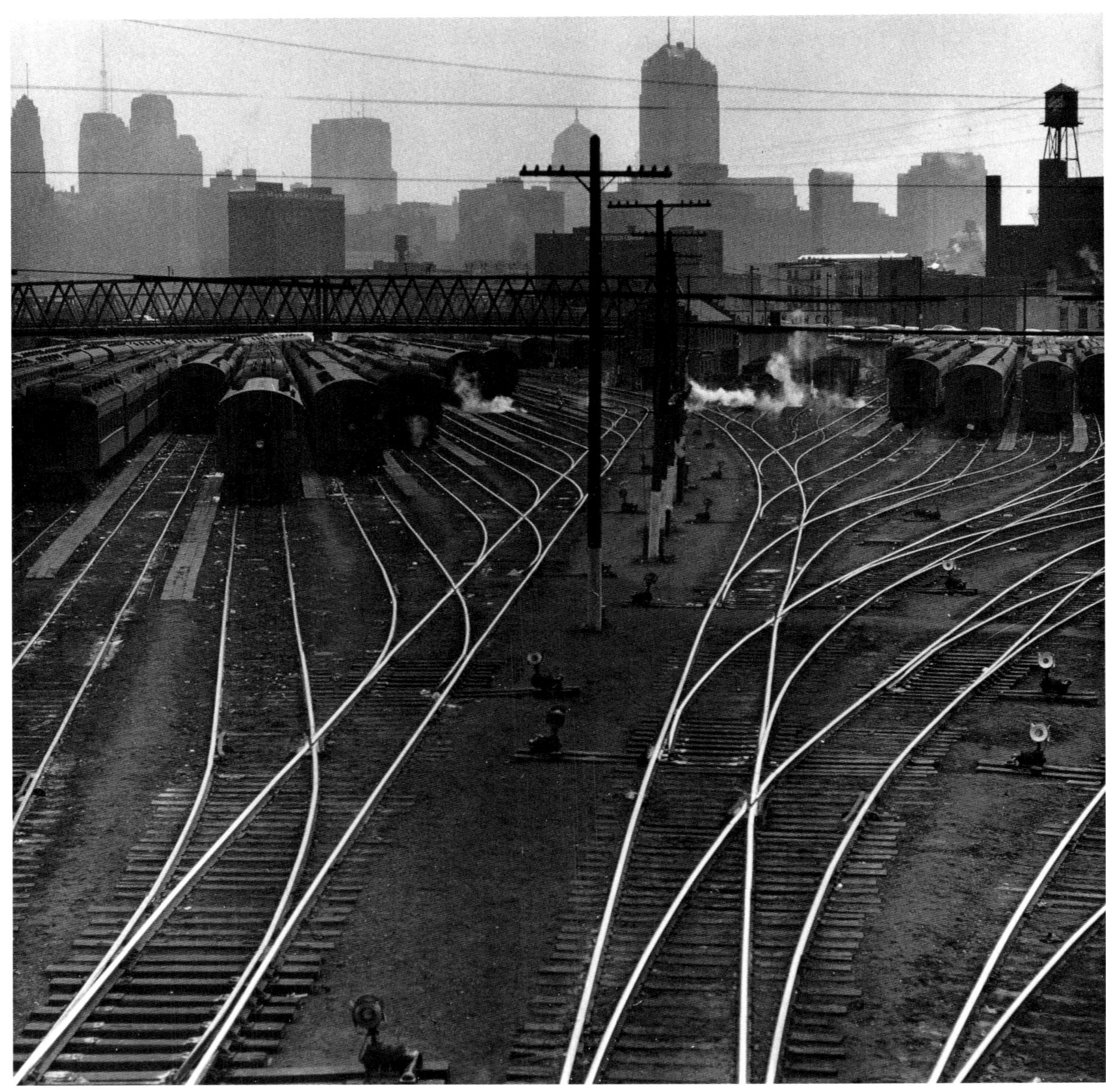

Freight Terminal, Chicago,
1957
I was captivated by the
pattern produced by the
meeting of the rails.

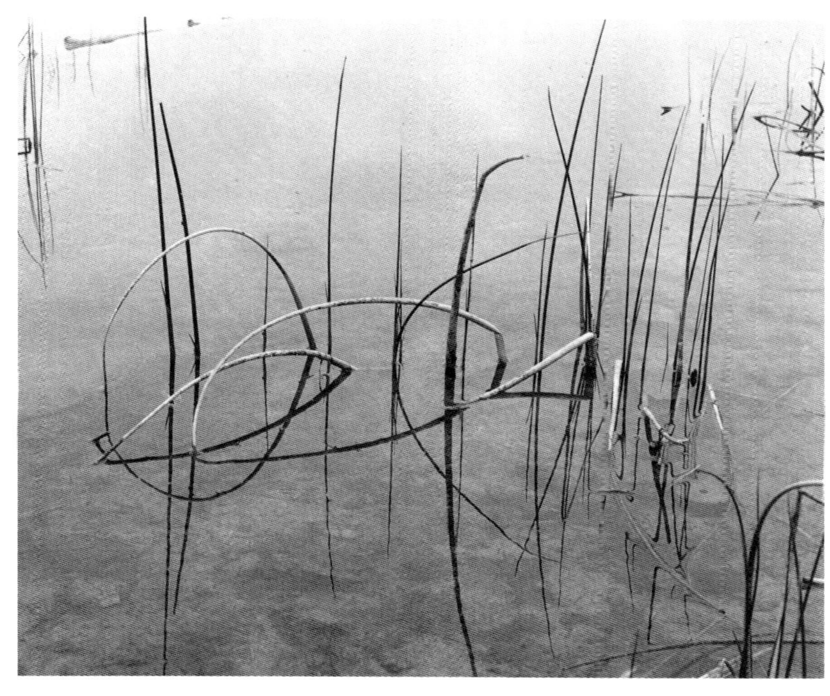

Reeds, Lake Michigan, 1956

*A walk along Lake Michigan
produced an image with
an almost Oriental feel.*

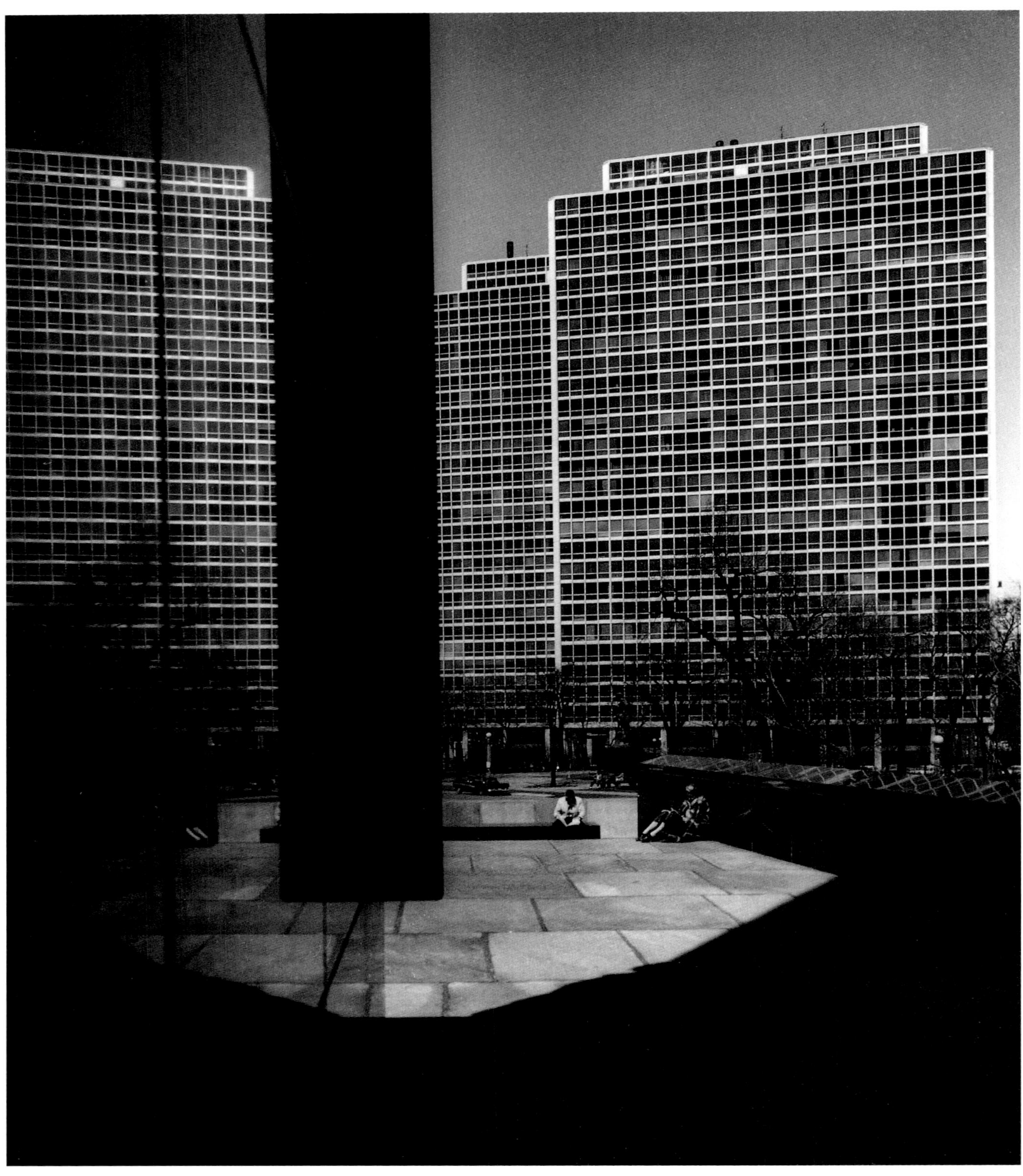

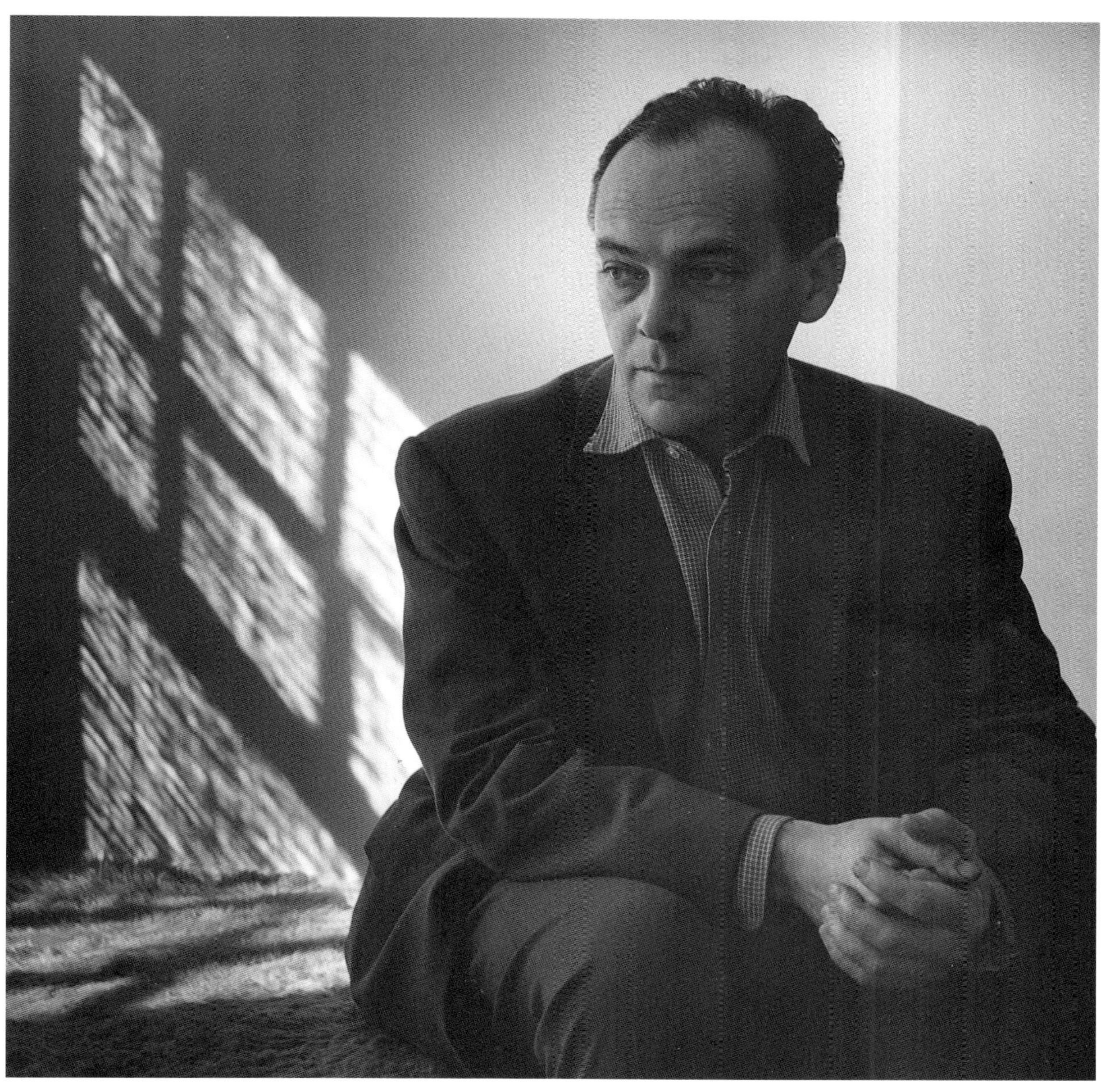

Commonwealth Promenade
Apartments, 1957
*This shot with the reflection of
the famous Mies van der Rohe
building took first prize in the
Chicago Modernization Photo
Contest.*

Gyorgy Kepes, Cambridge,
1958
*Kepes, a prominent Hungarian
designer and artist, worked
with Moholy-Nagy at the New
Bauhaus before founding the
Advanced Center for Visual
Studies at M.I.T.*

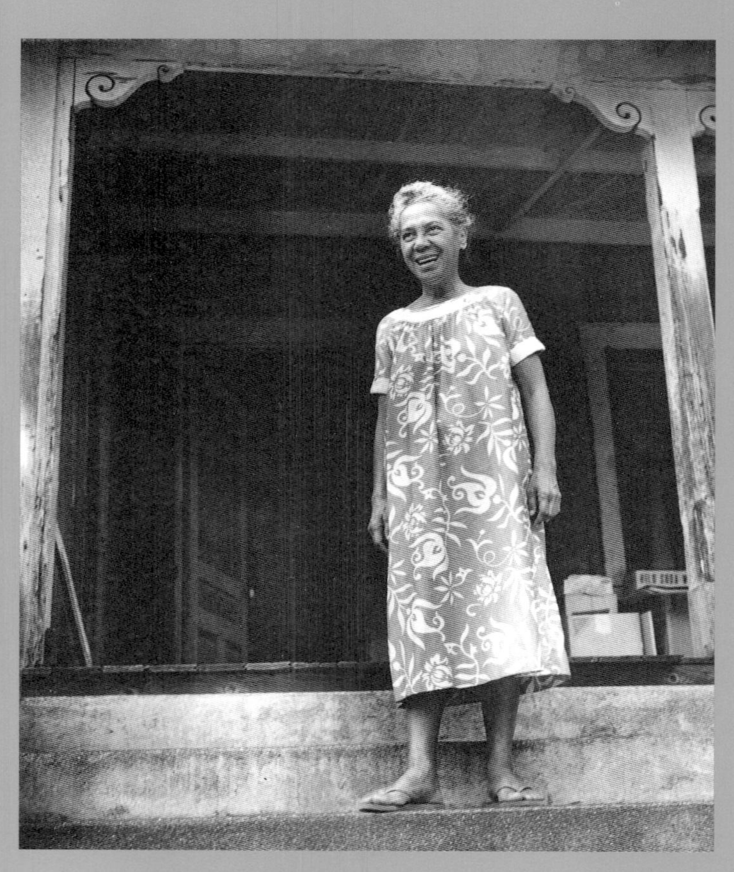

hawai'i

'Iolani Luahine on the steps of her family home in Nāpō'opo'o, Kona, 1975

After our move to Honolulu, I began studying the unique characteristics of the traditional dances of Hawai'i. Together with 'Iolani and Griffing, we began to develop a script and started shooting, with me directing and George Tahara as cameraman. We filmed all over the island of O'ahu. We had recorded 'Iolani's chants in the studio and replayed them so that she was shown dancing to her own voice in different locations. She was a remarkable woman, deeply religious and mystical, and at times very funny. Some of her dances were quite naughty. *Hula Ho'olaulea—Traditional Dances of Hawai'i* was completed in 1961. A premier was held at the Academy, and the film received very good reviews.

Our good friend Kawazoe notified me early in 1963 that he wanted to produce an hour-long 35 mm documentary film about the cultural history of Japan. Tokyo had been selected as the site of the 1964 Olympics, and he planned to present the film to foreign visitors during the event. Kawazoe was an idealistic man but also very patriotic: he would do anything to help Japan and raise its level of recognition in the world. Kawazoe was aware that I loved Japan and knew it well, and he decided I would be the best qualified to direct the film, which was to be sponsored by the Fuji Television Company with a sizable budget. I happily accepted the assignment and returned to Japan to begin the project with Kawazoe and a Japanese crew of fifteen. I worked with them for ten long months, all the way through to the final edit.

Making *Symbol and Myth* was my greatest filmmaking challenge in Japan. The situation was ideal. I had three months for preparation, including traveling the country far and wide to determine the best locations and the best artifacts. The only instruction the producer gave me was not to explain or analyze, but simply to address the hearts of the audience.

After the war, Kawazoe had become secretary to Prince Takamatsu (p. 89), the younger brother of Emperor Hirohito, and as a result, we received special permission to shoot restricted places and ceremonies that never before had been filmed. This included such sites as Ise Shrine, the holiest of Shinto shrines, and a sequence showing a night harvest ceremony performed by Shinto priests. For

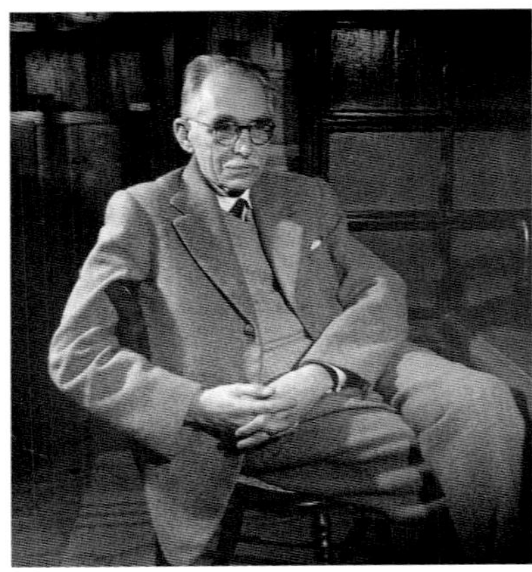

Bernard Leach, 1953

This portrait of Leach was taken during the filming of Arts of Japan.

this, I was told I was one of only three people who had ever witnessed the ceremony.

Some of the most interesting scenes were of the Emperor, who besides his role as symbolic head of the Shinto religion, worked as a marine biologist. Because he was considered of divine origin and commoners were not supposed to get close to him, I had to draw diagrams to show the court photographer what I wanted, and he then shot the scenes as I planned.

Another problem was filming the art objects—tomb figures, scrolls, and statues—that help tell the story of Japan's early history. This was a challenge because they were all precious national treasures. We had to devise a studio set-up inside the Shosoin, the archive inside the compound of the Ise Shrine, where these treasures were housed.

I approached a friend, Bernard Leach, a renowned British potter who had worked in Japan for a few years, and asked him to write a narration script. We had decided we did not need an explanation for the film, but we wanted some kind of poetic commentary to accompany the pictures. Bernard Leach understood what was needed and wrote a brief but beautiful narration.

The film, *Tenno—Symbol and Myth*, was first shown publicly on Japanese television on the Emperor's birthday, April 30, 1964. It was so well received by the Japanese that it was selected to be sent to the Venice Film Festival to represent Japanese documentary films, despite the fact that I, a foreigner, was its director.

After the 1964 Tokyo Olympics, Kawazoe came to Honolulu and organized a presentation of the film at the Japanese Consulate. Dean Sakamaki, of the University of Hawai'i, was especially impressed by the film and said to me, "Mr. Haar, you should come to the University of Hawai'i to teach photography." I told him I was flattered, but because I had learned English only during the time I had worked with the Americans in Japan, my English was still minimal. He convinced me I wouldn't need to talk much; it would be enough to show the students my photographs and teach them how to handle the camera. Several days later, I was hired to teach that summer.

I had a difficult time in the beginning. There were fifteen students in my first class, and we had only a small darkroom equipped with three enlargers. Because I couldn't let them all work in the darkroom at once, I was obliged to provide a lecture course. I couldn't find the right words and often lost my train of thought during the lectures. I noticed, however, that my limited English and heavy Hungarian accent were not as great a disadvantage as I had anticipated. Because the students had to listen more carefully, it seems they got more out of the lectures. As time passed, my English improved and so did my ability as a teacher. I was soon teaching forty-five students in beginning and advanced courses and began to enjoy teaching. When I reached the retirement age of sixty-five, the administration told me I could continue teaching until age seventy if I wanted to. By this time, though, I had seventy-five students in the two classes, and because I always tried to work individually with each student it was becoming a bit tiring. I decided to accept retirement from the university in 1974.

After moving to Hawai'i, I had begun photographing the different Asian groups who had transplanted themselves to this Island culture. I was particularly interested in the festivals and celebrations of the Japanese, Chinese, Korean, and Filipino cultures. Together with Jacob Fuehring, a noted pianist and teacher, and Harlow Dillingham, a descendent of the founder of the Dillingham Transportation Company, we worked on a script and formed a production company, Island Films. The film, entitled *Hawaii's Asian Heritage*, was completed in 1966 and received a C.I.N.E. (the Council on International Nontheatrical Events) Golden Eagle Award in Washington, D.C.

I achieved realization of another private ambition two years later. Hawai'i was rapidly changing, and I wanted to show some aspect of a community before this change called "progress." A painter, Kenneth Bushnell, informed me that 'A'ala, an old neighborhood of downtown Honolulu where he rented a studio, was going to be razed and converted into a park in the next few months. I hurriedly did some preliminary photographic studies of the area, then got together with Ken and his friend Steve Bartlett, a writer, to plan a documentary of the threatened community. The result was a twenty-minute experimental film, *Aala—Life and Death of a Community*, a historic document, as well as a lyrical poem in black and white.

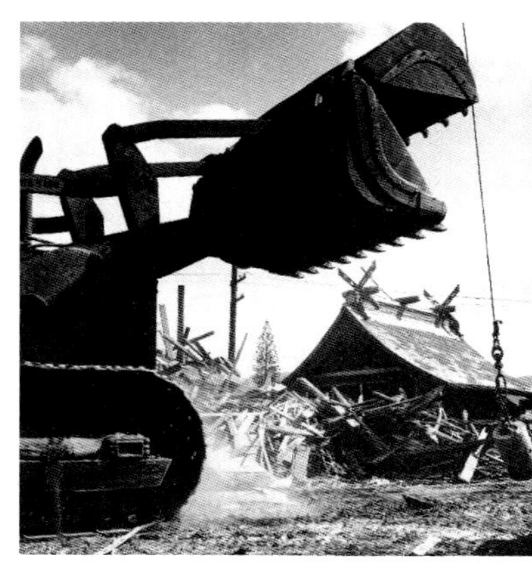

The destruction of 'A'ala gets under way, 1968.

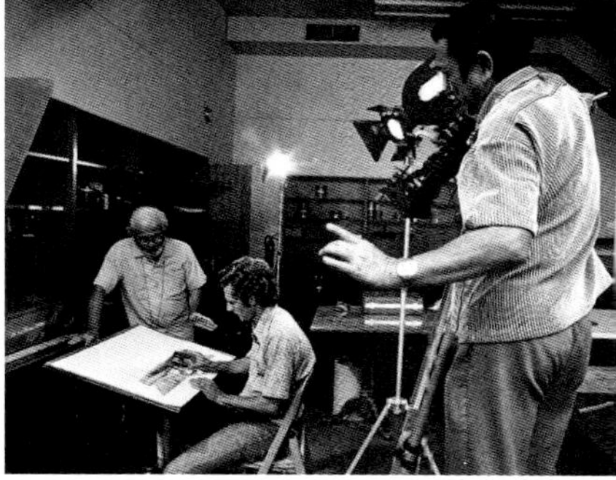

Directing Artists of Hawai'i, with cinematographer Joe Konno lining up a shot on artist Ron Kowalke. Tom Haar photo.

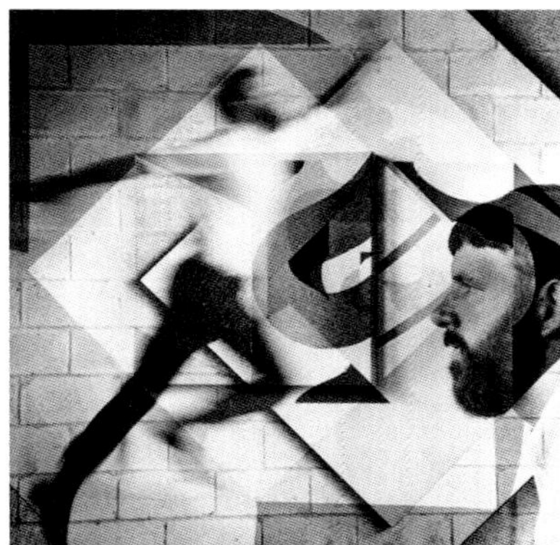

Ken Bushnell, 1968
A double print, this photograph was shot in the artist's studio in Honolulu.

In time, I had become acquainted with many artists in Hawai'i, among them Jean Charlot, Madge Tennent, Juliette May Fraser, and Tseng Yu-Ho. Most of them were associated with the University of Hawai'i at Mānoa. I knew a significant group of artists who lived in Hawai'i, a group any large city on the mainland would have been proud to embrace. I sent a proposal to the Hawai'i State Foundation on Culture and the Arts, or SFCA, to produce a book introducing the work of these talented artists to the world. The idea was accepted, and a committee was formed with the collaboration of Prithwish Neogy, professor of art history, to select eighteen artists for the book. This was an extremely difficult

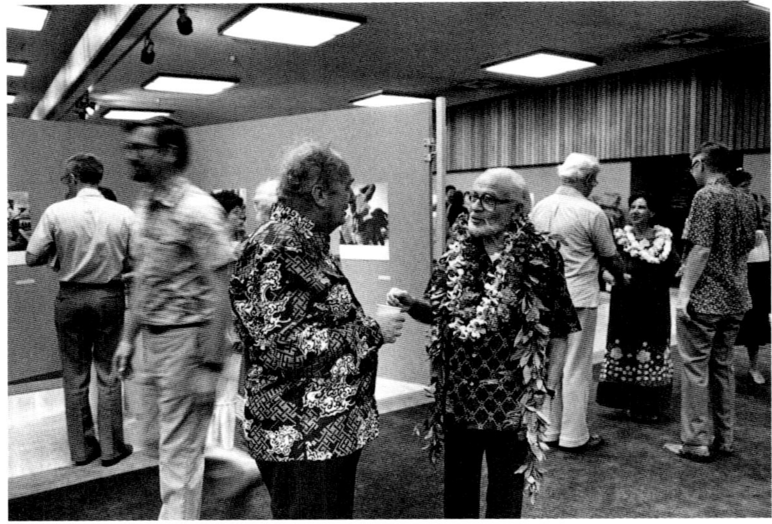

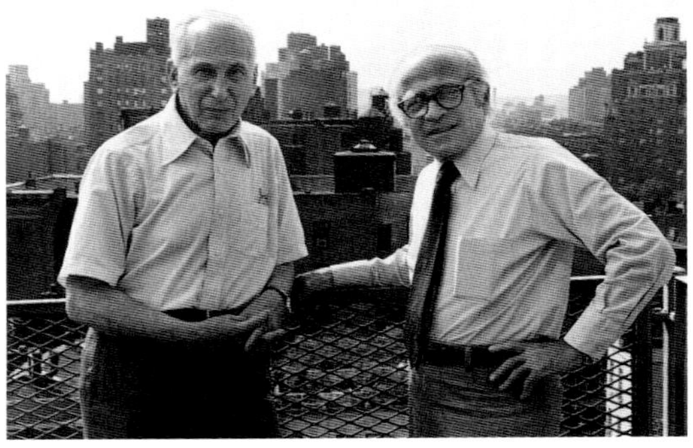

task because there were many more artists than we could include. When the book, entitled *Artists of Hawaiʻi*, was published, it was so popular that the SFCA decided to publish a second volume, presenting an additional eighteen artists.

It occurred to me that it would be even more educational and intimately revealing to produce a film showing the artists at work. Alfred Preis, director of the SFCA, liked the idea and requested a grant from the National Endowment for the Arts, sending the books we had already published as samples of the artists' work. The committee in Washington, D.C., viewed the artists of Hawaiʻi as special and their work of high quality, and they gave us the grant we had requested. This amount was matched locally by the SFCA and the Hawaiʻi Bicentennial Commission to finance a one-hour documentary film, made with technical help from KHET, the local Public Broadcasting television station. The film, titled *Artists of Hawaiʻi*, was divided into six segments: painting, sculpture, textiles, ceramics, printmaking, and design. It was edited in two different ways and could be shown as a whole or in segments, with each of the six parts used individually for teaching.

In 1983, Irene and I were approaching our fiftieth wedding anniversary. As I thought of this, I was also thinking of the fifty years I had worked as a photographer, and the idea came to me to put together a fifty-year retrospective exhibit. The date was set for January of 1984, and I arranged to use the large American Factors Exhibition Hall in downtown Honolulu for the show. Irene and I worked for two months making the enlargements for the 180-piece exhibit. My eldest son, Tom, who was following in my footsteps as a photographer and working in New York, came to help me set up and make the final arrangements.

We had an impressive opening night, with live music and a large crowd of visitors. This was, in reality, an overview of my life's work. I arranged the exhibit chronologically, starting with an early self-portrait drawing that I had done when I was fifteen years old. Then came my early photographs of Hungary, with some of my prize-winning pictures, and then pictures from Paris, Japan, Chicago, and Hawai'i.

During the three-week span of the exhibit, I received a notification from the Buddhist Honpa Hongwanji Mission of Honolulu that I had been designated a "Living Treasure of Hawai'i" for my artistic contribution to the community. They believed my work was of significant importance to the cultural climate of Hawai'i and invited me and five other artist nominees to an elaborate ceremony, which was attended by representatives from all of the different Buddhist denominations. Days later, the state Senate and then the House of Representatives invited us to the state Capitol, where the recognition ceremony was repeated.

About this time, I had the idea of making a book built around the pictures I had shot at various times of D. T. Suzuki, a Zen Buddhist scholar (p. 58). I first met him in 1950, when I visited him at his home in Kita-Kamakura. I did not know much about Zen at that time, but I was impressed by his simplicity and openness. When he agreed to allow me to take pictures of him, it turned into one of the most extraordinary portrait sessions I ever had. He let me take the photos without posing: he was almost unaware that I was there with the camera. His behavior was for me an example of what Zen teaches, that we have to get rid of our egos, our self-centeredness.

When Masao Abe, one of Suzuki's followers, was teaching at the University of Hawai'i as an exchange scholar, I approached him about working with me and editing a book on Suzuki. He enthusiastically accepted, and assembled from scholars all over the world a collection of articles about their appreciation of Suzuki and what they had learned from him, plus a few short articles by Suzuki himself. *A Zen Life: D. T. Suzuki Remembered* was published in 1986.

I am happy to live in Hawai'i. I have made many good friends here; in the past thirty-two years, the scope of my work has expanded because of the great variety of subject matter I have incorporated into my photographic work. Although Irene and I have been naturalized American citizens since 1965, we still return to Hungary every two or three years to visit our relatives and friends. Most recently, we went in the spring of 1989, when I had a retrospective exhibit at the Photographic Art Gallery in Budapest. The following year, I was honored with a Lifetime Achievement Award from the Hungarian Photographic Society.

I am eighty-four years old as I write this, and I feel grateful to Providence for the work I have accomplished and for the life I have had the opportunity to live. It is a great privilege to be alive. Life is a unique and wonderful experience. The past is always here with me. My photographs are memories that never go away.

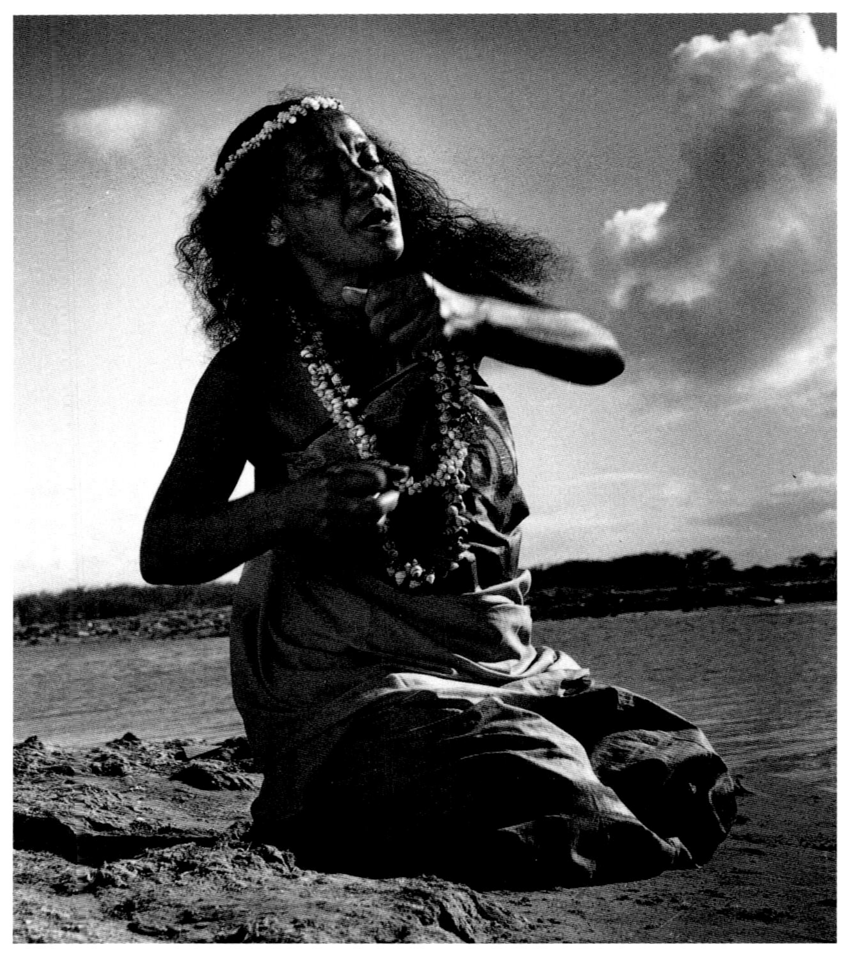

*'Iolani Luahine Dancing
a Seated Hula, 1961*
*It was a moment of wonder
to see this great dancer per-
forming the hula 'ili 'ili
(the pebble dance).*

*She was already a folk legend
and a living embodiment of the
elegiac spirit of the Hawaiian
people when I produced and
directed the documentary film*
Ho'olaulea: Traditional Dances
of Hawai'i.

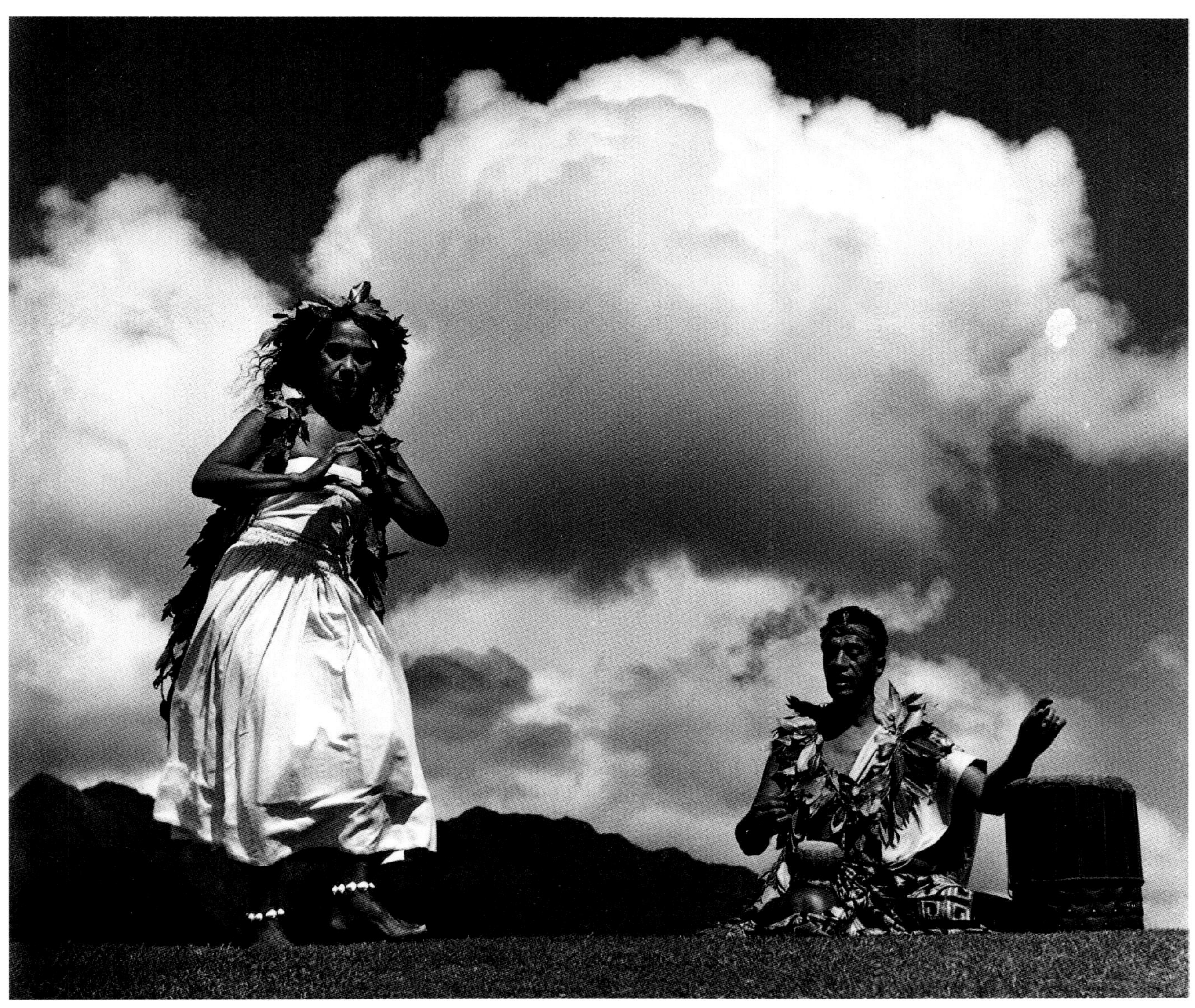

'Iolani Luahine and Tom Iona,
1961
While working with 'Iolani on
the film, I began to know her
more closely and realized that
she was more than a dancer.
She was rather a mystic, a
priestess of the sacred rite
of the hula.

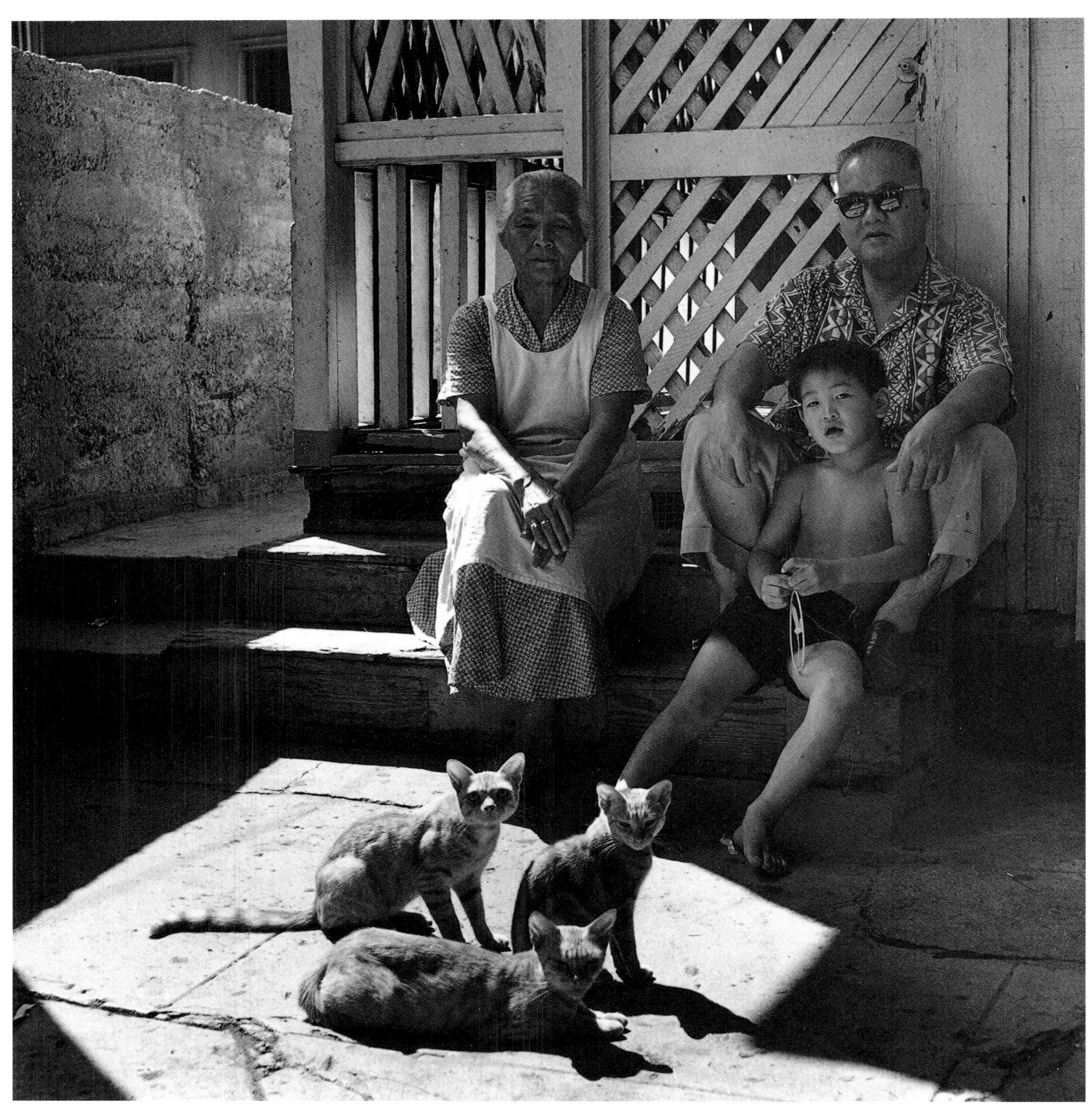

Chinatown Family, 1967

*Three generations of a family
rest on a hot summer's day
while I was researching the
documentary film on the 'A'ala
section of downtown Honolulu.*

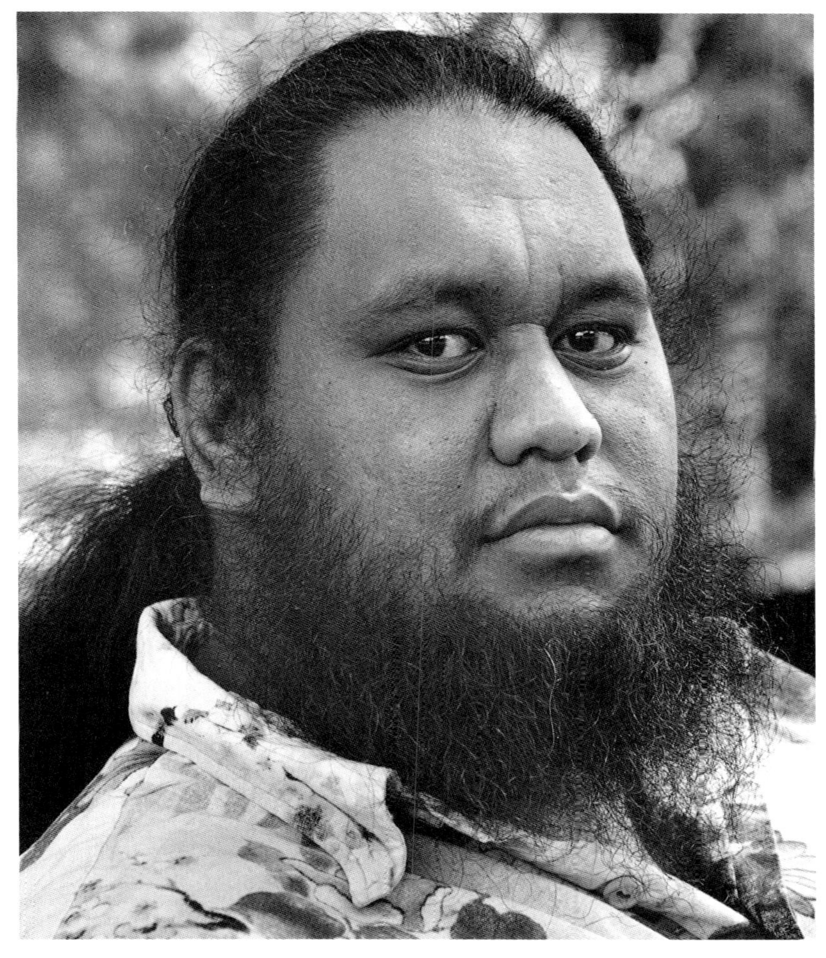

Hawaiian Man, 1968

While I was photographing

children playing at a park, I was

struck by the strength of the

features of this imposing

Hawaiian man.

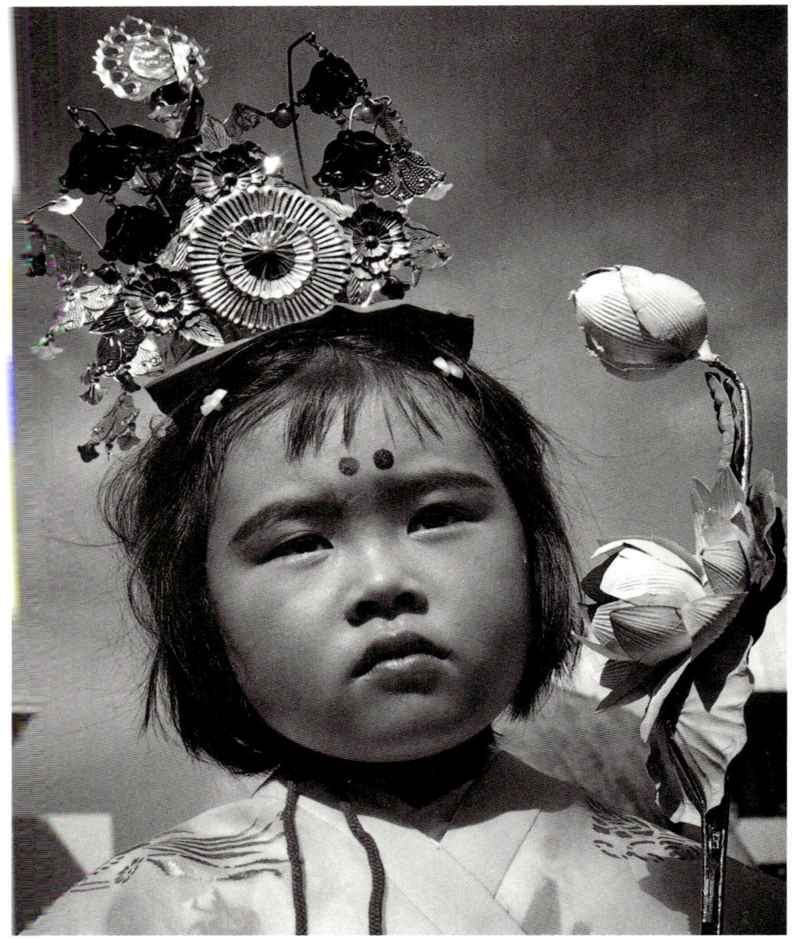

Buddha's Birthday Festival,
Hilo, 1968
A young Japanese American
girl was dressed up for a
Buddhist festival on the
island of Hawai'i.

Kamehameha Chorister, 1968
Every year, the students at The
Kamehameha Schools, a private
school for children of Hawaiian
lineage, participate in a choral
festival. This girl wears a haku,
or head, lei.

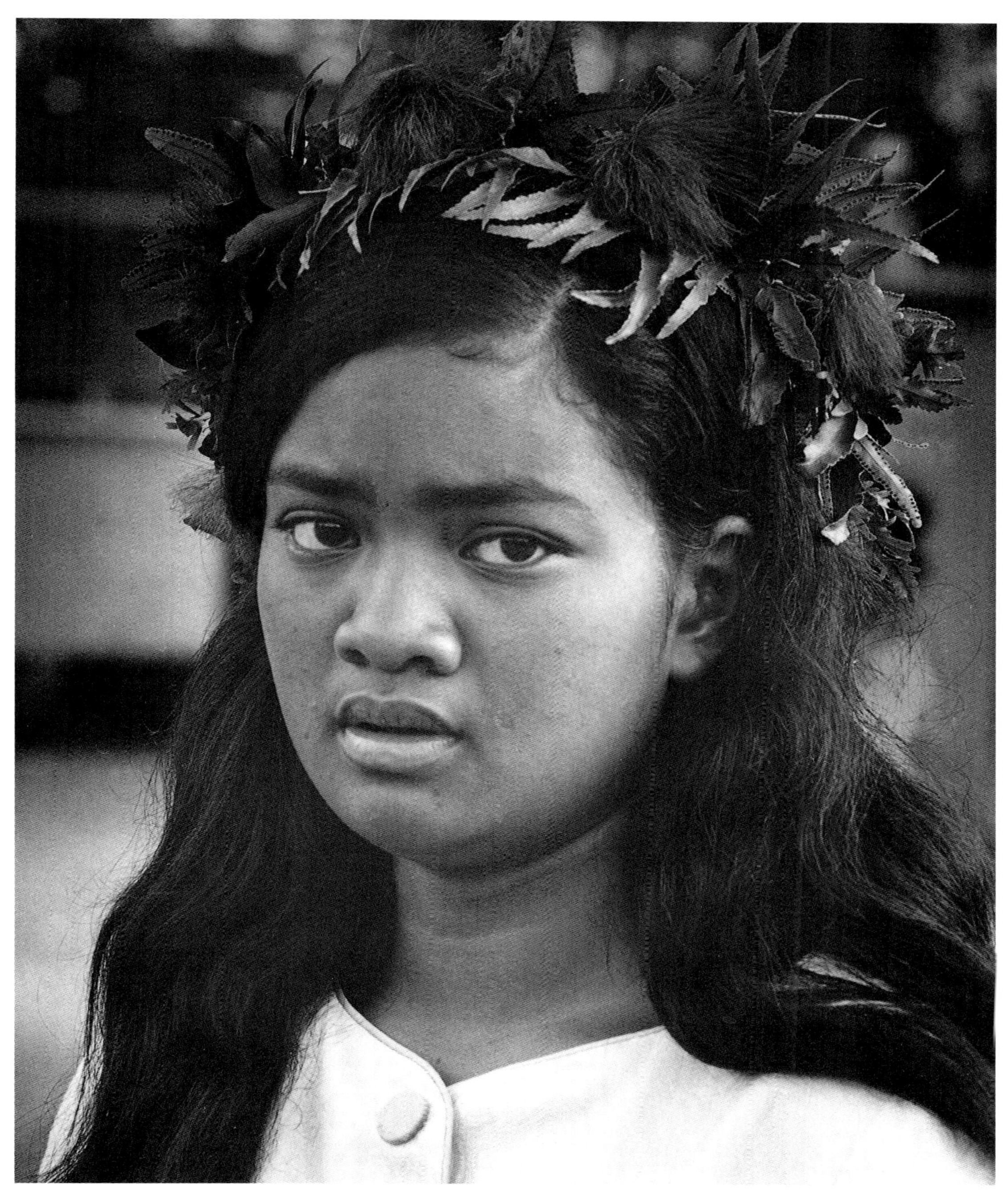

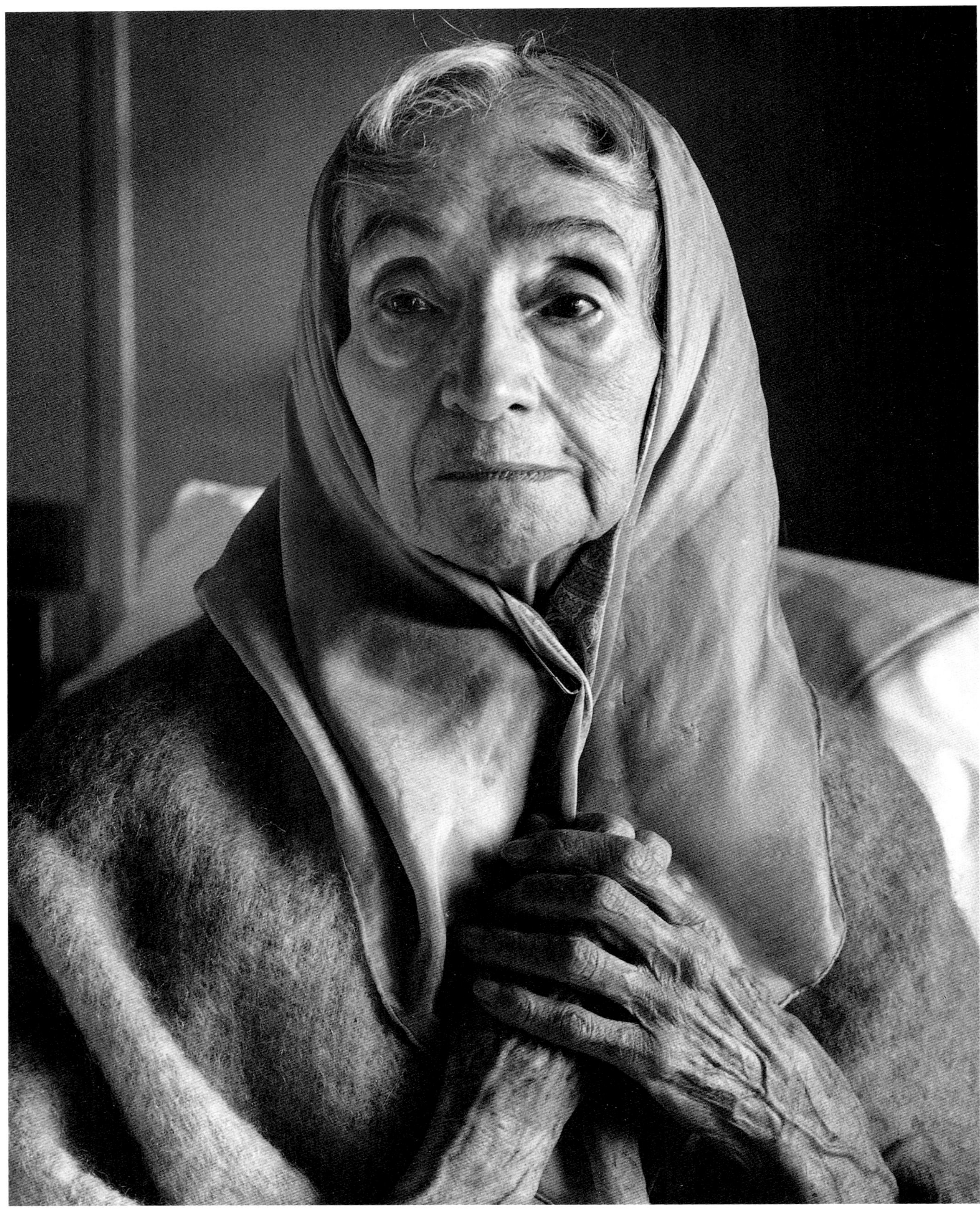

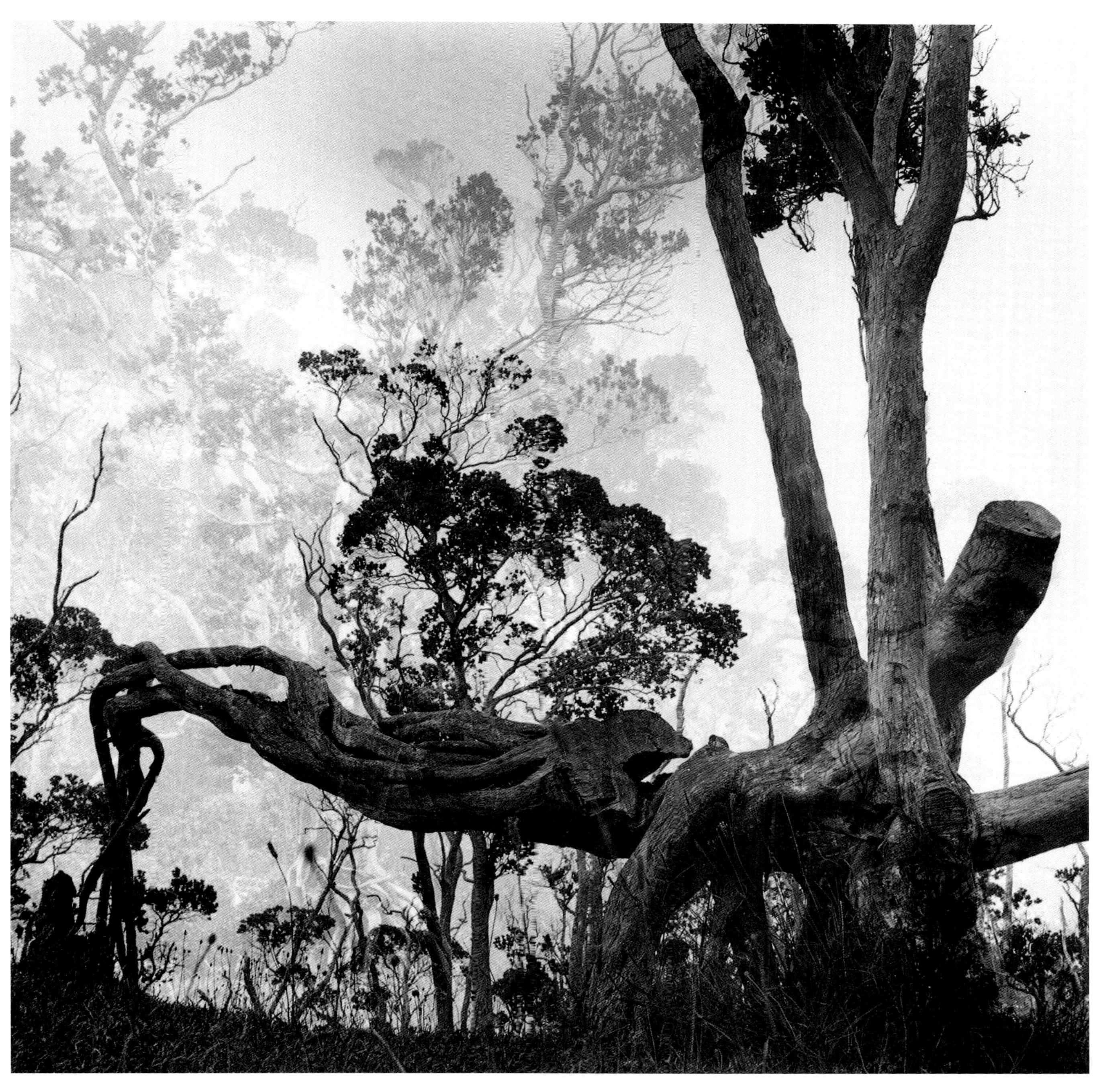

◄

Madge Tennent, 1970
Originally from England, this
renowned painter had turned
eighty when this portrait
was taken.

Kaua'i Forest, 1962
Exploring the oldest island
of the Hawaiian chain, I came
upon these windswept trees
high on a mountainside.

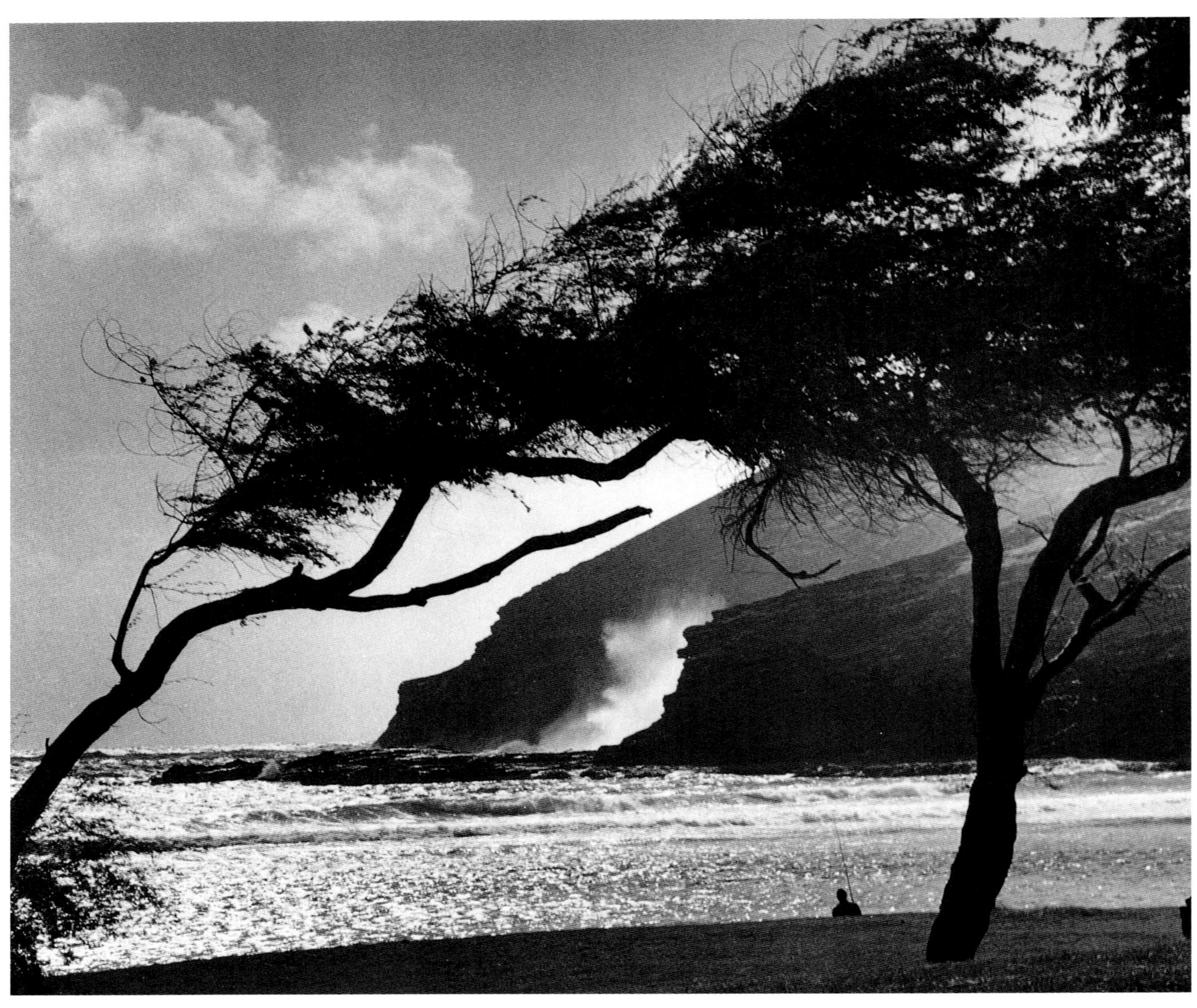

Hanauma Bay, Oʻahu, 1960
Hanauma Bay, famed for its
teeming marine life, was
formed from a volcanic crater.

Jean Charlot, 1970
I treasured my friendship with
this prolific painter, printmaker,
and writer. Originally from Paris,
Charlot had settled in Hawaiʻi
after working with the mural
renaissance movement in
Mexico for many years.

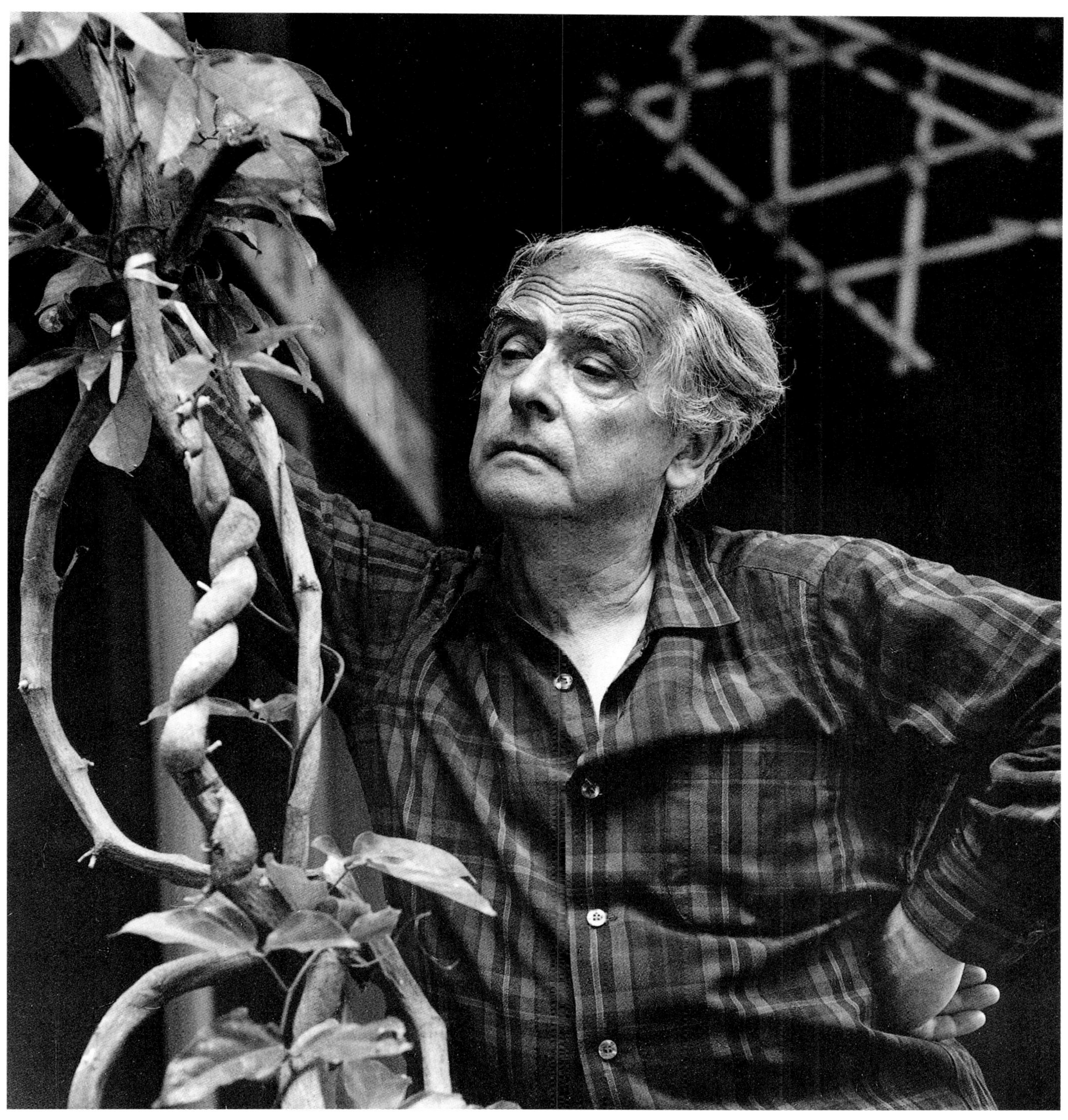

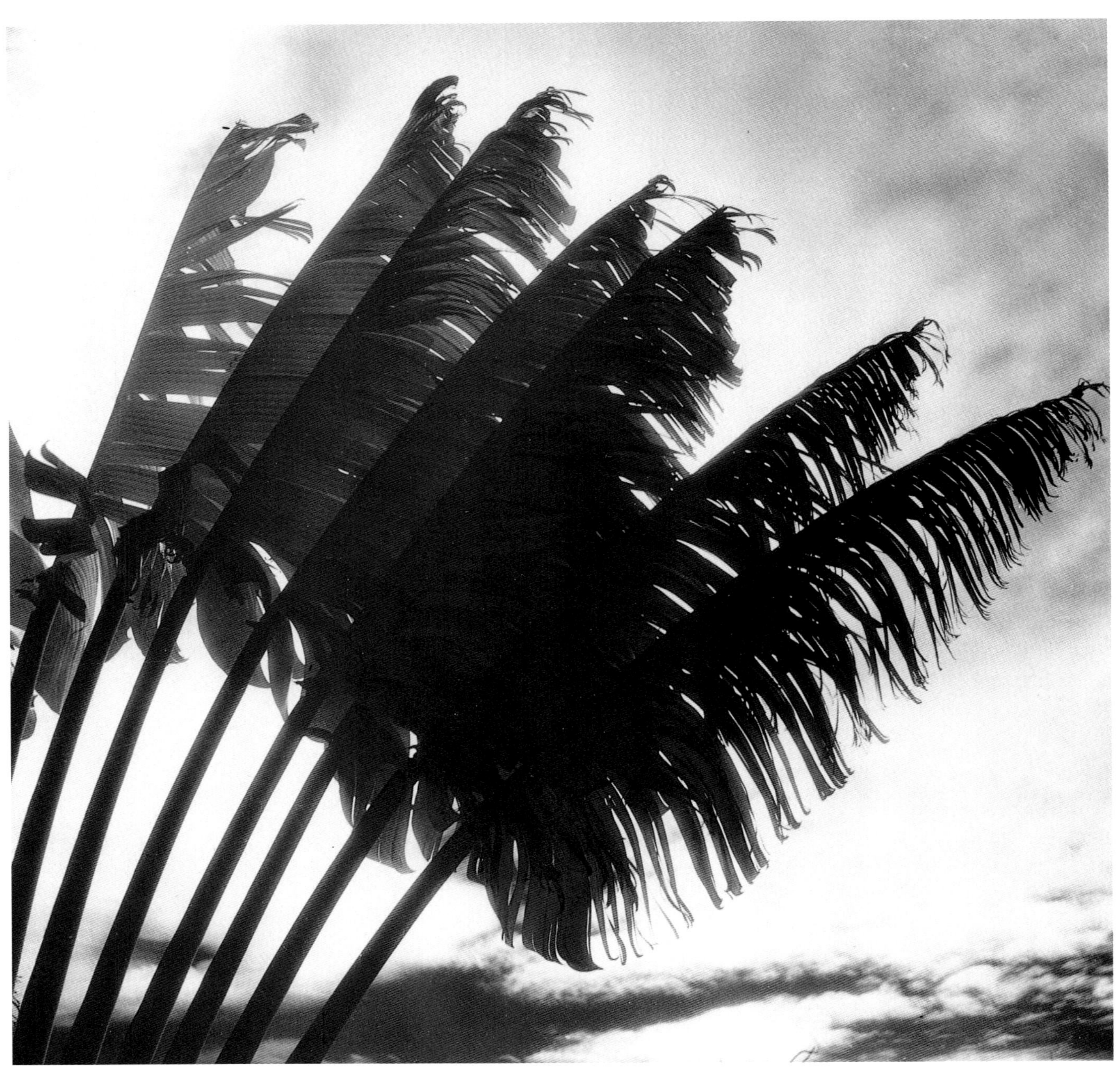

▶

Traveler's Palm, Hawai'i, 1962
Hawai'i has many varieties
of plants. This palm, with its
rhythmically spaced leaves,
originated in Madagascar.

Juliette May Fraser, 1973
Born in Honolulu, this painter,
printmaker, and muralist was
still producing works in her
mid-eighties, when this
picture was taken.
(Original in color)

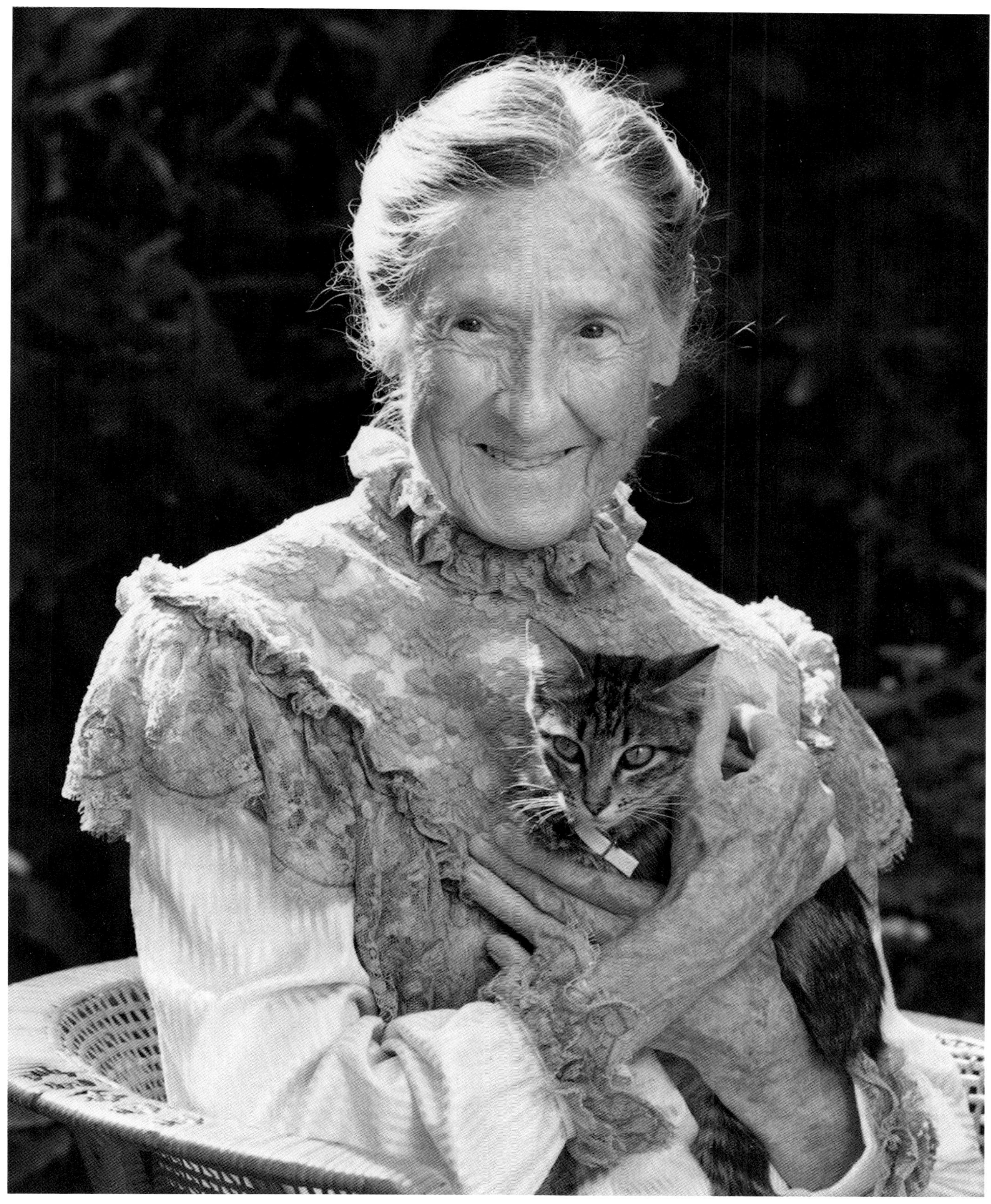

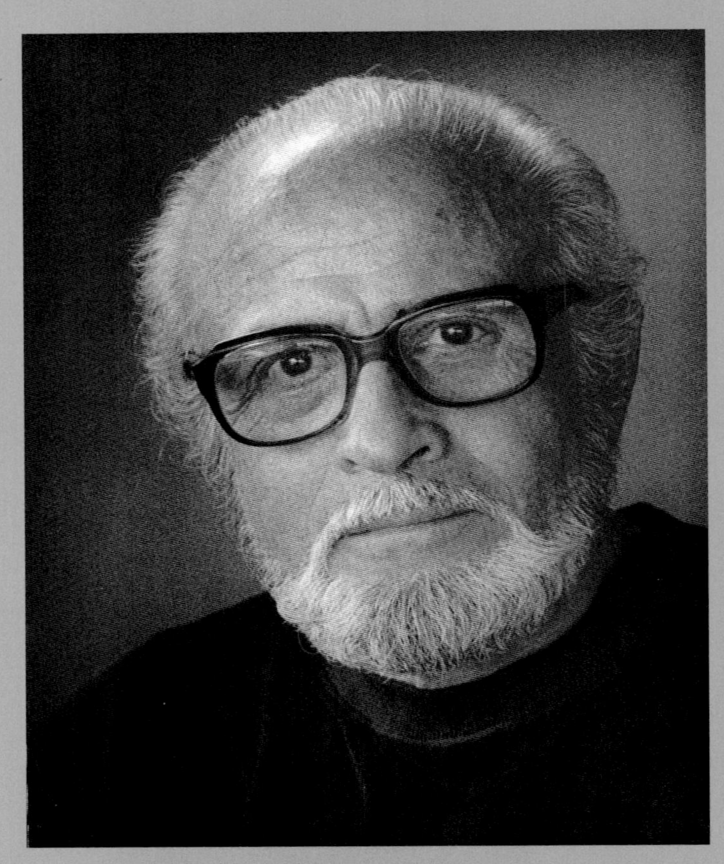

The late Alfred Preis, the first executive director of the Hawai'i State Foundation on Culture and the Arts, described Francis Haar, his career, and his work for the Fifty-Year Retrospective in 1984:

Francis Haar practiced his art of photography and filmmaking in three distinctly different worlds. He started his first studio in his native Budapest; later he moved to Paris and from there he was invited to Japan. After twenty years working in the Orient— interrupted by three years of activity in Chicago—he settled in Honolulu in 1960. He brought with him from these previous experiences priceless riches and memories, reflected in all of his contemporary work.

He emerged from the same artistic and cultural milieu and matrix which nurtured Laszlo Moholy-Nagy and Gyorgy Kepes, with whom he enjoyed a personal and artistic friendship. As with so many Hungarians, he became fluent and expert in the "Language of Vision" and enthralled with the "Vision of Motion." When expressing himself verbally, his Hungarian accent is unmitigated, but when speaking visually, in photography or in cinematography, his message resonates with overtones from Japan and reverberates with the cosmopolitan sophistication of European and American big-city environments. Like other sensitive and receptive newcomers to Hawai'i, he became deeply attracted to the study of Hawaiian culture. Ho'olaulea, a magnificent film on the traditional dances of Hawai'i, featuring the late 'Iolani Luahine, was produced and directed by him for the Honolulu Academy of Arts in 1961.

He became increasingly more enraptured with capturing in photos and on film the image of creativity and creation in the various media of the cultures of Hawai'i. This resulted in insightful photographs, exhibitions, films, and printed publications. These were always based on meticulous research and presented with flawless technique and superb craftsmanship.

Over the years, Francis Haar was honored with several outstanding awards and prizes, both nationally and internationally. His work is in such prestigious public collections as the Victoria and Albert Museum in London and the Museum of Modern Art in New York. He has had twenty-three one-man shows and fourteen major publications, including *Best of Old Japan* and *Japanese Theatre in Highlights*, both published by Charles Tuttle Company, Tokyo. Locally, he is known for *Legends of Hawaii*, volumes 1 and 2 of *Artists of Hawai'i*, and *'Iolani Luahine*.

Portrait of Francis Haar
by Irene, 1978

Francis Haar Chronology

1908	Born in Csernatfalu, Hungary
1924–1928	Studied at the National Academy of Industrial Arts, Budapest
1928–1931	Worked as designer at the Gerloczy firm of architects; taught himself photography
1931–1933	Drafted into the Hungarian Army
1934	Married Irene Papa
1934–1937	Operated his photo studio in Budapest
1937–1939	Operated his photo studio in Paris
1939	Went to Japan at the invitation of the Japan Foundation (Kokusai Bunka Shinkokai)
1940–1942	Operated his photo studio in Tokyo
1943–1946	Evacuated to Karuizawa, where he and his family spent the war years
1946–1948	Photographer with *Yank* magazine of the U.S. occupation forces in Japan, and subsequently filmmaker with the U.S. Public Health and Welfare Section
1948–1956	Operated his photo studio in Tokyo
1956–1959	Worked as photographer for the Container Corporation of America, Chicago
1959–1960	Operated his photo studio in Tokyo
1960	Moved to Hawai'i, started photo studio
1964–1974	Taught photography at the University of Hawai'i, Summer Session
1965–1975	Production photographer for the Kennedy Theater, the University of Hawai'i Drama Department
1997	Francis Haar passed away at the age of eighty-nine in Honolulu

One-Man Exhibitions

1940	First Retrospective, Shirokiya Department Store Gallery, Tokyo
1941	Shirokiya Department Store Gallery, Tokyo
1949	American Cultural Center, Tokyo
1952	Haar Photo Studio, Kamakura
1957	Chicago Public Library
1958	University of Chicago
1962	Honolulu Public Library
1967	Art Department, University of Hawai‘i
1968	Unitarian Church Gallery, Honolulu
1969	Graphics Gallery, Honolulu Academy of Arts
1972	Budapest Art Gallery, Hungary
1972	Princess Kaiulani Hotel, Honolulu
1973	American Savings and Loan Art Gallery, Honolulu
1975	Kennedy Theater, University of Hawai‘i
1983	Focus Gallery, Honolulu Academy of Arts
1983	Ramsay Gallery, Honolulu
1984	Fifty-Year Retrospective, Amfac Plaza Exhibition Room, Honolulu
1985	Tsukuba Museum of Photography, Japan
1987	Manoa Gallery, Honolulu
1989	Photographic Art Gallery, Budapest
1990	Graphics Gallery, Honolulu Academy of Arts
1991	Budapest Art Gallery, Hungary
1991	Gallery Saka, Tokyo

Group Exhibitions

1937	Hungarian Pavilion at the Paris World Exposition
1965–1983	Regular entries in the following annual juried exhibitions:
	Honolulu Printmakers
	Hawai'i Artists League
	Artists of Hawai'i
	Image Foundation
1971	*Mirella Belshe/Francis Haar*, Contemporary Arts Center of Hawai'i
1972, 1983	*Homage to the Native Land*, Mucsarnok Museum, Budapest
1977	Wailea Arts Center Gallery, Maui
1978	*Haar: Three Personal Visions*, Contemporary Arts Center of Hawai'i
1978	C. S. Wo's Annual Showcase, Honolulu
1981	*The Spirit of Hawaiian Dance*, Camera '81, Honolulu Hale
1984	*Twentieth-Century Photographs from Hawai'i Collections*, Honolulu Academy of Arts
1987	*Retrospective, 1967–1987*, State Foundation on Culture and the Arts, Honolulu
1988	*Munka*, Kassák Memorial Museum, Budapest
1991	Inaugural Exhibition, Hungarian Museum of Photography, Kecskemet
1997	*Collective Visions: 1967–1997*, Honolulu Academy of Arts
1997	*Portraits in Tribute*, Queen Emma Gallery, Honolulu
1997	*Mind to Mind, Hand to Hand*, Gallery on the Pali, Honolulu

Publications

1940	*Way to the Orient*, Arts Publishing Company, Tokyo
1941	*Hungarian Picture Book*, Benrido Publishing Company, Kyoto
1942	*Around Mount Fuji*, Benrido Publishing Company, Kyoto
1951	*The Best of Old Japan*, Charles E. Tuttle Company, Tokyo
1952	*Japanese Theatre in Highlights*, Charles E. Tuttle Company, Tokyo
1954	*Mermaids of Japan*, Kanameshobo Company, Tokyo
1954	*Geisha of Pontocho*, Tokyo News Service
1960	*The Tokyo You Should See*, Charles Tuttle Company, Tokyo
1969	*Foto Haar Ferenc*, Corvina Publishing Company, Budapest
1972	*Legends of Hawai'i*, Victoria Publishers, Honolulu
1974	*Artists of Hawai'i, Vol. 1*, University of Hawai'i Press, Honolulu
1977	*Artists of Hawai'i, Vol. 2*, University of Hawai'i Press, Honolulu
1985	*'Iolani Luahine*, Topgallant Publishing, Honolulu
1986	*A Zen Life: D. T. Suzuki Remembered*, John Weatherhill, Inc., Tokyo

Documentary Films

1948	*Hamajo Fishing Village*, Palmer Pictures
1950	*Picturesque Japan*, Japan Travel Bureau
1951	*Students Today—Japan's Tomorrow*, Australian Mission, Tokyo
1953	*Arts of Japan*, U.S. Information Agency, Tokyo
1954	*Awakening*, Sophia University, Tokyo
1955	*Japanese Calligraphy*, Belgian Education Ministry
1959	*Ukiyoe—Prints of Japan*, Art Institute of Chicago
1959	*Juvenile Delinquency in Chicago*, Chicago Public Television
1961	*Hula Ho'olaulea—Traditional Dances of Hawai'i*, Honolulu Academy of Arts

1962	*Pineapple Country Hawai‘i*, Pineapple Growers Association, Honolulu
1963	*The Other Language*, AID Far East Training Center, Hawai‘i
1964	*Tenno—Symbol and Myth*, Asuka Production with Fuji Television Company, Tokyo
1966	*Hawaii's Asian Heritage*, Island Films Production, Honolulu
1968	*Aala—Life and Death of a Community*, B.B.H. Productions, Honolulu
1976	*Artists of Hawai‘i*, Bicentennial Commission and Hawai‘i State Foundation on Culture and the Arts, Honolulu

APPENDIX F

Awards

1933, 1935	First Prize, National Photo Contest, Budapest
1959	First Prize, Metropolitan Improvement Photo Contest, Chicago
1963	Golden Eagle Award for *Pineapple Country Hawai‘i*, C.I.N.E., Washington, D.C.
1966	Golden Eagle Award for *Hawaii's Asian Heritage*, C.I.N.E., Washington, D.C.
1970	Photographic Award, *Educational Perspectives Magazine*, University of Hawai‘i
1982	Gift Print Award, Arts Council of Hawai‘i
1984	Living Treasure of Hawai‘i, Honpa Hongwanji and the Hawai‘i State Legislature
1991	Lifetime Achievement Award, Hungarian Photographic Society

APPENDIX G

Works in Public Collections

Victoria and Albert Museum, London

Museum of Modern Art, New York

Hawai‘i State Foundation on Culture and the Arts

The Contemporary Museum, Honolulu

Honolulu Academy of Arts

Hungarian Museum of Photography, Kecskemét

Television Programs about Francis Haar

"Francis Haar: The Artist and Japan" (Hawai'i PBS). 1971. Tom Howe, producer. Thirty minutes.

Hungarian Television (Magyar Televizio). "Családi magazin 4." 1987. László Szabó, producer/director. Ten minutes.

Spectrum KHET (Hawai'i PBS). 1987. Christopher Conybeare, producer/director. Eight minutes.

Treasures, Vol. 10. (Hawai'i KHON). 1988. Dennis Christianson, producer/director. Thirteen minutes.

Selected Contributions to Books, Periodicals, and Catalogues

Budapest. Photo illustrations. Hungary, 1933.

A Mi Életünkből. A selection of photographs. Budapest, Hungary: Munka Kör, 1934.

Gebrauchs Graphik (Germany). "Hungarian Advertising Art," photographs of packaging. Vol. 13, no. 8 (January 1936): 13

Budapester Rundschau (Germany). Vol. 3 (March 1936): 7, 8, 9, 16.

Commercial Art and Industry (U.K.). "Photographs by Haar." Vol. 20, no. 117 (March 1936): 114, 115.

Pesti Napló (Hungary). "Sunbathing" photo. August 30, 1936, p. 4.

A Pesti Városháza (Hungary). "View from the Basilica" photo. November 1936, p. 5.

Művészet (Hungary). Architectural photography. Vol. 2, no. 13 (1937): 162, 163.

Hungaria Magazin (Germany). Cover photo. February 1938, pp. 10, 12.

Gebrauchs Graphik (Germany). Photographs of packaging. Vol. 15 (July 1938): 37–43.

Art and Industry (U.K.). "Publicity in Hungary." Vol. 25, no. 147 (September 1938): 81, 90, 91.

The Studio (U.K.). Charles Rosner, "Francis Haar." Vol. 116, no. 548 (November 1938): 250, 251.

Kokokukai (Japan). "Hungary no Shogyo Bijutsu" (article on industrial arts in Hungary). November 1938, pp. 26, 27.

Magyar Fényképezés. Photo illustrations. Budapest, Hungary: Officina Press, 1939, photo nos. 8, 9, 66.

Se (Germany). March 26, 1939, pp. 10, 11.

Pesti Napló (Hungary). Photographs of Paris. April 16, 1939, pp. 5, 6.

Tükör (Hungary). Photographs of Paris. Vol. 7, no. 4 (April 1939): 246–249.

U.S. Camera (U.S.A.). Cover "Sunbathing" photo February–March, 1940.

Sakura no Kuni (Japan). Cover "Sunbathing" photo, interview, other photos. Vol. 8, no. 8 (August 1940): 1–4.

Insatsu (Japan). Cover "Boat on River" photo. August 25, 1940.

Shashin Shuho (Japan). "Nichi Doku I no atarashii ototo: Hungary." December 4, 1940, pp. 2–5.

Coronet (U.S.A.). "Little Old Lady" photo. Vol. 10, no. 2 (June 1941): 97.

Ungarn (Germany). "Ungarischer Photokünstler in Japan." January 1941, p. 312.

Híd (Hungary). "Egy Magyar Fotografus Japánban." January 10, 1941, pp. 12, 13.

Sentaku, Dento, Sozo (Japan). Charlotte Perriand and Junzo Sakakura. Catalogue for exhibit at Osaka Takashimaya, Japan, December 25, 1941, p. 21.

Missi (France). "Chez les Boudhistes ZEN," December 1949, pp. 306, 307.

Orient Photography (Japan). "Creative Expression in Amateur Photography." April 1954, pp. 26–28.

L'Art Sacré (France). July–August 1954, pp. 6, 7, 9–12, 15–18, 23, 25, 26, 29–31, 34, 35.

The Geijutsu Shincho (Japan). "Nihon no shodo," about Haar's film on Japanese calligraphy. December 1955, pp. 170–173.

The Geijutsu Shincho (Japan). "Kanko Nippon," about Japanese art and culture. January 1956, pp. 139–162.

Quadrum (Belgium). Pierre Alechinsky, "Calligraphie Japonaise." Photos from calligraphy film. May 1956, pp. 44–52.

Hungary Shibungaku Zenshu (Japan). Book of Hungarian poetry edited and translated by Juichiro Imaoka. Photographs of Budapest. Tokyo: Shinkigensha, February 1956, pp. v–vi, xii.

Sansai (Japan). "Geijutsu no fueki to ryuko," about traditional Japan. June 1956, pp. 2–6.

Japán élet Japán emberek, by Ferenc Zàgoni. Budapest, Hungary: Ifjúsági Könyvkiadó, 1956. Pp. 19, 55, 68, 103, 157, 159, 179, 221, 241.

The Geijutsu Shincho (Japan). "Shodo kara Zen Art E," review of calligraphy film. February 1957, pp. 40–43.

Art and Photography (U.S.A.). "What Happened to Refugee Photographers?" Vol. 8, no. 8–92 (February 1957): 4–8, 45, 46.

Weekend Magazine (U.S.A.). "Satoko Trains for a Life of Pleasure." Vol. 8, no. 35 (August 30, 1958): 6, 8, 9.

Photo (catalogue). International Exhibition of Photographic Art. Hungary: Corvina, 1958, p. 107.

The Beacon (U.S.A.). Cover photo and inside photos. Vol. 1, no. 8 (September 1961): 12, 13.

Bungei Shunju (Japan). Japanese portraits. September 1961, pp. 1–8.

Mele (U.S.A.). Cover photo. March 1966.

Honolulu (U.S.A.). Cover photo and inside photos for article "Courtship in Peking." Vol. 1, no. 3 (September 1966): 24–26.

A Mi Életünkből, 1932: Szociofoto Kiállítás (Hungary). Catalogue, Damjanich Múzeum, Szolnok. 1966, pp. 28, 29.

Educational Perspectives (U.S.A.). Cover photo and photos with article "Astronomy in the Museum's Science Education Program." Vol. 6, no. 1 (March 1967): 11–14.

Magyar Hírek (Hungary). Article on "Eyes of Haar" film showing. April 1967.

The Eastern Buddhist (Japan). Frontispiece photo of Daisetz Suzuki. Kyoto: Eastern Buddhist Society. Vol. 2, no. 1 (August 1967).

Educational Perspectives (U.S.A.). Articles and photos: "The Old Story-Teller" and "Photography as Communication." Vol. 8, no. 1 (March 1969): 3, 4, 22–25.

Orság Világ (Hungary). "A Távol-kelet szerelmese," August 6, 1969, pp. 23, 24.

Dance Magazine (U.S.A.). "Hula" and "A Dance Department with the Aloha Spirit." Vol. 43, no. 12 (December 1969): 58–63.

25 év (Hungary). Catalogue of the International Exhibition of Photographic Art, 1970, pp. 29, 30.

Fotóművészet (Hungary). "Haár Ferenc kiállitása." April 1972, pp. 43–46.

Mele (U.S.A.). Cover photo. March 1973.

Hamada: Potter (Japan). By Bernard Leach. Tokyo: Kodansha International, 1975, p. 86.

Bulletin (U.S.A.). "Jean Charlot," Georgia Museum of Art. Fall 1976: Frontispiece and pp. 23, 34.

The Art and Writing of Madge Tennent. Honolulu: Island Heritage, 1977, p. 21.

Alechinsky: Paintings and Writings (catalogue). Pittsburgh, Penna.: Carnegie Institute Museum of Art, 1977, pp. 202, 203.

Beyond East and West (U.K.). By Bernard Leach. London: Faber and Faber, 1978, pl. 1.

Kassák Lajos: Eijünk a mi idönkben (Lajos Kassák: We should be a part of our times). Book contains a chapter on Haar entitled "Egy Magyar Fotográfus Japánban" (A Hungarian photographer in Japan). Budapest, Hungary: Magvetö Könyvkiadó, 1978, pp. 220–223.

Washi: The World of Japanese Paper (Japan). Sukey Hughes. Tokyo: Kodansha International, 1978, pp. 61–63, 77, 78, 115, 116, 127, 143, 149, 167, 169, 170, 199, 200, 202, 204, 216, 225, 227.

Új Tükör (Hungary). "Egykori munkásfotós Honoluluban." Vol. 16 (January 14, 1979): 21.

Educational Perspectives (U.S.A.). Vol. 18, no. 2 (May 1979): 18, 19.

East-West Photo Journal (U.S.A.). Kabuki photo. Vol. 2, no. 6 (Fall 1981): 8.

Tény-kép (catalogue). "The History of Hungarian Photography from 1840 to 1981." Budapest, Hungary: Mücsarnok Art Gallery, 1981, pp. 28, 65.

East-West Photo Journal. Wally Ruckert. "Francis Haar." Vol. 3, no. 8 (Spring 1982): 12–17.

Hawai'i (U.S.A.). Photos of Juliette May Fraser. April 1982, pp. 34, 35.

Eastwest (U.S.A.). Geisha photo. Vol. 3, no. 9 (Summer 1982): 18.

Honolulu (U.S.A.). Juliette May Fraser photo. Vol. 17, no. 5 (November 1982): 96.

Something Like an Autobiography (Japan). Akira Kurosawa, translated by Audie Bock. New York: Alfred A. Knopf, 1982, p. 114.

Tisztelet A Szülöföldnek (catalogue). "Homage to the Native Land." Budapest, Hungary: Mücsarnok Art Gallery, 1983, p. 61.

Fotóművészet (Hungary). "Ut Kelet Es Nyugat Felé." January 1983, pp. 3–10.

Fotó (Hungary). "A 75 éves Haár Ferenc köszöntése." Vol. 30, no. 6 (June 1983): 240, 248–253.

Twentieth-Century Photographs from Hawai'i Collections (catalogue). Honolulu: Honolulu Academy of Arts, 1984, p. 62.

Aloha (U.S.A.). Steve Barth, "Francis Haar: Life in Focus." Vol. 13, no. 5 (September–October 1984): 58–62, 68.

Honolulu (U.S.A.). Brett Uprichard, "Francis Haar: A Lifetime of Images." Vol. 19, no. 5 (November 1984): 98–103, 173–175.

Artists of Hawai'i. Catalogue for a twelve-part educational TV series. Hawai'i Department of Education, 1985. Pp. 9, 17, 21, 25, 28, 41, 66, 69, 72.

Asahi Camera (Japan). Kotaro Iizawa, "Tsuchi No Niyoi Ga Suru Jokei." October 1985, p. 188.

Pierre Alechinsky: Margin and Center (catalogue). New York: Solomon R. Guggenheim Museum, 1987, p. 150.

Retrospective, 1967–1987 (catalogue). Hawai'i State Foundation on Culture and the Arts' Twentieth Anniversary Exhibition, 1987, p. 131.

Frameless Windows, Squares of Light. Poems by Cathy Song. Cover photo. New York: W. W. Norton, 1988.

Hawaii, 1959–1989. By Gavan Daws. Honolulu: Publishers Group Hawaii, 1989, pp. 84, 198.

Fotóművészet (Hungary). "Haar Ferenc a képeiröl." March 1989, pp. 14–21.

Új Tükör (Hungary). "A Honolului Mester." Vol. 26, no. 25 (June 18, 1989): 20, 21.

Fotó (Hungary). "A két Haár." Vol. 36, no. 9 (September 1989): 384, 393–397.

A Fénykép Varázsa. "The Magic of Photography." Budapest, Hungary: Association of Hungarian Photographers, 1989, p. 288.

Jean Charlot: A Retrospective (catalogue). Honolulu: University of Hawai'i Art Gallery, 1990, p. 31.

Fotóművészet (Hungary). "A két Haár." March 1991, pp. 21–26.

Shukan Bunshun (Japan). "Nippon No Omono." September 1991, pp. 13–20.

Fotográfiák Kassák Lajosról (catalogue). Budapest, Hungary: Kassák Museum, 1992, nos. 65–68, 72–76, 78, 83.

Testimony to the Invisible. James F. Lawrence, editor. West Chester, Penna: Chrysalis Books, 1995, p. 172.

Swedenborg: Buddha of the North. By D. T. Suzuki. West Chester, Penna: Swedenborg Foundation, 1996, pp. 2, 76.

Collective Visions, 1967–1997 (catalogue). Honolulu: Hawai'i State Foundation on Culture and the Arts' Thirtieth Anniversary Exhibition, 1997, p. 26.

A Hawai'i Anthology. Joseph Stanton, editor. Hawai'i State Foundation on Culture and the Arts, 1997, p. 177.

Sanko Inoue (catalogue): Portrait of Inoue. Japan: Hiratsuka Art Museum, 1998.

Photographs: Made in Hungary (catalogue). Hungary: Hungarian Museum of Photography, 1998, pp. 116, 117.

Nā Wāhine Kapu: Divine Hawaiian Women. By Lilikalā Kame'eleihiwa. Cover photo. Honolulu, Hawai'i: 'Ai Pōhaku Press, 1999.